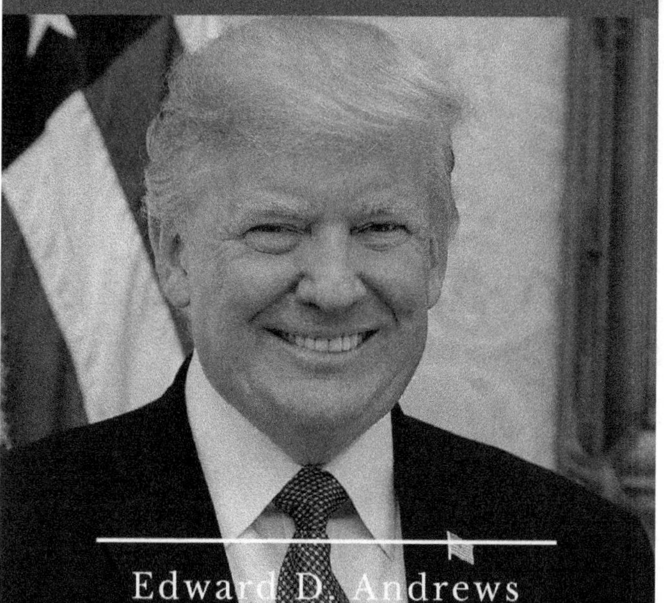

Obama
Donald Trump U.S.A. page 65

The apostasy or falling away and man revealed after restraint
129

UNITED STATES OF AMERICA IN BIBLE PROPHECY

THE KINGS OF THE NORTH & SOUTH OF DANIEL AND THE SEVEN KINGS OF REVELATION

Edward D. Andrews

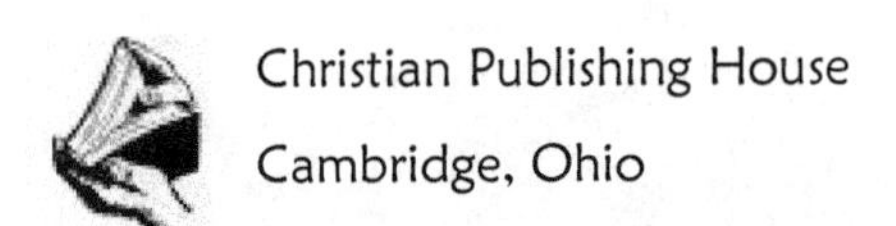

Christian Publishing House

Cambridge, Ohio

Unless otherwise indicated, Scripture quotations are from the Updated American Standard Version of the Holy Scriptures, 2017 edition (UASV).

UNITED STATES OF AMERICA IN BIBLE PROPHECY: THE KINGS OF THE NORTH & SOUTH OF DANIEL AND THE SEVEN KINGS OF REVELATION by Edward D. Andrews

ISBN-13: **978-1-945757-77-8**

ISBN-10: **1-945757-77-9**

HOLY
BIBLE

Table of Contents

INTRODUCTION

The first chapter will defend the authorship of Daniel and the time of his writing the book. It is imperative that the reader study this chapter. Why? Because Daniel either wrote the prophetic apocalyptic book that bears his name in the sixth century B.C.E. before the time of his prophecies, meaning that he is a legitimate prophet of God; or another fraudulent author penned the book in the second century B.C.E., which would be after most of the prophecies of the book, meaning it is simply repeating historical facts as prophecies.

The second chapter is an introduction on how a reader is to interpret a prophetic book based on the conservative, evangelical the historical-grammatical method of biblical interpretation (objective), as opposed to the liberal to moderate the historical-critical method of biblical interpretation (subjective). Chapters 3-6 cover the battle between the kings of the south and the kings of the north. While this will eventually culminate into a discussion of the United States of America, it is important that you take note of the kings of the south and the north beforehand, to see how detailed Daniel is in his prophetic message. Chapter 8 will cover what role the United States has played in the last days and how the election of Donald J. Trump as president was timely. Chapter 9-11 will identify the Antichrist, while chapter 12-13 will cover the Man of Lawlessness, with chapter 14 dealing with the Mark of the Beast. Finally, we close out AMERICA IN BIBLE PROPHECY explaining the signs of the end of the age.

AMERICA 1 Authorship of Daniel and Revelation Defended

Daniel Misjudged

You have a critical body that has formulated an opinion of the Bible, especially prophetic books, long before they have ever looked into the evidence. The liberal critical scholar is antisupernatural in their mindset. In other words, any book that would claim to have predicted events hundreds of years in advance are simply misrepresenting itself, as that foreknowledge is impossible. Therefore, the book must have been written after the events, yet written in such a way, as to mislead the reader that it was written hundreds of years before.

This is exactly what these critics say we have in the book of Daniel. However, what do we know about the person and the book itself? Daniel is known historically as a man of uprightness in the extreme. The book that he penned has been regarded highly for thousands of years. The context within says that it is authentic and true history, penned by Daniel, a Jewish prophet, who lived in the seventh and sixth centuries B.C.E. The chronology within the book shows that it covers the time period of 616 to 536 B.C.E., being completed by the latter date.

The New Encyclopædia Britannica acknowledges that the book of Daniel was once "generally considered to be true history, containing genuine prophecy." However, the *Britannica* asserts that in truth, Daniel "was written in a later time of national crisis—when the Jews were suffering severe persecution under [Syrian King] Antiochus IV Epiphanes." This encyclopedia dates the book between 167 and 164 B.C.E. *Britannica* goes on to assert that the writer of the book of Daniel does not prophesy the future but merely presents "events that are past history to him as prophecies of future happenings."

How does a book and a prophet that has enjoyed centuries of a reputable standing, garner such criticism? It actually began just two-hundred years after Christ, with Porphyry, a philosopher, who felt threatened by the rise of Christianity. His way of dealing with this new religion, was to pen fifteen books to undercut it, the twelfth being against Daniel. In the end, Porphyry labeled the book as a forgery, saying that it was written by a second-century B.C.E. Jew. Comparable attacks came in the 18th and 19th centuries. German scholars, who were prejudiced against the supernatural, started modern objections to the Book of Daniel.

As has been stated numerous times in this section, the higher critics and rationalists start with the presupposition that foreknowledge of future events is impossible. As was stated earlier in the chapter on Isaiah, the **important truth for the Bible critic is** the understanding that in all occurrences, prophecy pronounced or written in Bible times meant something to the people of the time it was spoken or written to; it was meant to serve as a guide for them. Frequently, it had specific fulfillment for that time, being fulfilled throughout the lifetime of that very generation. This is actually true; the words always had some application to the very people who heard them. However, the application could be a process of events, starting with the moral condition of the people in their relationship with Jehovah God, which precipitated the prophetic events that were to unfold, even those prophetic events that were centuries away.

However, it must be noted that while Daniel and Isaiah are both prophetic books, Daniel is also known as an apocalyptic book, as is the book of Revelation. This is not to say that Isaiah does not contain some apocalyptic sections (e.g., Isa 24–27; 56–66) What is assumed by the critical scholar here is that there is a rule that a prophet is understood in his day, to be only speaking of the immediate concerns of the people. They are looking at it more like a proclamation, instead of a future event that could be centuries away. Before addressing this concern, let us define apocalyptic for the reader:

Apocalyptic

This is a term derived from a Greek word meaning "revelation," and used to refer to a pattern of thought and to a form of literature, both dealing with future judgment (eschatology).

Two primary patterns of eschatological thought are found in the Bible, both centered in the conviction that God will act in the near future to save his people and to punish those who oppress them. In prophetic eschatology, the dominant form in the OT, God is expected to act within history to restore man and nature to the perfect condition which existed prior to man's fall. Apocalyptic eschatology, on the other hand, expects God to destroy the old imperfect order before restoring the world to paradise.

Origins of Apocalypticism

In Israel, apocalyptic eschatology evidently flourished under foreign domination.

From the early 6th century B.C., prophetic eschatology began to decline and apocalyptic eschatology became increasingly popular. The Book of Daniel, written during the 6th century B.C., is the earliest example of apocalyptic literature in existence.[1]

The problem with the modern critic is that he is attempting to look at the Biblical literature through the modern-day mindset. His first error is to believe that a prophetic book was viewed only as a proclamation of current affairs. The Jewish people viewed all prophetic literature just as we would expect, as a book of prophecy. The problem today is that many are not aware of the way they viewed the prophetic literature. While we do not have the space to go into the genre of prophecy and apocalyptic literature extensively, it is recommended that you see Dr. Stein's book in the bibliography at the end of the chapter.

Some Rules for Prophecy

- One needs to identify the beginning and end of the prophecy.
- The reader needs to find the historical setting.
- The Bible is a diverse book when it comes to literary styles: narrative, poetic, prophetic, and apocalyptic; also containing parables, metaphors, similes, hyperbole, and other figures of speech. Too often, these alleged errors are the result of a reader taking a figure of speech as literal, or reading a parable as though it is a narrative.
- Many alleged inconsistencies disappear by simply looking at the context. Taking words out of context can distort their meaning.
- Determine if the prophet is foretelling the future. On the other hand, is he simply proclaiming God's will and purpose to the people. (If prophetic, has any portion of it been fulfilled?)
- The concept of a second fulfillment should be set aside in place of implications.
- Does the New Testament expound on this prophecy?
- The reader needs to slow down and carefully read the account, considering exactly what is being said.

---

[1] Walter A. Elwell and Barry J. Beitzel, *Baker Encyclopedia of the Bible* (Grand Rapids, Mich.: Baker Book House, 1988), 122.

- The Bible student needs to understand the level that the Bible intends to be exact in what is written. If Jim told a friend that 650 graduated with him from high school in 1984, it is not challenged, because it is all too clear that he is using rounded numbers and is not meaning to be exactly precise.
- Unexplained does not equal unexplainable.

Digging into the ancient Jewish mindset, we find that it is dualistic. It views all of God's creation, either on the side of God or Satan. Further, the Jewish mind was determined that regardless of how bad things were, God would come to the rescue of his people. The only pessimistic thinking was their understanding that there had to be a major catastrophe that precipitated the rescue. In combining this way of thinking, they believed that there are two systems of things: (1) the current wicked one that man lives in, and (2) the one that is to come, where God will restore things to the way it was before Adam and Eve sinned. Jehovah impressed upon his people, to see His rescue as imminent. The vision that comes to Daniel in the book of Daniel and John in the book of Revelations, comes in one of two ways: (1) in a dreamed vision state or (2) the person in vision is caught up to heaven and shown what is to take place. Frequently, Isaiah, Daniel and John did not understand the vision; they were simply to pen what they saw. (Isa 6:9-10; 8:16; 29:9-14; 44:18; 53:1; Dan 8:15–26; 9:20–27; 10:18–12:4; Rev 7:13–17; 17:7–18) The people readily recognized the symbolism in most of the prophetic literature, and the less common symbolisms in apocalyptic literature were far more complex, which by design, heighten the desire to interpret and understand them. There are two very important points to keep in mind: (1) some were not meant to be understood fully at the time, and (2) only the righteous ones would have insight into these books, while the wicked would refuse to understand the spiritual things.

Daniel 8:26-27 Updated American Standard Version (UASV)

[26] The vision of the evenings and the mornings that has been told is true,[2] but seal up the vision,[3] for it refers to many days from now."[4]

[27] And I, Daniel, was exhausted and sick for days. Then I got up and carried out the business of the king, and I was disturbed over the vision and no one could understand it.[5]

---

[2] Lit *truth*; Heb., *'emet*

[3] I.e., keep the vision secret; Heb., *satar*

[4] Lit *for to days many*; I.e., to the distant future

[5] Lit *make* me *understand*

Daniel 10:14 Updated American Standard Version (UASV)

[14] Now I have come to give you an understanding of what will happen to your people in the end of the days, for it is a vision yet for the days to come."

Daniel 12:3-4 Updated American Standard Version (UASV)

[3] And the ones who are wise will shine brightly like the brightness of the expanse of heaven; and those who turn many to righteousness, like the stars forever and ever. [4] But as for you, O Daniel, conceal these words and seal up the book until the time of the end; many will go to and fro,[6] and knowledge will increase."

Daniel 12:9-10 Updated American Standard Version (UASV)

[9]He said, "Go your way, Daniel, for the words are shut up and sealed until the time of the end. [10]Many shall purify themselves and make themselves white and be refined, but the wicked shall act wickedly. And none of the wicked shall understand, but those who are wise shall understand.

2 Corinthians 4:3-4 Updated American Standard Version (UASV)

[3] And even if our gospel is veiled, it is veiled to those who are perishing. [4] In their case the god of this world has blinded the minds of the unbelievers, to keep them from seeing the light of the gospel of the glory of Christ, who is the image of God.

One of the principles of interpreting prophecy is to understand judgment prophecies. If a prophet declares judgment on a people, and they turn around from their bad course, the judgment may be lifted, which does not negate the trueness of the prophetic judgment message. There was simply a change in circumstances. There is a principle that most readers are not aware of:

Jeremiah 18:7-8 Updated American Standard Version (UASV)

[7] At one moment I might speak concerning a nation or concerning a kingdom to uproot, to tear down, and to destroy it; [8] and if that nation which I have spoken against turns from its evil, I will also feel regret over[7] the calamity that I intended to bring against it.

---

[6] I.e. examine the book thoroughly

[7] Lit *repent of*, .e., *I will change my mind concerning*, or *I will think better of*, or *I will relent concerning*

Another principle that needs to be understood is the language of prophecy. It uses imagery that is common to the people, with the exception of the highly apocalyptic literature. One form of imagery is the cosmic.

Isaiah 13:9-11 Updated American Standard Version (UASV)

[9] Behold, the day of Jehovah is coming,
cruel, with wrath and burning anger,
to make the land a desolation;
and he will destroy its sinners from it.
[10] For the stars of the heavens and their constellations
will not flash forth their light;
the sun will be dark when it rises,
and the moon will not shed its light.
[11] And I will punish the world for its evil,
and the wicked for their iniquity;
I will put an end to the arrogance of the proud,
and lay low the haughtiness of tyrants.

It is often assumed that this sort of imagery is talking about the end of the world, and this is not always the case. Using Isaiah 13 as our example, it is talking about a pronouncement against Babylon, not the end of the world, as can be seen in verse 1. This type of terminology is a way of expressing that God is acting in behalf of man. At times, figurative language can come across as contradicting for the modern-day reader. For example, in chapter 21 of Revelation the walls of Jerusalem are described as being 200 feet thick. The walls are an image of safety and security for the New Jerusalem. However, in verse 25 we read that the gates are never shut. This immediate leads to the question of why have walls that cannot be penetrated, and then leave the gates open? Moreover, if gates are the weakest point to defend, why have twelve of them (vs. 12)? To the modern militaristic mind, this comes off as contradictory, but not to the Jewish-Christian mind of the first-century. Both present the picture of safety. It is so safe that you can leave the gates open. What about the idea of a "fuller meaning" that the prophet was not aware of? As we saw in the above there would be symbolism meant for a day far into the future, but generally speaking, most prophets proclaimed a message that was applicable to their day, and implications for another day. Dr. Robert Stein addresses this issue:

> There are times when a prophetic text appears to have a fulfillment other than what the prophet himself apparently expected. (The following are frequently given as examples: Matt. 1:22–23; 2:15, 17–18; John 12:15; 1 Cor. 10:3–4.) Is it possible that a prophecy may have a deeper meaning or "fuller" sense than the prophet envisioned? . . . Rather than appealing to a "fuller sense" distinct and different from that of the biblical author,

however, it may be wiser to see if the supposed sensus plenior is in reality an implication of the author's conscious meaning. Thus, when Paul in 1 Corinthians 9:9 quotes Deuteronomy 25:4 ("do not muzzle an ox while it is treading out the grain") as a justification for ministers of the gospel living off the gospel, this is not a "fuller" meaning of the text unrelated to what the author sought to convey. Rather, it is a legitimate implication of the willed pattern of meaning contained in Deuteronomy 25:4. If as a principle animals should be allowed to share in the benefits of their work, how much more should the "animal" who is made in the image of God and proclaims the Word of God be allowed to share in the benefits of that work! Thus, what Paul is saying is not a fuller and different meaning from what the writer of Deuteronomy meant. On the contrary, although this specific implication was unknown to him, it is part of his conscious and willed pattern of meaning. Perhaps such prophecies as Matthew 1:22–23 and 2:15 are best understood as revealing implications of the original prophecies in Isaiah 7:14 and Hosea 11:1. Whereas in Isaiah's day the prophet meant that a maiden would give birth to a son who was named "Immanuel," that willed meaning also allows for a virgin one day to give birth to a son who would be Immanuel. Whereas God showed his covenantal faithfulness by leading his "son," his children, back from Egypt to the promised land in Moses' day so also did he lead his "Son," Jesus, back from Egypt to the promised land. [8]

Getting back to Daniel, we can clearly see that his book is prophetic and the only Old Testament apocalyptic book at that, which makes him a special target for the Bible critic. The critic has deemed that Daniel did not pen the book that bears his name, but another writer penned the words some centuries later.[9] These attacks have become such a reality that most scholars accept the late date of 165 B.C.E., by a pseudonym. As we have learned throughout this book, it is never the majority that establishes something as being true, simply for the fact of being the majority; it is the evidence. If the evidence proves that Daniel did not write the book, then the words are meaningless, and the hope that it contains is not there.

---

[8] Robert H. Stein, *A Basic Guide to Interpreting the Bible: Playing by the Rules* (Grand Rapids, MI: Baker Books, 1994), 97.

[9] Some Bible critics attempt to lessen the charge of forgery by saying that the writer used Daniel as a false name (pseudonym), just as some ancient noncanonical books were written under assumed names. In spite of this, the Bible critic Ferdinand Hitzig held: "The case of the book of Daniel, if it is assigned to any other [writer], is different. Then it becomes a forged writing, and the intention was to deceive his immediate readers, though for their good."

For example, take the allegation made in *The Encyclopedia Americana:* "Many historical details of the earlier periods [such as that of the Babylonian exile] have been badly garbled" in Daniel. Really? We will take up three of those alleged mistakes.

Claims That Belshazzar Is Missing From History

Daniel 5:1, 11, 18, 22, 30 Updated American Standard Version (UASV)

[1] Belshazzar the king made[10] a great feast for a thousand of his nobles, and he was drinking wine in the presence of the thousand.

[11] There is a man in your kingdom in whom is a spirit of the holy gods;[11] and in the days of your father, enlightenment, insight and wisdom like the wisdom of the gods were found in him. And King Nebuchadnezzar, your father, your father the king, appointed him chief of the magic-practicing priests, conjurers, Chaldeans and diviners.

[18] You. O king, the Most High God granted the kingdom and the greatness and the glory and the majesty to Nebuchadnezzar your father.

[22] "But you, his son[12] Belshazzar, have not humbled your heart, although you knew all of this,

[30] That same night Belshazzar the Chaldean king was killed.

In 1850 German scholar Ferdinand Hitzig said in a commentary on the book of Daniel, confidently declaring that Belshazzar was "a figment of the writer's imagination."[13] His reasoning was that Daniel was missing from history, only found in the book of Daniel itself. Does this not seem a bit premature? Is it so irrational to think that a person might not be readily located by archaeology, a brand new field at the time, especially from a period that was yet to be fully explored? Regardless, in 1854, there was a discovery of some small cylinders in the ancient city of Babylon and Ur, southern Iraq. The cuneiform documents were from King Nabonidus, and they included a prayer for "Belshazzar my firstborn son, the offspring of my heart." This discovery was a mere four years after Hitzig made his rash judgment.

---

[10] I.e., held

[11] Spirit of ... gods Aram., *ruach-'elahin';* Or possibly *the Spirit of the holy God*

[12] Or *descendant*

[13] *Das Buch Daniel.* Ferdinand Hitzig. Weidman (Leipzig) 1850.

Of course, not all critics would be satisfied. H. F. Talbot made the statement, "This proves nothing." The charge by Talbot was that Belshazzar was likely a mere child, but Daniel has him as being king. Well, this critical remark did not even stay alive as long as Hitzig's had. Within the year, more cuneiform tablets were discovered, this time they stated he had secretaries, as well as a household staff. Obviously, Belshazzar was not a child! However, more was to come, as other tablets explained that Belshazzar was a coregent king while Nabonidus was away from Babylon for years at a time.[14]

One would think that the critic might concede. Still disgruntled, some argued that the Bible calls Belshazzar, the son of Nebuchadnezzar, and not the son of Nabonidus. Others comment that Daniel nowhere mentions the name of Nabonidus. Once again, both arguments are dismantled with a deeper observation. Nabonidus married the daughter of Nebuchadnezzar, making Belshazzar the grandson of Nebuchadnezzar. Both Hebrew and Aramaic language do not have words for "grandfather" or "grandson"; "son of" also means "grandson of" or even "descendant of." (See Matthew 1:1.) Moreover, the account in Daniel does infer that Belshazzar is the son of Nabonidus. When the mysterious handwriting was on the wall, the horrified Belshazzar offered the *third* place in his kingdom, to whoever could interpret it. (Daniel 5:7) The observant reader will notice that Nabonidus held first place in the kingdom, while Daniel held the second place, leaving the third place for the interpreter.

Darius the Mede

One would think that the critic would have learned his lesson from Belshazzar. However, this is just not the case. Daniel 5:31 reads: "and Darius the Mede received the kingdom, being about sixty-two years old." Here again, the critical scholar argues that Darius does not exist, as he has never been found in secular or archaeological records. Therefore, *The New Encyclopædia Britannica* declares that this Darius is "a fictitious character."

There is no doubt that in time; Darius will be unearthed by archaeology, just as Belshazzar has. There is initial information that allows for inferences already. Cuneiform tablets have been discovered that shows Cyrus the Persian did not take over as the "King of Babylon" directly after

[14] When Babylon fell, Nabonidus was away. Therefore, Daniel was correct in that Belshazzar was the king at that time. Critics still try to cling to their Bible difficulty by stating that no secular records state that Belshazzar was a king. When will they quit with this quibbling? Even governors in the Ancient Near East were stated as being kings at times.

the conquest. Rather he carried the title "King of the Lands."[15] W. H Shea suggests, "Whoever bore the title of 'King of Babylon' was a vassal king under Cyrus, not Cyrus himself." Is it possible that Darius is simply a title of a person that was placed in charge of Babylon? Some scholars suggest a man named Gubaru was the real Darius. Secular records do show that Cyrus appointed Gubaru as governor over Babylon, giving him considerable power. Looking to the cuneiform tablets again, we find that Cyrus appointed subgovernors over Babylon. Fascinatingly, Daniel notes that Darius selected 120 satraps to oversee the kingdom of Babylon. – Daniel 6:1.

We should realize that archaeology is continuously bringing unknown people to light all the time, and in time, it may shed more light on Darius. However, for now, and based on the fact that many Bible characters have been established, it is a little ridiculous to consider Darius as "fictitious," worse still to view the whole of the book of Daniel as a fraud. In fact, it is best to see Daniel as a person, who was right there in the midst of that history, giving him access to more court records.

After Belshazzar (King of Babylon), Sargon (Assyrian Monarch), and the like have been assailed with being nonexistent, the Bible critic and liberal scholars do the same with Darius the Mede, and Mordecai in the book of Esther. This illustrates the folly of assigning boundless confidence in the ancient secular records, while we wait in secular sources to validate Scripture. Most outside of true conservative Christianity carry the presupposition that the Bible is myth, legend and erroneous until secular sources support it.

Bible critics argued profusely that Belshazzar was not a historical person. Then, evidence came in that substantiated Belshazzar, and the Bible critic just move on to another like Sargon, saying that he was not a real historical person, as though they had never raised such an objection for Belshazzar. Then, evidence came in that substantiated Sargon and the Bible critic would silently move on yet again. This is repeated time after time.

The Bible critics, liberal and moderate Bible scholars believe the Bible is wrong until validated by secular history. They move the goal post of trustworthiness as they please, so that Scripture will never be authentic and true, it will never be trustworthy, and to theses one, it is not the inspired, fully inerrant Word of God, as far as they are concerned.

---

[15] This evidence is found in royal titles in economic texts, which just so happens to date to the first two years of Cyrus' rule.

Why do we continue to cater to these ones, as though we need to appease them somehow?

King Jehoiakim

Daniel 1:1 Updated American Standard Version (UASV)

[1] In the third year of the reign of Jehoiakim king of Judah, Nebuchadnezzar king of Babylon came to Jerusalem and besieged it.

Jeremiah 25:1 Updated American Standard Version (UASV)

[1] The word that came to Jeremiah concerning all the people of Judah, in the fourth year of Jehoiakim the son of Josiah, king of Judah (that was the first year of Nebuchadnezzar king of Babylon),

Jeremiah 46:2 Updated American Standard Version (UASV)

[2] About Egypt, concerning the army of Pharaoh Neco king of Egypt, which was by the Euphrates River at Carchemish, which Nebuchadnezzar king of Babylon defeated in the fourth year of Jehoiakim the son of Josiah, king of Judah:

The Bible critic finds fault with Daniel 1:1 as it is not in harmony with Jeremiah, who says "in the fourth year of Jehoiakim the son of Josiah, king of Judah (that was the first year of Nebuchadnezzar king of Babylon)." The Bible student who looks a little deeper will find that there is really no contradiction at all. Pharaoh Necho first made Jehoiakim king in 628 B.C.E. Three years would pass before Nebuchadnezzar succeeded his father as King in Babylon, in 624 B.C.E. In 620 B.C.E., Nebuchadnezzar conquered Judah and made Jehoiakim the subordinate king under Babylon. (2 Kings 23:34; 24:1) Therefore, it is all about the perspective of the writer and where he was when penning his book. Daniel wrote from Babylon; therefore, Jehoiakim's third year would have been when he was made a subordinate king to Babylon. Jeremiah on the other hand, wrote from Jerusalem, so he is referring to the time when Jehoiakim was made a subordinate king under Pharaoh Necho.

This so-called discrepancy really just adds more weight to the fact that it was Daniel, who penned the book bearing his name. In addition, it must be remembered that Daniel had Jeremiah's book with him. (Daniel 9:2) Therefore, are we to believe that Daniel was this clever forger, and at the same time, he would contradict the well-known book of Jeremiah, especially in verse 1?

Positive Details

There are many details in the book of Daniel itself, which give credence to its authenticity. For example, Daniel 3:1-6 tells us that Nebuchadnezzar set up a huge image of gold, which his people were to worship. Archaeology has found evidence that credits Nebuchadnezzar with attempts to involve the people more in nationalistic and religious practices. Likewise, Daniel addresses Nebuchadnezzar's arrogant attitude about his many construction plans. (Daniel 4:30) It is not until modern-day archaeology uncovered evidence that we now know Nebuchadnezzar was the person who built much of Babylon. Moreover, his boastful attitude is made quite evident by having his name stamped on the bricks. This fact would not have been something a forger from 167-63 B.C.E. would have known about because the bricks hadn't at that time been unearthed.

The writer of Daniel was very familiar with the differences between Babylonian and Medo-Persian law. The three friends of Daniel were thrown into the fiery furnace for disobeying the Babylonian law, while Daniel, decades later under Persian law, was thrown into a lion's pit for violating the law. (Daniel 3:6; 6:7-9) Archaeology has again proven to be a great help, for they have uncovered an actual letter that shows the fiery furnace was a form of punishment. However, the Medes and Persians would have not used this form of punishment; as fire was sacred to them. Thus, they had other forms of capital punishment.

Another piece of inside knowledge is that Nebuchadnezzar passed and changed laws as he pleased. Darius on the other hand was unable to change a law once it was passed, even one that he himself had commissioned. (Daniel 2:5, 6, 24, 46-49; 3:10, 11, 29; 6:12-16) Historian John C. Whitcomb writes: "Ancient history substantiates this difference between Babylon, where the law was subject to the king, and Medo-Persia, where the king was subject to the law."

Daniel 5:1-4 Updated American Standard Version (UASV)

[1] Belshazzar the king made[16] a great feast for a thousand of his nobles, and he was drinking wine in the presence of the thousand.

[2] Belshazzar, when he tasted the wine, commanded that the vessels of gold and of silver that Nebuchadnezzar his father[17] had taken out of the temple in Jerusalem be brought, that the king and his nobles, his wives, and his concubines might drink from them. [3] Then they brought the gold vessels that had been taken out of the temple, the house of God which was in

---

[16] I.e., held

[17] Or *predecessor*; also verses 11, 13, 18

Jerusalem; and the king and his nobles, his wives and his concubines drank from them. 4 They drank the wine and praised the gods of gold and silver, of bronze, iron, wood and stone.

Archaeology has substantiated these kinds of feasts. The fact that stands out is the mention of women being present at the feast, the "wives, and his concubines" were present as well. Such an idea would have been repugnant to the Greeks and Jews of 167-67 B.C.E. era. This may very well be why the Greek Septuagint version of Daniel removed the mention of these women.[18] This so-called forger of Daniel would have live during this same time of the Septuagint.

Do External Factors Prove Daniel Is A Forgery?

Even the place of Daniel in the canon of the Hebrew Old Testament is evidence against his having written the book, so says the critics. The Jewish scribes (like Ezra) of ancient Israel arranged the books of the Old Testament into three groups: the Torah, the Prophets, and the Writings. Naturally, we would expect that Daniel would be found among the Prophets, yet they placed him among the Writings. Therefore, the critic makes the argument that Daniel had to of been an unknown when the works of the prophets were being collected. Their theory is that it was placed among the writings, because these were collected last.

However, not all Bible scholarship agree that the ancient scribes placed Daniel in the Writings, and not the Prophets. However, even if it is as they claim, Daniel was added among the Writings; this does nothing to prove that it was penned at a later date. Old Testament Bible scholar Gleason L. Archer states that . . .

> It should be noted that some of the documents in the Kethubhim [Writings] (the third division of the Hebrew Bible) were of great antiquity, such as the book of Job, the Davidic psalms, and the writings of Solomon. Position in the Kethubhim, therefore, is no proof of a late date of composition. Furthermore the statement in Josephus (Contra Apionem. 1:8) quoted previously in chapter 5 indicates strongly that in the first century A.D., Daniel was included among the prophets in the second division of the Old Testament canon; hence it could not have been assigned to the Kethubim until a later period. 349 The Masoretes may have been influenced in this reassignment by the

---

[18] Hebrew scholar C. F. Keil writes of Daniel 5:3: "The LXX. have here, and also at ver. 23, omitted mention of the women, according to the custom of the Macedonians, Greeks, and Romans."

> consideration that Daniel was not appointed or ordained as a prophet, but remained a civil servant under the prevailing government throughout his entire career. Second, a large percentage of his writings does not bear the character of prophecy, but rather of history (chaps. 1-6), such as does not appear in any of the books of the canonical prophets.350 Little of that which Daniel wrote is couched in the form of a message from God to His people relayed through the mouth of His spokesman. Rather, the predominating element consists of prophetic visions granted personally to the author and interpreted to him by angels.[19]

The critic also turns his attention to the Apocryphal book, Ecclesiasticus, by Jesus Ben Sirach, penned about 180 B.C.E., as evidence that Daniel did not pen the book that bears his name. Ecclesiasticus has a long list of righteous men, of which, Daniel is missing. From this, they conclude that Daniel had to of been an unknown at the time. However, if we follow that line of reasoning; what do we do with the fact that the same list omits: Ezra and Mordecai, good King Jehoshaphat, and the upright man Job; of all the judges, except Samuel.[20] Simply because the above faithful and righteous men are missing from a list in an apocryphal book, are we to dismiss them as having never existed? The very idea is absurd.

Sources in Favor of Daniel

> Ezekiel's references to Daniel must be considered to be one of the strongest arguments for a sixth-century date. No satisfactory explanation exists for the use of the name Daniel by the prophet Ezekiel other than that he and Daniel were contemporaries and that Daniel had already become widely known throughout the Babylonian Empire by the time of Ezekiel's ministry.[21]

---

[19] Archer, Gleason (1996-08-01). A Survey of Old Testament Introduction (Kindle Locations 7963-7972). Moody Publishers.

[20] If we turn our attention to the Apostle Paul's list of faithful men and women found in Hebrews chapter 11; it does appear to mention occasions recorded in Daniel. (Daniel 6:16-24; Hebrews 11:32, 33) Nevertheless, the list by Paul is not an exhaustive list either. Even within his list, Isaiah, Jeremiah, and Ezekiel are not named in the list, but this scarcely demonstrates that they never existed.

[21] Stephen R. Miller, vol. 18, *Daniel*, electronic ed., Logos Library System; The New American Commentary (Nashville: Broadman & Holman Publishers, 2001), 42-43.

We have in chapter 9 a series of remarkable predictions which defy any other interpretation but that they point to the coming of Christ and His crucifixion [about] A.D. 30, followed by the destruction of the city of Jerusalem within the ensuing decades. In Dan. 9:25–26, it is stated that sixty-nine heptads of years (i.e., 483 years) will ensue between a "decree" to rebuild the walls of Jerusalem, and the cutting off of Messiah the Prince. In 9:25–26, we read: "Know therefore and understand, that from the going forth of the commandment to restore and to build Jerusalem unto the Messiah the Prince shall be seven weeks, and threescore and two weeks.... And after threescore and two weeks shall Messiah be cut off, but not for himself: and the people of the prince that shall come shall destroy the city and the sanctuary."[22]

The Greatest Evidence for Daniel

First of all, we have the clear testimony of the Lord Jesus Himself in the Olivet discourse. In Matt. 24:15, He refers to "the abomination of desolation, spoken of through [*dia*] Daniel the prophet." The phrase "abomination of desolation" occurs three times in Daniel (9:27; 11:31; 12:11). If these words of Christ are reliably reported, we can only conclude that He believed the historic Daniel to be the personal author of the prophecies containing this phrase. No other interpretation is possible in the light of the preposition *dia*, which refers to personal agency. It is significant that Jesus regarded this "abomination" as something to be brought to pass in a future age rather than being simply the idol of Zeus set up by Antiochus in the temple, as the Maccabean theorists insist.[23]

While this has certainly been an overview of the evidence in favor of the authenticity of Daniel, there will never be enough to satisfy the critic. One professor at Oxford University wrote: "Nothing is gained by a mere answer to objections, so long as the original prejudice, 'there cannot be supernatural prophecy,' remains." What does this mean? It means that the critic is blinded by his prejudice. However, God has given them the choice of free will.

---

[22] Gleason Leonard Archer, *A Survey of Old Testament Introduction*, 3rd. ed.]. (Chicago: Moody Press, 1998), 445.

[23] Gleason Leonard Archer, *A Survey of Old Testament Introduction*, 3rd. ed.]. (Chicago: Moody Press, 1998), 444.

The Bible critics are ever so vigilant today. They are more prepared than most Christians, and witness about their doubts far more than your average Christian witnesses about his or her faith.

1 Peter 3:15 Updated American Standard Version (UASV)

[15] but sanctify Christ as Lord in your hearts, always being prepared to make a defense[24] to anyone who asks you for a reason for the hope that is in you; yet do it with gentleness and respect;

Peter says that we must be prepared to make a *defense*. The Greek word behind the English "defense" is *apologia* (apologia), which is actually a legal term that refers to the defense of a defendant in court. Our English apologetics is just what Peter spoke of, having the ability to give a reason to any who may challenge us, or to answer those who are not challenging us but who have honest questions that deserve to be answered.

To whom was the apostle Peter talking? Who was Peter saying needed always to be prepared to make a defense? Was he talking only to the pastors, elders, servants, or was he speaking to all Christians? Peter opens this letter saying, "to the chosen who are residing temporarily in the dispersion in Pontus, Galatia, Cappadocia, Asia, and Bithynia." Who are these "chosen" ones? The College Press NIV Commentary gives us the answer,

The Greek text does not include the word "God's," but the translation is a fair one since the clear implication is that God did the choosing. The word Peter uses has a rich biblical heritage. The Jews found their identity and the basis of their lives in the fact that they were God's chosen people (see, e.g., Deut 7:6–8). The New Testament frequently identifies Christians as elect or chosen. In 1 Peter 2:9 Peter will identify Christians as "a chosen people," using the same word ἐκλεκτός (*eklektos*) here translated "elect." The same word is also used of Christ in 2:4 and 6 (where it is translated "chosen"). Christians are chosen or elect through the chosen or elect One, Jesus Christ. The idea that Christians are God's chosen people is fundamental to Peter's thinking, as is apparent in 1:13–2:10. Peter is already laying the foundation for his appeals to these Christians to live up to their holy calling. (Black and Black 1998)

The "chosen who are residing temporarily in the dispersion" were Christians, who were living among **non**-Christian Jews and Gentiles. This letter, then, is addressed to all Christians, but the context of chapters 1:3 to 4:11 is mostly addressed to newly baptized Christians. Therefore, all Christians are obligated to 'be prepared to make a defense to anyone who asks us for a reason for the hope that is in us.' Yes, we are all required to

---

[24] Or *argument*; or *explanation*

defend our hope successfully. If any have not felt they were up to the task, this author by way of Christian publishing House are publishing books to help along those lines. Here is what is available at present, including this publication you are reading,

CONVERSATIONAL EVANGELISM, [Second Edition] by Edward D. Andrews

THE CHRISTIAN APOLOGIST: Always Being Prepared to Make a Defense [Second Edition] By Edward D. Andrews

CHRISTIAN APOLOGETIC EVANGELISM: Reaching Hearts with the Art of Persuasion by Edward D Andrews

THE EVANGELISM HANDBOOK: How All Christians Can Effectively Share God's Word in Their Community, [SECOND EDITION], by Edward D. Andrews

These first-century Christians in Asia Minor were in a time of difficulty. They were at the time of Peter's letter; about 62-64 C.E. going through some trials, not knowing that many far more severe lie in the not too distant future. Within a few years, the persecution of Christians by Emperor Nero would begin. These new converts had given up former religions, idols, cults and superstitions, their 'the futile ways inherited from your forefathers.' (1 Pet. 1:18) These one's were taking of their old person, and bringing their lives in harmony with God's Word, such as 'malice and deceit and hypocrisy and envy and slander.' (1 Pet. 2:1) Now they were 'no longer living for the lusts of men, but for the will of God.' (1 Pet. 4:2) Their former pagan friends now hated these new Christians, because 'they were surprised when these chosen ones do not join them in the same flood of debauchery, and they maligned them.' (1 Pet. 4:4) In fact, Peter informs us that Satan, the Devil is enraged when one is converted from their former life of debauchery, conformed instead to the Word of God. Peter warned them, "Be sober-minded; be watchful. Your adversary the devil prowls around like a roaring lion, seeking someone to devour." 1 Peter 5:8

Christians have never really had it easy in defending their hope. Peter counsels these new ones, who have next to no experience in coping with trials and persecutions to rejoice, albeit distressed by numerous trials. "**Keep your conduct among the Gentiles honorable**, so that when they speak against you as evildoers, they may see your good deeds and glorify God on the day of visitation." (1 Pet. 2:12) "The end of all things is at hand; therefore **be self-controlled and sober-minded for the sake of your prayers.**" 1 Pet. 4:4) "Be sober-minded; be watchful" in the midst of men who continue "living in sensuality, passions, drunkenness, orgies, drinking parties, and lawless idolatry." (1 Pet. 4:3) They should be united under Christ as they 'Have purified their souls by their obedience to the truth for a sincere brotherly love, love one another earnestly from a pure heart." (1 Peter 1:22) "Above all, [they were to] keep loving one another earnestly, since love covers a multitude of sins. Show hospitality to one another without grumbling. As each has received a gift, use it to serve one another, as good stewards of God's varied grace." (1 Pet 4:8-10) 'Finally, all of them, had unity of mind, sympathy, brotherly love, a tender heart, and a humble mind. They did not repay evil for evil or reviling for reviling, but on the contrary, they blessed, for to this they were called, that you may obtain a blessing.' (1 Pet. 3:8-9) If they heeded this counsel, it would have kept them from falling or drifting back into their former ways.

There was one more obligation, if they were to preserve on the right path of conduct, namely, being prepared to make a defense for their hope. "It was revealed to [the prophets] that they were serving not themselves but you, in the things that have now been announced to you through those who preached the good news to you by the Holy Spirit sent from heaven, things into which angels long to look. Therefore, preparing your minds for action, and being sober-minded, set your hope fully on the grace that will be brought to you at the revelation of Jesus Christ." (1 Pet. 1:12-13) Peter went on to tell them that they were "a chosen race, a royal priesthood, a holy nation, a people for his own possession, that you may proclaim the excellencies of him who called you out of darkness into his marvelous light." (1 Pet. 2:9) When should they "proclaim these excellencies"? He writes, "but in your hearts honor Christ the Lord as holy, **always being prepared** to make a defense to anyone who asks you for a reason for the hope that is in you; yet do it with gentleness and respect." 1 Peter 3:15

The world in which we live today is much more vast than that of the first-century up unto the 21st-century. The trials and persecution today are much more intense, which unfortunately we ca watch around the world, by way of the media and social media. The greatest threat to Christianity is Islam, which has been an ardent enemy of Christianity since the seventh-century C.E. They are slaughtering Christians the world over. They view Christians as the big Satan and the Jews as little Satan. In their theology, they are looking to turn the world into one big Islamic state, governed by the Quran. For the more radical aspects of Islam, it is convert to Islam or be killed as an infidel.

The second greatest threat to tradition and conservatism is liberal Christianity. Their continued dissecting of the Scriptures until Moses did not pen the first five books, Isaiah is not the author of the book that bears his name, nor is Daniel the author of the book that bears his name, and the Bible is full of myths and legends, errors and contractions.

Then, as we have seen throughout this publication, there are moderate and liberal Bible scholars, who are advocates of Historical Criticism

Methodology, and its sub-criticisms: Source Criticism, Tradition Criticism, Form Criticism, Redaction Criticism, among others.

2 Timothy 2:24-25 Updated American Standard Version (ASV)

[24] For a slave of the Lord does not need to fight, but needs to be kind to all, qualified to teach, showing restraint when wronged, [25] instructing his opponents with gentleness, if perhaps God may grant them repentance leading to accurate knowledge [*epignosis*][25] of the truth,

Look at the Greek word (*epignosis*) behind the English "knowledge" from above. "It is more intensive than *gnosis*, knowledge, because it expresses a more thorough participation in the acquiring of knowledge on the part of the learner."[26] The requirement of all of the Lord's servants is that they be able to teach, but not in a quarrelsome way, but in a way to correct opponents with mildness. Why? The purpose of it all is that by God, yet through the Christian teacher, one may come to repentance and begin taking in an accurate knowledge of the truth.

> Some Christians see apologetics as pre-evangelism; it is not the gospel, but it prepares the soil for the gospel.[27] Others make no such distinction, seeing apologetics, theology, philosophy, and evangelism as deeply entwined facets of the gospel.[28] Whatever its relation to the gospel, apologetics **is an extremely important enterprise that can profoundly impact unbelievers** and be used as the tool that clears the way to faith in Jesus Christ. (Bold mine.)
>
> Many Christians did not come to believe as a result of investigating the Bible's authority, the evidence for the resurrection, or as a response to the philosophical arguments for God's existence. They responded to the proclamation of the gospel. Although these people have reasons for their belief, they are deeply personal reasons that often do not make sense to unbelievers. **They know the truth but are not necessarily equipped to share or articulate the truth in a way that is understandable** to those who have questions about their faith. It

---

[25] *Epignosis* is a strengthened or intensified form of *gnosis* (*epi,* meaning "additional"), meaning, "true," "real," "full," "complete" or "accurate," depending upon the context. Paul and Peter alone use *epignosis.*

26. Spiros Zodhiates, *The Complete Word Study Dictionary: New Testament,* Electronic ed. (Chattanooga, TN: AMG Publishers, 2000, c1992, c1993), S. G1922.

[27] Norman Geisler and Ron Brooks, When Skeptics Ask (Grand Rapids: Baker Books, 1996), 11.

[28] Greg Bahnsen, Van Til Apologetic (Phillipsburg, NJ: Presbyterian and Reformed, 1998), 43.

is quite possible to believe something is true without having a proper understanding of it or the ability to articulate it. (Bold mine.)

Christians who believe but do not know why are often insecure and comfortable only around other Christians. Defensiveness can quickly surface when challenges arise on issues of faith, morality, and truth because of a lack of information regarding the rational grounds for Christianity. At its worst, this can lead to either a fortress mentality or a belligerent faith, precisely the opposite of the Great Commission Jesus gave in Matthew 28:19–20. The Christian's charge is not to withdraw from the world and lead an insular life. Rather, we must be engaged in the culture, to be salt and light.

The solution to this problem requires believers to become informed in doctrine, the history of their faith, philosophy, logic, and other disciplines as they relate to Christianity. Believers must know the facts, arguments and theology and understand how to employ them in a way that will effectively engage the culture. Believers need Christian apologetics. One of the first tasks of Christian apologetics provides information. A number of widely held assumptions about Christianity can be easily challenged with a little information. This is even true for persons who are generally well-educated.[29]

The ability to reason with others will take time, practice and patience. For example, if someone reasons with others successfully, that person must be reasonable. In a discussion about the historicity about Jesus, a believer knows the other person denying the existence of Jesus is wrong. Moreover, believers possess a truckload of evidence to support this position. However, it is best sometimes to not unload the truck by dumping the entire load at a listener's feet in one conversation, or in one breath. Being reasonable does not mean that a believer compromises the truth because he or she does not unload on the listener.

The other person will likely make many wrong statements in the conversation, and we should let most of them go unchallenged; rather, focus on a handful of the most crucial pieces of evidence and do not get lost by refuting every wrong statement. He may make bold condemnatory statements about many Christian beliefs, but we need to remain calm and not make a big deal of those statements. Listen carefully to the other person, and stay within the boundaries of the evidence in the conversation. For

---

[29] Powell, Doug (2006-07-01). *Holman QuickSource Guide to Christian Apologetics* (Holman Quicksource Guides) (p. 6-7). B&H Publishing. Kindle Edition.

example, in a conversation on the historicity of Jesus when the listener states, "The New Testament manuscripts were completely corrupted in the copying process for a millennium, to the point that we do not even have the supposed Word of God." The evidence for the historicity of Jesus rests in the first and second century, so it would be a fool's errand to get into an extensive side subject about the restoration of the New Testament text, which took place over the centuries that followed the first two centuries C.E. There will be another day to talk about the history of the Greek New Testament, but today focus on the historicity of Jesus Christ.

God has given humanity free will, meaning each human has the right to choose, even if that choice is unwise. Believers have the assignment of proclaiming "the good news of the kingdom," as well as "making disciples" of redeemable humankind. Therefore, we must not pressure, coerce, or force people to accept the truth of that "Good News." However, all Christians have an obligation to reason with anyone by respectfully, gently, and mildly overturning their false reasoning, in the attempt that being used by God we may save some.

Evidence that Revelation Is Authentic and Inspired

1 Revelation of Jesus Christ which gave to him the God to show
'Αποκάλυψις Ἰησοῦ , ἣν ἔδωκεν αὐτῷ ὁ θεὸς δεῖξαι
to the slaves of him
τοῖς δούλοις αὐτοῦ,
which (things it is binding to occur in quickness and he showed by signs
ἃ δεῖ γενέσθαι ἐν , καὶ ἐσήμανεν
having sent off through the angel of him to the slave of him
ἀποστείλας διὰ τοῦ ἀγγέλου αὐτοῦ τῷ δούλῳ αὐτοῦ Ἰωάνει,

1 Ἀποκάλυψις Ἰησοῦ Χριστοῦ ἣν ἔδωκεν αὐτῷ ὁ θεὸς
Revelation of Jesus Christ that gave to him the God

δεῖξαι τοῖς δούλοις αὐτοῦ ἃ δεῖ γενέσθαι ἐν τάχει ,
to show to the slaves of him what is necessary to become in quickness

καὶ ἐσήμανεν ἀποστείλας διὰ τοῦ ἀγγέλου αὐτοῦ τῷ
and he signified having delegated through the messenger of him to the

δούλῳ αὐτοῦ **Ἰωάννῃ**,
slave of him **John**
[30]

[30] Eberhard Nestle et al., *The Greek New Testament*, 27th ed. (Deutsche Bibelgesellschaft: Stuttgart, 1993), Re 1.

Revelation 1:1 Updated American Standard Version (UASV)

1 The revelation of Jesus Christ, which God gave him, to show his slaves the things that must shortly take place; and he sent his angel and presented it in signs through him to his slave **John**,

Who is John that is referred to as the author of Revelation? The account above from 1:1 tells us that he was a slave of Jesus Christ and 1:9 tells us, "I John, **your brother** and a **sharer with you in the tribulation** and kingdom and the patient endurance that are in Jesus, was **on the island called Patmos** because of the word of God and the testimony about Jesus." This being so vague means that the author must have been well-known to his readers as no further identification was necessary. The most well-known John was the apostle John. Papias, who wrote in the first part of the second century C.E., is said to have held the book to be of apostolic origin. Says Justin Martyr, of the second century, "There was a certain man with us, whose name was John, one of the apostles of Christ, who prophesied, by a revelation that was made to him."[31]

Some have argued that the apostle John's other writings contained tremendous emphasis on love, which they use to suggest that he could have written Revelation. However, a different genre of writing called for a very forceful and dynamic writing style. If we recall it was John and his brother James, who were filled with indignation against the Samaritans of a certain city, to the point where they wanted to call down fire from heaven. That is why they were given the surname "Boanerges, that is, "Sons of Thunder" (Mark 3:17; Luke 9:54) Again, this departure in writing style should cause no difficulty when we remember that in Revelation the subject matter has changed. What John was shown in these visions is unlike anything he had ever seen before. Moreover, it is the Holy Spirit that gave him his subject matter. In addition, we must keep in mind the exraordinary harmony of the book with the rest of the prophetic Scriptures indisputably proves it to be an authentic, fully inerrant part of the inspired Word of God.[32] Lastly, Dr. Norman L. Geisler writes,

---

[31] Justin Martyr *Dialogue with Trypho* 81, in *The Ante-Nicene Fathers*, ed. Alexander Roberts and James Donaldson, vol. 1, *The Apostolic Fathers, Justin Martyr, and Irenaeus* (reprint, Grand Rapids: Eerdmans, n.d.), p. 240. Note that the elapsed time between John's death (presumably in a.d. 98) and Justin Martyr's comment is less then forty years, when eyewitnesses could still testify to the veracity of his statement. Irenaeus (Eusebius *Eccl. Hist.* 3.39.5–6) writes that the apostle John lived "until the times of Trajan," who was emperor from 98 to 117.

[32] Geisler writes, "External Evidence (1) Justin Martyr called the author 'A certain man among us, whose name was John, one of the apostles of Christ ...' (Justin, Against Heresies). (2) Irenaeus, an early resident of Asia, cited it as John's writing. (3) The Shepherd of Hernias refers to it. (4) The early Muratorian canon includes it in the Bible. (5) Other early Fathers cited it as coming from John the apostle, including Tertullian, Hippolytus, Clement of

No one else but the apostle John could use just his name, John, and have his book accepted. (3) It is the only hook, other than the Gospel of John (also written by the apostle John), to refer to Christ as the Word (Logos) in the personal sense (John 1:1; Rev. 19:13). (4) The basic style and content use of the Greek fit the apostle John.' (5) The vocabulary has a strong overlap, with 416 words in the Gospel the same as 913 separate words in Revelation. (6) The author's detailed knowledge of the land and events fits the apostle John (chaps. 1-3).[33]

When we look at the earliest evidence, the late date of 95 C.E. fits the apostle John alone, as he lived to 100 C.E., which was twenty-five years after the destruction of Jerusalem. This would have been toward the end of the reign of Emperor Domitian (81-96 C.E.). In verification of this, Irenaeus (born between 120 C.E. and 140 C.E.; died about 200 C.E.) in his "Against Heresies" says of the Apocalypse, "For that was seen no very long time since, but almost in our day, towards the end of Domitian's reign.[34] both Eusebius and Jerome agree with this testimony.

Roman Emperor Titus (79-81 C.E.) was the brother of Domitian. It was then general Titus, who formerly had directed the effective assault on Jerusalem, destroying the city. Domitian became the emperor at the death of Titus, fifteen years before the book of Revelation was penned. He commanded that he be worshiped as god and took the title "*Dominus et Deus noster ('our Lord and God').*"[35] The first-century Christian could not and would not in worship of false gods, as they refused to compromise their faith. It was at the end of Domitian's reign when extremely severe persecution was being handed out to the Christians that John was exiled to Patmos by Domitian. It was in 96 C.E. that Domitian was assassinated, wherein he was succeeded by the more tolerant emperor Nerva, who was the one to release John from Patmos. John wrote down these visions that he saw while he was imprisoned on Patmos.

Alexandria, Origen, Athanasius, and Augustine. (6) Later voices to reject John's authorship did so on dogmatic grounds, largely because they opposed John's millennialism (chap. 20) and used an allegorical method of interpretation. (7) The alleged assertion by Papias that John was martyred before AU) 70 is contradicted by many other sources (see points 1-6) and is subject to other interpretations." – Norman Geisler. *A Popular Survey of the New Testament*, (pp. 310-311).

[33] Norman Geisler. *A Popular Survey of the New Testament*, (p. 310).

[34] Irenaeus of Lyons, "Irenæus against Heresies," in *The Apostolic Fathers with Justin Martyr and Irenaeus*, ed. Alexander Roberts, James Donaldson, and A. Cleveland Coxe, vol. 1, The Ante-Nicene Fathers (Buffalo, NY: Christian Literature Company, 1885), 559–560.

[35] Grant R. Osborne, *Revelation*, Baker Exegetical Commentary on the New Testament (Grand Rapids, MI: Baker Academic, 2002), 513.

AMERICA 2 Interpreting Prophecy

Most understand the word "prophecy" to be another word for prediction. The Hebrew, *navi* and the Greek *prophētēs* (prophet), carry the meaning of one who is a proclaimer of God's message and need not necessarily be foretelling of the future. He may very well be proclaiming a moral teaching, an expression of a divine command or judgment, but they also mean a foretelling of something to come. Below, we will be considering the secondary meaning of prophecy, one who for *foretells* the future, not the primary meaning, one who *forth tells* the will and purpose of God, i.e. a proclaimer. Just as it is true of all these genres, there are principles that both writer and reader were aware of, and need be explained. We, however, are far removed from their time and need to be introduced to these principles.

The Prophetic Judgment of Nineveh

Deuteronomy 18:20-22 Updated American standard Version (UASV)

[20] But the prophet who speaks a word presumptuously in my name which I have not commanded him to speak, or which he speaks in the name of other gods, that prophet shall die.' [21] You may say in your heart, 'How will we know the word which Jehovah has not spoken?' [22] When a prophet speaks in the name of Jehovah, if the word does not come to pass or come true, that is a word that Jehovah has not spoken; the prophet has spoken it presumptuously; you shall not be afraid of him.

Jonah 3:4-5 Updated American standard Version (UASV)

[4] And Jonah began to go into the city a journey of one day, and he cried out and said, "Yet forty days, and Nineveh shall be overthrown!" [5] And the people of Nineveh believed God. They called for a fast and put on sackcloth, from the greatest of them to the least of them.

Jonah 3:10 Updated American standard Version (UASV)

[10] When God saw their deeds, that they turned from their wicked way, then God relented concerning the calamity which he had said he would do to them, and he did not do it.

Based on Deuteronomy 18:20-222, does Jonah 3:4-5 and 10 not prove that Jonah was a false prophet. No, both Jonah and the Ninevites were aware of a principle that is often overlooked by the modern-day reader. Both Jeremiah and Ezekiel give the answer or the principle that readers of that time would have understood about judgment prophecy. Jeremiah explicitly explains the rule of judgment prophecies, when he writes,

Jeremiah 18:7-8 Updated American standard Version (UASV)

[7] At one moment I might speak concerning a nation or concerning a kingdom to uproot, to tear down, and to destroy it; [8] and if that nation which I have spoken against turns from its evil, I will also feel regret over[36] the calamity that I intended to bring against it.

The opposite is true as well,

Jeremiah 18:9-10 Updated American standard Version (UASV)

[9] Or at another moment I might speak concerning a nation or concerning a kingdom to build up or to plant it; [10] if it does evil in my eyes by not obeying my voice, then I will feel regret over[37] the good with which I had promised to bless it.

Yes, if one turns back from their evil ways, endeavoring to obey God's Word, he will not receive the condemnatory judgment that he deserves. That a previous wicked deed will not be held against them, God states,

Ezekiel 33:13-16 Updated American standard Version (UASV)

[13] When I say to the righteous one: "You will surely keep living," and he trusts in his own righteousness and does injustice, none of his righteous acts will be remembered, but he will die for the wrong that he has done. [14] "'And when I say to the wicked one: "You will surely die," and he turns away from his sin and does what is just and righteous, [15] and the wicked one returns what was taken in pledge and pays back what was taken by robbery, and he walks in the statutes of life by not doing what is wrong, he will surely keep living. He will not die. [16] None of his sins that he has committed will be remembered against him. He has practiced justice and righteousness; he shall surely live.

Regardless of all that one has done throughout their life, it is their standing in God's eyes at the time of the divine judgment, which God

---

[36] Lit *repent of*; .e., *I will change my mind concerning*; or *I will think better of*, or *I will relent concerning*

[37] Lit *repent*; I.e., *I will change my mind concerning*; or *I will think better of*, or *I will relent concerning*

considers. Therefore, God goes on to say through Ezekiel, "None of his sins that he has committed will be remembered against him."

Supposed Unfulfilled Prophecy

In the days when Micah was prophesying, c. 777-717, the king, the heads of the Jerusalem government, the religious leaders, the priests, and some prophets, were deserving of nothing but death. All were guilty of causing the life of their fellow countrymen, all for the sake of greed. They were guilty of false worship, bribery, lies, and wicked behavior. These leaders used false prophets, who were not true spokesmen of God. Therefore, the real prophet, Micah, shouted,

Micah 3:12 Updated American Standard Version (UASV)

[12] Therefore because of you
Zion shall be plowed as a field;
Jerusalem shall become a heap of ruins,
and the mountain[38] of the house as a high place in a forest.

The destruction occurred in the late seventh-century B.C.E., just as it was prophesied. As we can see below, Micah 3:12 was quoted over a century later in Jeremiah 26:18.

Jeremiah 26:16-19 Updated American Standard Version (UASV)

[16] Then the officials and all the people said to the priests and the prophets, "This man is not worthy of death; for he hath spoken to us in the name of Jehovah our God." [17] Then rose up certain of the elders of the land, and spoke to all the assembly of the people, saying, [18] "Micah the Morashtite prophesied in the days of Hezekiah king of Judah; and he spoke to all the people of Judah, saying: 'Thus says Jehovah of hosts,

"'Zion shall be plowed as a field;
Jerusalem shall become a heap of ruins,
and the mountain of the house a wooded height.'

[19] Did Hezekiah king of Judah and all Judah put him to death? Did he not fear Jehovah and entreat the favor of Jehovah, and Jehovah changed his mind about the misfortune, which he had pronounced against them? But we are committing a great evil against our own souls."

Is this another unfulfilled prophecy? Did not Jeremiah himself say, "Jehovah changed his mind about the misfortune, which he had

---

[38] I.e., *the temple mount*

pronounced against them"? Verse 19 of Jeremiah [chapter 26] "indicates that Micah's preaching may have been instrumental in the revival under King Hezekiah (see 2 Kgs 18:1–6; 2 Chr 29–31)." (Barker and Bailey 2001, 82) The New American Commentary authors go on to say,

> Lamentations describes the awful fulfillment of this prophecy (see Introduction, p. 30).[39] It is ironic that those who thought they were the builders of Zion (v. 10) actually turned out to be, in a sense, its destroyers. The Lord, because of their breach of covenant, used King Nebuchadnezzar's Neo-Babylonian army to raze Jerusalem and its temple. They were reduced to a "mound of ruins" (translating the Hb. word *ʿîyyîn*) similar to an archaeological tell and to Ai (see also comments on 1:6), foreshadowing the Roman destruction of a.d. 70. Jerusalem became a place suitable only for wild animals. And the temple mount that thronged with worshipers became as deserted as when Abraham almost offered Isaac there on Mount Moriah (Gen 22:2, 14). (Barker and Bailey 2001, 82)

Yes, there is no reason to view Micah's words as an unfulfilled prophecy. What we have here is a following of the above rule, with a qualifying clause, so to speak. As God said through Jeremiah, "If at any time I say that I am going to uproot, break down, or destroy any nation or kingdom, but then that nation turns from its evil, I will not do what I said I would." (17:7-8) However, "if I say that I am going to plant or build up any nation or kingdom, but then that nation disobeys me and does evil, I will not do what I said I would." In other words, the king, the governmental leaders and the priests heeded Micah's warning, repented, and were forgiven for a time, with the judgment prophecy lifted. However, they fell back into their former ways, even more grievously than before. Therefore, Micah's prophecy was reinstated. It is as Jeremiah said in 26:19, "But we are committing a great evil against our own souls." Therefore, Jeremiah was saying, Micah prophesied, the people repented, God forgave them, and now Micah's words will be carried out, because of the current generation of God's people 'committing a great evil against their own souls.'

As we can see from the above, judgment prophecies are based on a continued wrong course by those receiving condemnation. However, both the condemned and the one proclaiming the prophecy knew that the judgment would be lifted if they reversed course, and repented. This was even expressed by Jonah himself. "But it displeased Jonah exceedingly, and he was angry. And he prayed to Jehovah and said, "O Jehovah, is not this

---

[39] Cf. Lam 1:1, 4, 6, 18–19; 2:2, 6, 9–10, 20; 5:17–18, etc.

what I said when I was yet in my country? That is why I made haste to flee to Tarshish; for I knew that you are a gracious God and merciful, slow to anger and abounding in steadfast love, and relenting from disaster." (4:1-2) However, it is also true, if one goes in the opposite direction after having repented, returning to the sinful ways, the judgment will be reinstated.

Prophetic Language

The prophet is much like the poet, in that he is given a license to express himself in nonliteral language. Generally, he is working with images that are far more effective than words themselves.

Matthew 24:29-31 Updated American Standard Version (UASV)

The Coming of the Son of Man

[29] "But immediately after the tribulation of those days the sun will be darkened, and the moon will not give its light, and the stars will fall from heaven, and the powers of the heavens will be shaken. [30] And then will appear in heaven the sign of the Son of Man, and then all the tribes of the earth will mourn, and they will see the Son of Man coming on the clouds of heaven with power and great glory. [31] And he will send forth his angels with a great trumpet call, and they will gather his chosen ones from the four winds, from one end of heaven to the other.

The above cosmic terminology need not be taken literally. It is a part of their toolkit, which enables them to make it clear that God is acting on behalf of humans. (See Dan. 2:21; 4:17, 25, 34–35; 5:21) The sun is not going to be darkened, the moon will not stop giving its light, the stars are not going to fall from the heavens, nor will the heavens be shaken. What is being communicated here is that following the tribulation when God is going to judge humans, the righteous will receive life, and the unrighteous will cut off from life. (34-45) While we do not take cosmic terminology literally, we do discover its meaning, and this is what we are to take literally.

Acts 2:14-21 Updated American Standard Version (UASV)

Peter's Sermon at Pentecost

[14] But Peter, standing with the eleven, lifted up his voice and declared to them, "Men of Judea and all who dwell in Jerusalem, let this be known to you, and give ear to my words. [15] For these men are not drunk, as you

suppose, since it is only the third hour of the day;[40] [16] but this is what was spoken of through the prophet Joel

[17] "'And it shall be in the last days, God says,
that I will pour out my Spirit on all flesh,
and your sons and your daughters shall prophesy,
  and your young men shall see visions,
  and your old men shall dream dreams;
[18] and even on my male slaves and on my female slaves
  I will pour out some of my Spirit in those days, and they will prophesy.
[19] And I will show wonders in the heavens above
  and signs on the earth below,
  blood, and fire, and vapor of smoke;
[20] the sun shall be turned to darkness
  and the moon to blood,
  before the great and glorious day of the Lord comes.
[21] And it shall come to pass that everyone who calls upon the name of the Lord will be saved.'[41]

In all occurrences, prophecy proclaimed in Bible times had meaning to the people who heard it; it served for their guidance as well as each generation up unto the time of its fulfillment. Usually, it had some fulfillment in that time, in numerous instances being fulfilled during the days of that very generation. In looking at Peters quote from Joel, it must be asked; did they see those cosmic events on Pentecost? Yes, the cosmic terminology is expressing that God was acting on behalf of those first Christians. A new era was being entered, and God did pour out His Spirit, and sons and daughters did prophesy, both in proclaiming a message and in the foretelling of further events. However, let us delve even deeper into prophecy and how they are to be interpreted. Before moving on, let us briefly offer what we have learned this far:

- Judgment prophecies could be lifted, set aside if the parties affected repent and turnaround from their former course.
- On the other hand, if God has promised blessings but then that person or group disobeys him and does evil, he will not do what he had said he would do.

---

[40] I.e. 9 a.m.

[41] A quotation from Joel 2:28-32

- Then again, if one has repented, turned around, and a judgment prophecy has been lifted, it can be reinstated if that person or group returns to their former evil ways.
- Prophets have a license to use prophetic language, cosmic terminology that evidences that God is working or acting within humanity.
- While we do not take cosmic terminology literally, we do discover its meaning, and this is what we are to take literally.

Interpreting Prophecy

If we are to understand and interpret prophecy correctly, we must first have a grasp of the figurative language, types, and symbols. We have already dealt with figurative language back in the CHRISTIAN PUBLISHING HOUSE BLOG Interpreting Figurative Language,[42] and typology is dealt with throughout this book. In addition, the reader should carefully consider New Testament Writers Use of the Old Testament.[43]

We will follow the same interpretation process here that we would elsewhere, grammatical-historical interpretation, which attempts to ascertain what the author meant by the words that he used, which should have been understood by his original readers. (Stein 1994, 38-9) It was the primary method of interpretation when higher criticism's Historical-Critical Method was in its infancy back in the 19th century (Milton Terry), and remains the only method of interpretation for true conservative scholarship in the later 20th century into the 21st century.

Grammatical Aspect

When we speak of interpreting the Bible grammatically, we are referring to the process of seeking to determine its meaning by ascertaining four things: (a) the meaning of words (lexicology), (b) the form of words (morphology), (c) the function of words (parts of speech), and (d) the relationships of words (syntax). In the meaning of words (lexicology), we are concerned with (a) etymology- how words are derived and developed, (b) usage how words are used by the same and other authors, (c) synonyms

---

[42] https://christianpublishinghouse.co/2016/10/28/interpreting-figurative-language/

[43] https://christianpublishinghouse.co/2016/12/07/interpreting-new-testament-writers-use-of-the-old-testament/

and antonyms -how similar and opposite words are used, and (d) context-how words are used in various contexts.

In discussing the form of words (morphology), we are looking at how words are structured and how that affects their meaning. For example, the word eat means something different from ate, though the same letters are used. The word part changes meaning when the letter "s" is added to it to make the word parts. The function of words (parts of speech) considers what the various forms do. These include attention to subjects, verbs, objects, nouns, and others, as will be discussed later. The relationships of words (syntax) are the way words are related or put together to form phrases, clauses, and sentences. (Zuck 1991, 100-101)

Historical Aspect

By "historical" we mean the setting in which the prophet's book was written and the circumstances involved in the writing. ... taking into consideration the circumstances of the writings and the cultural environment. We must keep in mind that even though many of the prophetic utterances were meant for the generation, in which they were spoken, or shortly thereafter. Even if it is not the immediate generation, all prophetic utterances had some type of meaning to the prophet's generation, be it hope in some future person or event, or the knowledge of a judgment that is coming or could come as a result of their behavior. For example, maybe the Israelites are under persecution and oppression by the surrounding nations, and the prophecy is for a protector that is to rise up, and set matters straight. Even though they do not know, who the protector is, or the exact time of his appearance, they do know that God cannot lie, nor has he ever lied, and so, they can have hope and faith in his words. Moreover, they would have also known that if they fell back into false worship, God could withdraw his prophetic message of a savior.

The context in which a given Scripture passage is written influences how that passage is to be understood. Context includes several things:

- the verse(s) immediately before and after a passage
- the paragraph and book in which the verses occur
- the dispensation in which it was written
- the message of the entire Bible
- the historical-cultural environment of that time when it was written. (Zuck 1991, 77)

We will end this chapter here. However, our next chapter, chapter 10, will walk the reader through a portion of a prophetic book. We have chosen the book of Isaiah (66:1-14), which is a favorite of many, even viewed as the fifth Gospel, because it speaks of the coming Messiah so much.

AMERICA 3 The Kings of the South and the North

Daniel 11:1-9 (530 – 226 B.C.E.)

Daniel 8:17, 19, 26 Updated American Standard Version (UASV)

[17] So he came near where I stood. And when he came, I was frightened and fell on my face; but he said to me, "Understand, O son of man, that **the vision is for the time of the end.**" [19] And he said, "Look, I am making known to you what will happen in **the period of the wrath**, for it refers to **the appointed time of the end.** [26] The vision of the evenings and the mornings that has been told is true,[44] but **seal up the vision,**[45] for it refers to **many days from now.**"[46]

"The period of the wrath," has "the basic idea [of] experiencing or expressing intense anger. The word is parallel to *qāṣap*, except that its expression takes a more specific form, especially of denunciation."[47]

Daniel 12:4, 9, 13 Updated American standard Version (UASV)

[4] But as for you, O Daniel, **conceal these words** and **seal up the book** <u>**until**</u> **the time of the end**; many shall run to and fro,[48] and **knowledge will increase.**" [9] He said, "Go your way, Daniel, for the words are **shut up** and **sealed until the time of the end.** [13] But go your way till the end; and you shall rest and shall stand in your allotted place at **the end of the days.**"

The "time of wrath," connects it to "time of the end," and says: "It refers certainly to God's time of judgment on Israel at the time of Antiochus Epiphanes; but it refers also to God's future time of judgment during the great tribulation, in the last half of which the little horn of Daniel's first vision will bring even worse affliction" (Wood, Daniel, p. 106).

Campbell adds:

> It should also be noted that the expression "time of the end" occurs in Daniel 12:4 where it clearly means the time approaching Christ's Second Coming. The conclusion, then, is that we are to see an Antiochus Epiphanes a dread picture and symbol of

---

[44] Lit *truth*; Heb., *'emet*

[45] I.e., keep the vision secret; Heb., *satar*

[46] Lit *for to days many*; I.e., to the distant future

[47] Leon J. Wood, "568 זַעַם," ed. R. Laird Harris, Gleason L. Archer Jr., and Bruce K. Waltke, *Theological Wordbook of the Old Testament* (Chicago: Moody Press, 1999), 247.

[48] I.e. examine the book thoroughly

Antichrist to come in the end time, or Tribulation" (Campbell, 126).

Kelly, West, Seiss, Pentecost, and Walvoord all support this dual reference approach to our passage. Walvoord says, "The entire chapter is historically filled in Antiochus, but to varying degrees foreshadowing typically the future world ruler who would dominate the situation at the end of the times of the Gentiles (Walvoord, Daniel, p. 196).

Archer, though hesitant, throws his considerable weight with this position as well:

> This interpretation has much to commend it, for Daniel makes clear through the assignment of the symbol of the "little horn" both to Antiochus of Kingdom III and to Antichrist of the latter-day phase of Kingdom IV that they bear to each other the relationship of type-antitype. Insofar as Epiphanes prefigured the determined effort to be made by the Beast to destroy the biblical faith, that prophecy that described the career of Antiochus also pertained to "the time of the end." Every type has great relevance for its antitype. But the future dealings of Antichrist can only be conjectured or surmised. Therefore, our discussion will be confined to the established deeds of Antiochus Epiphanes (Archer, p. 106).[49]

Some Bible scholars rightly understand these references to end times, as an increased understanding of the prophecies in the book of Daniel at that times. "Understandably **Daniel** and his immediate readers could not have comprehended all the details of the prophecies given in this book (cf. v. 8). Not until history continued to unfold would many be able to understand these prophetic revelations. But God indicated that an increased understanding of what Daniel had written would come. People today, looking back over history, can see the significance of much of what Daniel predicted. And in **the time of the end** (cf. v. 9, and note "the end" and "the end of the days" in v. 13) the words of this book that have been sealed (kept intact) will be understood by **many** who will seek to gain **knowledge** from it. This will be in the Tribulation (cf. 11:40, "the time of the end"). Even though Daniel's people may not have fully understood this book's prophecies, the predictions did comfort them. They were assured that God

[49] Anders, Max. *Holman Old Testament Commentary - Daniel* (p. 232). B&H Publishing.

will ultimately deliver Israel from the Gentiles and bring her into His covenanted promises."[50]

It is "the third year of Cyrus king of Persia," and hence about 536 B.C.E., shortly after the Jews' return to Jerusalem. After a three-week fast, Daniel is by the bank of the Hiddekel (the Tigris) river. (Dan. 10:1, 4; Gen. 2:14) An angel appears to him and explains

Daniel 10:13-14 Updated American Standard Version (UASV)

[13] The prince of the kingdom of Persia withstood me twenty-one days, but Michael, one of the chief princes, came to help me, for I was left there with the kings of Persia, [14] Now I have come to give you an understanding of what will happen to your people in the end of the days, for it is a vision yet for the days to come."

Chapter 10 of the book of Daniel precedes the final vision that was given to Daniel, the battles between The Kings of the South and the North.

Daniel 11:1 Updated American Standard Version (UASV)

11 "And as for me, in the first year of Darius the Mede [539/538 B.C.E.], I stood up to confirm and strengthen him.

This opening verse of chapter 11 could just as easily be seen as the closing verse of chapter 10. This is the angel still speaking here, not Daniel, and he is referring to his reign as the starting point of the prophetic message, as Darius was no longer living. God's angel continued,

Daniel 11:2 Updated American Standard Version (UASV)

[2] And now I will show you the truth. Behold, three more kings shall arise in Persia, and a fourth shall be far richer than all of them. And when he has become strong through his riches, he shall stir up all against the kingdom of Greece.

Just who were these Persian rulers?

---

[50] J. Dwight Pentecost, "Daniel," in *The Bible Knowledge Commentary: An Exposition of the Scriptures*, ed. J. F. Walvoord and R. B. Zuck, vol. 1 (Wheaton, IL: Victor Books, 1985), 1373.

As to whether the Jews remained God's chosen people after the rejection of Jesus Christ, the Son of God, see this author's CPH Blog article, MODERN ISRAEL IN BIBLE PROPHECY: Are the Natural Jews Today Still God's Chosen People?

https://christianpublishinghouse.co/2017/03/27/modern-israel-in-bible-prophecy-are-the-natural-jews-today-still-gods-chosen-people/

or http://tiny.cc/mdippy

The **three more kings shall arise in Persia** refer to Cyrus (539–529 B.C.E.), Cambyses (529–522 B.C.E.), and Darius I (Hystaspes) (521–486 B.C.), with Bardiya not being considered because he ruled for only seven months. The fourth was the son and successor of Darius, Xerxes I (485–465 B.C.). He was the King Ahasuerus who married Esther, who was richer than all who preceded him. With his wealth and power, he embarked on a campaign against Greece.

Daniel 11:3-4 Updated American Standard Version (UASV)

[3] And a mighty king will arise, and he will rule with great dominion and do as he wills. [4] And as soon as he has **stood up,**[51] his kingdom shall be broken and divided toward the four winds of heaven, but not to **his posterity, nor according to the authority** with which he ruled, for his kingdom shall be plucked up and go to others besides these.

Twenty-year-old Alexander "**stood up**" as king of Macedonia in 336 B.C.E. He did become "a mighty king," known the world over today as Alexander the Great. "Between 334 and 330 B. Alexander conquered Asia Minor, Syria, Egypt, and the land of the Medo-Persian Empire. His conquests extended as far as India."[52] Alexander was not quite 33 years old when malaria coupled with alcoholism took his life in Babylon in 323 B.C.E.

The great empire of Alexander the Great was not passed onto "**his posterity.**" Alexander's brother Philip III Arrhidaeus reign lasted less than seven years, as he and his wife Eurydice were murdered at the order of Olympias, Alexander's mother, in 317 B.C.E. Alexander's son Alexander IV ruled until 311 B.C.E., wherein he was killed at the hands of Cassander, one of his father's generals. Alexander has an illegitimate son Heracles, who then sought to rule in his father's name but was murdered in 309 B.C.E. Thus, we see that Alexander the Great rose up as a mighty king and ruled with great dominion, yet his kingdom was short lived but was not to go to his posterity because they could not rule with his authority.

Rather Alexander's kingdom was literally "broken and divided toward the four winds of heaven," that is, "his kingdom was divided among his four generals (cf. 8:22): Seleucus (over Syria and Mesopotamia), Ptolemy (over Egypt), Lysimacus (over Thrace and portions of Asia Minor), and Cassander (over Macedonia and Greece). This division was anticipated

---

[51] Or *risen*

[52] J. Dwight Pentecost, "Daniel," in *The Bible Knowledge Commentary: An Exposition of the Scriptures*, ed. J. F. Walvoord and R. B. Zuck, vol. 1 (Wheaton, IL: Victor Books, 1985), 1367–1368.

through the four heads of the leopard (7:6) and the four prominent horns on the goat (8:8)."[53]

Daniel 11:5-6 Updated American Standard Version (UASV)

[5] "Then the king of the south will be strong, but one of his princes will be stronger than he and will rule, and his authority will be a greater dominion. [6] After some years they will make an alliance, and the daughter of the king of the south will come to the king of the north to make an agreement. But she will not retain the strength of her arm, and he and his arm will not endure, but she will be given up, along with those who brought her in, he who fathered her, and he who supported her in those times.

The titles "the king of the south" and "the king of the north" refer to kings south and north of Daniel's people, who had been freed from Babylonian captivity and was now restored to the land of Judah. The first "king of the south" was a general who had served under Alexander, Ptolemy I Soter of Egypt (304-283 B.C.E.). Another general of Alexander was Syrian King Seleucus I Nicator (304-281 B.C.E) "and his authority will be a greater dominion," who assumed the role of "the king of the north."

From the initial "king of the south" and the "king of the north" "conflicts arose between the kingdoms of the Ptolemies (Egypt) and the Seleucids (Syria)."[54] Because Antiochus I, the son and successor of his father Seleucus I Nicator did not wage a significant war against the king of the south, the prophecy did not mention him. However, his successor, Antiochus II, fought a very long war against Ptolemy II, the son of Ptolemy I. Therefore, Ptolemy II and Antiochus II constituted the king of the south and the king of the north respectively. Antiochus II married Laodice, and they had a son named Seleucus II, while Ptolemy II had a daughter named Berenice. In about 250 B.C.E., "the daughter of the king of the south will come to the king of the north to make an agreement." In order to make this alliance Antiochus II divorced his wife Laodice and married Berenice, "the daughter of the king of the south."

We are told (11:6) she will not retain the strength of her arm, that is the supporting power of her father, Ptolemy II. When he died in 246 B.C.E., she did no longer had the support and power of her father, as his "arm will not endure" with her husband. Bernice "will be given up, along with those

---

[53] J. Dwight Pentecost, "Daniel," in *The Bible Knowledge Commentary: An Exposition of the Scriptures*, ed. J. F. Walvoord and R. B. Zuck, vol. 1 (Wheaton, IL: Victor Books, 1985), 1368.

[54] Stephen R. Miller, *Daniel*, vol. 18, The New American Commentary (Nashville: Broadman & Holman Publishers, 1994), 293.

who brought her in, he who fathered her, and he who supported her in those times.

But, and he and his arm will not endure, but she shall be given up, along with those who brought her in, he who fathered her, and he who supported her in those times. Antiochus II rejected Bernice; after that, he remarried Laodice, and named their son as his successor. As Laodice had planned, she succeeded "in murdering Antiochus, Berenice, and their child. Thus their 'power' did 'not last.' Laodice then ruled as queen regent during the minority of her son, Seleucus II Callinicus (246–226 B.C.)."[55] J. Dwight Pentecost tells us, "Laodice, whom Antiochus had divorced in order to marry Berenice, had Berenice killed (she was **handed over**). Laodice then poisoned Antiochus II and made her son, Seleucus II Callinicus, king (246–227)."[56] How would the next Ptolemaic king respond to all of this?

Daniel 11:7-9 Updated American Standard Version (UASV)

[7] "And **one from the sprout of her roots** will stand up in his position, and he will come to the army and come against **the fortress of the king of the north**, and he will deal with them and will prevail. [8] Also their gods, with their **metal images,**[57] with their precious vessels of silver and of gold, he will take captive to Egypt; and for some years he will stand off from the king of the north, [9] Then the latter will come into the realm of the king of the south but will return to his own land.

"One from the sprout" of Berenice's parents, or "roots," was her brother. At his father's death, he 'stood up' as the king of the south, the Egyptian Pharaoh Ptolemy III Euergetes (246–221 B.C.E.). He wasted no time in the vengeance of his sister's murder. He attacked Syrian King Seleucus II, who Laodice had used to murder Berenice and her son, he came against "the fortress of the king of the north." Ptolemy III took the fortified part of Antioch, capturing the major cities of Antioch and Seleucia and dealt a deathblow to Laodice.

Some 200 years earlier, Persian King Cambyses II had conquered Egypt and carried home Egyptian gods, "their metal images" or "their molten statues." Here we have Ptolemy III plundering the former royal capital Susa, where he recovered these "gods," taking them captive, carrying home the spoils of war. He also brought back as spoils of war a great many "precious

---

[55] IBID, 293–294.

[56] J. Dwight Pentecost, "Daniel," in *The Bible Knowledge Commentary: An Exposition of the Scriptures*, ed. J. F. Walvoord and R. B. Zuck, vol. 1 (Wheaton, IL: Victor Books, 1985), 1368.

[57] Or *molten statues*

vessels of silver and of gold." And Ptolemy III "for some years he will stand off from the king of the north," to quell revolt at home.

However, the king of the north, Syrian King Seleucus II, attempted to strike back. "In 242 Seleucus II attempted to invade Egypt, but was forced to withdraw. For the rest of his reign he was too busy with other problems to engage in further conflict with Egypt."[58] Seleucus II with only a small remnant of his army was forced to "return to his own land." At his death, his son Seleucus III succeeded him. "This was the beginning of the seesaw battle between the two nations."[59]

---

[58] John H Walton, *Zondervan Illustrated Bible Backgrounds Commentary (Old Testament): Isaiah, Jeremiah, Lamentations, Ezekiel, Daniel*, vol. 4 (Grand Rapids, MI: Zondervan, 2009), 562.

[59] Walvoord, John. Daniel (The John Walvoord Prophecy Commentaries) (Kindle Location 6113). Moody Publishers.

AMERICA 4 The Kings of the South and the North

Daniel 11:10-20 (226 – 175 B.C.E.)

Daniel 11:10-13 Updated American Standard Version (UASV)

[10] "His sons will wage war and assemble a multitude of great forces, which will keep coming and overflow and pass through, and again will wage war up to his fortress. [11] Then the king of the south, moved with rage, will come out and fight against the king of the north. And he will raise a great multitude, but it will be given into his hand. [12] And when the multitude is **taken away**, his heart will be lifted up, and he will cast down tens of thousands, but he will not prevail. [13] For the king of the north will again raise a multitude, greater than the former, and after some years[60] he will come on with a great army and many supplies.

Seleucus III reign was short lived, for in less than three years he was assassinated. His brother, Antiochus III, came to the Syrian throne. After he had dealt with the rebellions in Media and Asia Minor, Antiochus III gathered a great military force for an attack on the king of the south, who was by then Ptolemy IV. "Antiochus III ... was called the "Great" because of his military successes, and in 219–218 B.C. he campaigned in Phoenicia and Palestine, part of the Ptolemaic Empire ("as far as his [the king of the South's] fortress")."[61]

Massing a military force of 75,000, the king of the south, Ptolemy IV, moved northward against the enemy, the king of the north. We are told that the Syrian king of the north, Antiochus III raised "a great multitude [68,000], but it will be given into his hand." Antiochus III suffered defeat at the coastal city of Raphia, not far from Egypt's border.[62] A "multitude is taken away" by Ptolemy IV, the king of the south, 10,000 Syrian infantrymen and 300 cavalrymen into death and he took 4,000 as prisoners. The kings then made a truce agreement whereby Antiochus III kept his Syrian seaport of Seleucia but lost Phoenicia and Coele-Syria. Because of this victory, the 'heart of the Egyptian king of the south was

---

[60] Lit *at the end of the times, years*

[61] Stephen R. Miller, *Daniel*, vol. 18, The New American Commentary (Nashville: Broadman & Holman Publishers, 1994), 294.

[62] "According to Polybius, Ptolemy's forces consisted of 70,000 infantry, 5,000 cavalry, and 73 elephants; whereas Antiochus's army had 62,000 infantry, 6,000 cavalry, and 102 elephants. When the battle ended [in 217 B.C.], Ptolemy had won a great victory over the Syrians at Raphia (located in Palestine)." – Stephen R. Miller, Daniel, vol. 18, The New American Commentary (Nashville: Broadman & Holman Publishers, 1994), 295.

lifted up,' especially toward the one true God of the Jews. Judah remained under the control of Ptolemy IV. Nevertheless, he did not take advantage of the strong position that he held, trying to stay on top of this victory against the Syrian king of the north, so in the end 'he did not prevail.

But rather, Ptolemy IV turned to a life of depravity and corruption, and his five-year-old son, Ptolemy V, became the next king of the south some years before the death of Antiochus III. "fifteen years later (202 b.c.) Antiochus III again invaded Ptolemaic territories with a huge army. The occasion for this invasion was the death of Ptolemy IV in 203 B.C. and the crowning of his young son (between four and six years of age), Ptolemy V Epiphanes (203–181 B.C.), as the new king. Antiochus III took full advantage of the opportunity and attacked Phoenicia and Palestine; by 201 B.C. the fortress in Gaza had fallen to the Syrians."[63]

Daniel 11:14 Updated American Standard Version (UASV)

[14] "In those times many will rise against the king of the south, and the **violent among your own people** will lift themselves up in order to fulfill the vision, but they will stumble.[64]

"In those times many [did] rise against the king of the south." Not only did the king of the south have to face the forces of Antiochus III, as well as his Macedonian ally, the young king had many problems at home in Egypt. The young king of the south was facing a revolt because his guardian Agathocles, who ruled in his name, dealt haughtily with the Egyptians. Danial 11:14b tells us "the violent among your own people will lift themselves up in order to fulfill the vision." However, this "vision" of ending the Gentile dominion of their homeland was false and they 'were going to stumble.'

Daniel 11:15-16 Updated American Standard Version (UASV)

[15] And the king of the north will come and throw up a siege rampart and capture a **fortified city**. And the arms of the south will not stand, nor will his select men; and they will have no power to stand. [16] The one coming against him will do as he pleases, and no one will stand before him; he will **stand in the land of the beauty**,[65] with destruction in his hand.

Military forces under Ptolemy V, or "arms of the south," surrendered to assault from the north. At Paneas (Caesarea Philippi), Antiochus III drove Egypt's General Scopas and 10,000 "select men," into Sidon, "a fortified

---

[63] Stephen R. Miller, *Daniel*, vol. 18, The New American Commentary (Nashville: Broadman & Holman Publishers, 1994), 295.

[64] Or *will fail*

[65] I.e. Palestine

city." There Antiochus III would "throw up a siege rampart," taking that Phoenician seaport in 199 B.C.E. "He then retreated to Sidon on the Phoenician coast. Antiochus's forces pursued the Egyptians and besieged Sidon. General Scopas finally surrendered in 198 B.C.E."[66] Antiochus would "do as he pleases" because "no one [the Egyptian king of the south] will stand before him." Antiochus III then marched against Jerusalem, the capital of "the land of the beauty," namely, Judah, "with destruction in his hand."

Daniel 11:17 Updated American Standard Version (UASV)

[17] He will **set his face** to come **with the full force of his kingdom**, and there will be **equitable terms**; and he will perform them; he will give him the daughter of women to destroy her. But she will not stand for him, or be for him.

The king of the north, Antiochus III, "set his face" to completely control Egypt "with the full force of his kingdom." But rather he chose in the end to make "equitable terms" of peace with the king of the south, Ptolemy V. When Antiochus III and King Philip V of Macedonia join in a league or alliance against the young Egyptian king, attempting to take over his territories, the guardians of Ptolemy V went to Rome for protection, causing Antiochus III to change his plan. In this alliance of peace Antiochus III gave his daughter, Cleopatra I "the daughter of women," in marriage to Ptolemy V, hoping his daughter would be an inside spy so as to make Egypt subject to Syria. However, the scheme failed because Cleopatra I "[would] not stand for him, or be for him," but rather she sided with her husband. She "became staunchly loyal to her husband, even encouraging him to make an alliance with Rome against her father."[67]

Gleason L. Archer offers insight into this masterful scheme gone bad, "As it turned out, however, after the marriage finally took place in 195 [B.C.E.], Cleopatra became completely sympathetic to her husband, Ptolemy V, and the Ptolemaic cause, much to the disappointment of her father, Antiochus. Therefore, when she gave birth to a royal heir, who became Ptolemy VI, this gave no particular advantage or political leverage to her father. When Ptolemy V died in 181, Cleopatra was appointed queen regent by the Egyptian government, because they all loved and appreciated her loyalty to their cause. But she herself died not long after, and this meant the end of all possible Seleucid influence on Egyptian affairs. Yet by that time Antiochus himself, who died in 187 B.C., was gone." (Archer, The

---

[66] Stephen R. Miller, *Daniel*, vol. 18, The New American Commentary (Nashville: Broadman & Holman Publishers, 1994), 296.

[67] John H Walton, *Zondervan Illustrated Bible Backgrounds Commentary (Old Testament): Isaiah, Jeremiah, Lamentations, Ezekiel, Daniel*, vol. 4 (Grand Rapids, MI: Zondervan, 2009), 564.

Expositor's Bible Commentary, Vol. 7: Daniel and the Minor Prophets 1985, 132-33)

Daniel 11:18-19 Updated American Standard Version (UASV)

[18] Afterward he will **turn his face back to the coastlands** and will capture many. But a **commander** will put a stop to his reproach against him; he will turn his reproach upon him. [19] Then he will turn his face back toward the fortresses of his own land, but he will stumble and fall, and will not be found.

Antiochus would "turn his face back to the coastlands. The "coastlands" were those of Macedonia, Greece, and Asia Minor. Antiochus is an effort to repeat the accomplishments of Alexander the Great, sought to conquer and control Greece. However, Greece had other plans, as they turned to Rome for help. Rome formally declared war on him. This put Antiochus in battle on several fronts: Macedonia, Rome, and Greece. "The Romans defeated [Antiochus] at Thermopylae in 191 [B.C.E.] and then crushed him at the Battle of Magnesia in 190 [B.C.E.]. This forced him back east across the Taurus Mountains. The commander who defeated him was Lucius Scipio. By the Treaty of Apmea in 189 [B.C.E.] Antiochus became a vassal of Rome, had to send twenty hostages to Rome, and paid a huge indemnity. This left him humiliated and short of funds."[68]

Daniel 11:20 Updated American Standard Version (UASV)

[20] "Then there will stand up in his position one who causes an exactor to pass through the glory of his kingdom, but in a few days he will be broken, though not in anger nor in warfare.

God's angel foretold, "There will stand up in his position [***that of Antiochus III***] one who causes an exactor [the tax collector Heliodorus] to pass through the glory of his kingdom, but in a few days he will be broken, though not in anger nor in warfare." (Daniel 11:20) The one who was to "standing up" in this manner was Seleucus IV Philopator. (187–175 B.C.E.) "Seleucus IV reigned only 'a few years' and was not killed by an angry mob ("in anger") like his father or 'in battle.' Heliodorus, his tax collector and prime minister, evidently seeking to gain the throne for himself, poisoned the king (possibly abetted by Antiochus IV)."[69]

---

[68] John H Walton, *Zondervan Illustrated Bible Backgrounds Commentary (Old Testament): Isaiah, Jeremiah, Lamentations, Ezekiel, Daniel*, vol. 4 (Grand Rapids, MI: Zondervan, 2009), 564.

[69] Stephen R. Miller, *Daniel*, vol. 18, The New American Commentary (Nashville: Broadman & Holman Publishers, 1994), 297.

AMERICA 5 The Kings of the South and the North

Daniel 11:21-35 (175 – 164 B.C.E.)

Daniel 11:21 Updated American Standard Version (UASV)

[21] And there will stand up in his place **a despicable one**, and they have not conferred the majesty of the kingdom; and he will come in during a time of security and seize the kingdom by intrigue.

Antiochus IV Epiphanes (175–163 B.C.E.) had been a political hostage in Rome Since the defeat of Antiochus III at Magnesia. However, in 175 B.C.E. the oldest son of Seleucus IV, Demetrius I, was sent to Rome in replacement of Antiochus IV. Arriving home, Antiochus IV assumed power as a co-ruler with Antiochus III, the latter here dying in 170 C.E., leaving Antiochus IV to rule alone on the throne. Antiochus IV Epiphanes was certainly "a despicable one," for his severe persecution of the Jews, massacring thousands, and he became the greatest threat to the pure worship within Israel since Abraham left Haran for the Promise Land. Antiochus IV assumed the title Epiphanes, which means the "Manifest One," or "Illustrious One," clearly evidencing his haughty spirit.

Daniel 11:22-24 Updated American Standard Version (UASV)

[22] Armies shall be **utterly swept away** before him and broken, even **the leader of the covenant**. [23] And after an alliance is made with him, he will act deceitfully, and he will rise and he will become powerful by means of a little nation. [24] **In a time of tranquility** he will enter the richest parts of the province, and he will accomplish what his fathers and their fathers have not done; he will distribute plunder, booty and possessions among them, and he will **devise his schemes against strongholds**, but only for a time.

At the tender age of six Ptolemy VII (Philometor) took the throne at the age of six under control of his mother Cleopatra in 181 B.C.E., as it was she who controlled the kingdom. Shortly after that he move on Palestine with a huge military force and was soundly defeated by Antiochus Epiphanes who destroyed, in the process, "the leader of the covenant." The Egyptian armies were utterly swept away by the invading forces of Antiochus, as if it were by a flood. Antiochus gave the order to murder "the leader of the covenant, Onias III, which was carried out by his own defecting brother Menelaus about 171 B.C.E.

Walvoord tells us, "The reference to the "prince of the covenant" prophesied the deposing and eventual murder of the high priest Onias, which was ordered by Antiochus in 172 B.C. and indicates the troublesome times of his reign.39 The high priest bore the title "prince of the covenant" because he was de facto the head of the theocracy at that time. In 11:28 and 11:32 the term "covenant" is used for the Jewish state. Antiochus sold the office of high priest to Onias's brother, Jason, who sought to Hellenize the Jewish state."[70]

However, Stephen R. Miller sees the "prince of the covenant differently, saying, "Montgomery identifies the "prince [leader] of the covenant" as the high priest Onias III, who was assassinated in 170 B.C. (Daniel, 451; also Lacocque, Daniel, 226; Hartman and Di Lella, Daniel, 295; Wood, Daniel, 295). In context with the defeat of the Egyptian army, it is best to see this "prince" as its leader. The entire phrase is indefinite and can be rendered 'a prince of a covenant.' He goes on to say, "Ptolemy is called 'a prince [leader] of the covenant' because he agreed (made a covenant) to become an ally of Antiochus if the Syrians would help him regain his throne in Egypt, which had been taken by his younger brother, Ptolemy VII Euergetes II (Physcon). Antiochus was delighted to make such a pact, for he felt that it would give him a foothold in Egypt. So with Syrian help, Ptolemy regained his throne. Later Ptolemy broke this agreement and allied himself with his brother Ptolemy VII to dislodge Antiochus's troops from Pelusium, a fortress on the border of Egypt."[71]

In verse 24 we find Antiochus Epiphanes taking from the rich Egyptian places he could strike and giving to the poor and his own forces, to gain support and strengthen his control over the empire, as well as build up to take over Egypt.

Daniel 11:25-28 Updated American Standard Version (UASV)

[25] And he will **stir up his power and his heart against the king of the south** with a great army; and the king of the south shall wage war with an exceedingly great and mighty army, but he will not stand, for plots will be devised against him. [26] Even **those who eat** his food will break him; and his army will be swept away, and many will fall down slain. [27] As for both kings, their heart will be inclined to do what is evil, and **they will speak lies** to each other at the same table; but it will not succeed, for the end is still to come at the appointed time. [28] Then he will return to his land with many possessions, but his heart will be set **against the holy covenant**, and he will take action and he will return to his own land.

---

[70] Walvoord, John. Daniel (The John Walvoord Prophecy Commentaries) (Kindle Locations 6232-6237). Moody Publishers.

[71] Stephen R. Miller, *Daniel*, vol. 18, The New American Commentary (Nashville: Broadman & Holman Publishers, 1994), 299.

Antiochus set out to attacked Ptolemy VI Philometer in 170 B.C.E., the king of Egypt (c. 186 – 145 B.C.E.), who had become his enemy. Antiochus was able to defeat an Egyptian army near Pelusium, and then he captured Memphis but was not in a position to take Alexandria. Miller tells us that "Cumulatively these things prevented Ptolemy from successfully 'standing' against the Syrians. 'Those who eat from the king's provisions' (v. 26) were Ptolemy's trusted counselors, who unwisely urged the young king to recapture Syria and Palestine, thus incurring the wrath of Antiochus."[72]

Antiochus Epiphanes 'spoke lies,' as he pretended to help Ptolemy Philometer regain the throne in Egypt, which was then by Ptolemy Euergetes. Both kings "they will speak lies to each other at the same table." Antiochus had Philometer as king at Memphis, while he had Euergetes reigned at Alexandria. However, things did not go as planned because the two Egyptian kings decided up a joint rule, which greatly angered the Syrian. "Antiochus's successful first campaign against Egypt in 169 B.C. is the background for v. 28. After plundering Egypt, the king returned home by way of Palestine and found an insurrection in progress (cf. 1 Macc. 1:16–28; 2 Macc. 5:1–11). He put down the rebellion, massacring eighty thousand men, women, and children (2 Macc. 5:12–14) and then looted the temple with the help of the evil high priest, Menelaus (cf. 2 Macc. 5:15–21). The persecution of the Jews by this evil tyrant had now escalated to calamitous proportions."[73] These sources outside of the Scriptures are not inspired books of the Bible. However, First and Second Maccabees are historical accounts of the Jewish struggle for independence during the second-century B.C.E. These are the most valuable of the Old Testament Apocryphal works because of the historical information they supply for this period.

Daniel 11:29-30 Updated American Standard Version (UASV)

[29] "At the appointed time he will return and he will **come into the south**, but it will not be as it was before. [30] For **ships** of Kittim[74] will **come against him**; therefore he will be disheartened and will return and become enraged at the holy covenant and take action; so he will come back and show regard for those who forsake the holy covenant.

Here again, for the third time, we find Antiochus invading Egypt against the co-rulers about 168 B.C.E., "but it will not be as it was before,

---

[72] Stephen R. Miller, *Daniel*, vol. 18, The New American Commentary (Nashville: Broadman & Holman Publishers, 1994), 300.

[73] Stephen R. Miller, *Daniel*, vol. 18, The New American Commentary (Nashville: Broadman & Holman Publishers, 1994), 300.

[74] I.e. Cyprus

for a Roman fleet of ships from Cyprus sided with Egypt this time, frustrating the attack by Antiochus. "When he tried to play for time, the Roman envoy drew a circle around him in the sand and insisted on an answer before he stepped out of it. Humiliated, he withdrew from Egypt."[75] Antiochus left Egypt in a fit of rage, taking his anger out on the Israelites as he headed back home. He despised the Jews God and their Mosaic Law, so he showed favor to the apostate Jews, yes Antiochus showed "regard for those who forsake the holy covenant."

Miller tells us that "In 167 B.C., Antiochus turned his humiliation into anger against the Jewish people ("the holy covenant") once more (cf. 1 Macc 1:29–40; 2 Macc 6:1–6). He sent Apollonius (2 Macc 5:23–26), the head of his mercenaries and the "chief collector of tribute" (1 Macc 1:29), to Jerusalem. Apollonius pretended to come in peace, but on the Sabbath Day, he suddenly attacked, massacring many people and plundering the city (cf. 1 Macc. 1:30–32; cf. 2 Macc. 5:25–26). But he rewarded those apostate Jews like the high priest Menelaus, who supported his Hellenistic policies (cf. 1 Macc. 1:1, 43; 2 Macc. 4:7–17)."[76]

Daniel 11:31-32 Updated American Standard Version (UASV)

[31] Forces from him will stand up, **desecrate the sanctuary** fortress, and do away with the continual sacrifice. And they will set up the **abomination**[77] **that causes desolation.** [32] And those who act wickedly against the covenant, he will pollute by means of smooth words; but **the people who know their God** will prevail and act effectively.

The soldier of Antiochus worked in conjunction with the apostate Jews, guarding the temple, halting pure worship of the one true God. In addition, other Antiochus troops were sent out on the Sabbath to slaughter Jewish men, women, and children. The soldiers "desecrate the sanctuary," banned circumcision, and done away with away with "the continual sacrifice" (i.e., daily sacrifices), as well as offering up in sacrifice a big on God's altar. (1 Macc. 1:44–54) Moreover, on Chislev (Dec. 15, 167 B.C.E.) the Syrians even made compulsory worship of an idol statue in honor of the Olympian god Zeus in the temple. The Jews called it "the abomination that causes desolation." **Abomination**: (Heb. *shiqquts*) It means abhorrence,

---

[75] John H Walton, *Zondervan Illustrated Bible Backgrounds Commentary (Old Testament): Isaiah, Jeremiah, Lamentations, Ezekiel, Daniel*, vol. 4 (Grand Rapids, MI: Zondervan, 2009), 565.

[76] Stephen R. Miller, *Daniel*, vol. 18, The New American Commentary (Nashville: Broadman & Holman Publishers, 1994), 301.

[77] **Abomination**: (Heb. *shiqquts*) It means abhorrence, an object to abhor, horror, monster, filth. The sense of *shiqquts* is a detestable thing, also implying that it can make a person unclean. – 2 Ki 23:13; Ez. 5:11; 11:21; Dan. 9:27; 11:31; Hos. 9:10.

an object to abhor, horror, monster, filth. The sense of *shiqquts* is a detestable thing, also implying that it can make a person unclean. In other words, the Syrians ruined pure worship of the one true God in the temple by introducing an abhorrent, detestable, filthy object (the Olympian god Zeus) in the temple. The soldiers of Antiochus further profaned the temple by spreading sow's broth on the altar. (1 Macc. 1:44-54) Both Daniel and Jesus said this barbarism was only a preview of the abomination that was to come – Daniel 9:27; Matthew 24:15.

The Abomination of Desolation

Matthew 24:15 Update American Standard Version (UASV)

15 "Therefore when you see the abomination of desolation, which was spoken of through Daniel the prophet, standing in the holy place (let the reader understand),

Matthew 24:13 reads, "But **the one who endures** <u>to the end</u> will be saved." Matthew 24:14 said, "this gospel of the kingdom will be proclaimed throughout the whole world as a testimony to all nations, **and then** <u>**the end will come**</u>." Matthew 24:15 begins with the Greek word *hotan* "whenever" followed by *oun* "therefore, which reads in English, "Therefore when," which connects what preceded, "**the end**," and leads into what follows. Let us take a moment to investigate verse 15.

In verse 3-14, Jesus outlined the signs of "the end of the age." Here in Mathew 24:15, Jesus begins with "**Therefore when** you see the abomination of desolation, which was spoken of through Daniel the prophet, standing in the holy place (let the reader understand)." If we look at the corresponding accounts in Mark and Luke, they offer us additional insights. Mark 13:14 says, "standing where it ought not to be." Luke 21:20 adds Jesus' words, "But when you see Jerusalem surrounded by armies, then know[78] that its desolation has come near." The complete picture is an "abomination" "standing in the holy place," i.e., "where it ought not be," namely, "Jerusalem surrounded by armies,"

This is a reference to the Roman army, which assaulted Jerusalem and its temple starting in 66 C.E., under General Cestus Gallus. The temple was the "holy place," and the abomination was the Roman army "standing where it ought not to be." As for the "desolation," this came in 70 C.E. when General Titus of the Roman army completely desolated Jerusalem and its temple. Specifically, what was this "abomination"? Moreover, in what sense was it "standing in the holy place"?

---

[78] Or *then recognize*

Jesus had urged the readers to *understand.* What was it that they were to *understand*? They were to *understand* that "which was spoken of through Daniel the prophet," i.e., Daniel 9:27. Part "b" of verse 27 reads "And upon the wing of abominations shall come the one causing desolation, even until a complete destruction, one that is decreed, is poured out on the one causing desolation." – Daniel 9:26-27; see also Daniel 11:31; 12:11.

> The *abomination of desolation* is an expression that recurs in Daniel with some variation in wording (Daniel 8:13; 9:27; 11:31; 12:11), where most scholars agree that there is a reference to the desecration perpetrated by Antiochus Epiphanes when he built an altar to Zeus in the temple and offered swine and other unclean animals on it as sacrifices (cf. 1 Macc. 1:41–61).[79]

We can have it but one of two ways, as Jesus' words were a clear reference to the Roman armies of 66–70 C.E. It may very well be that Daniel's prophecy points to Antiochus Epiphanes "who in 167 [B.C.E., 200-years before Jesus uttered his prophecy] plundered the temple, ordered the sacrificial system to cease, and polluted the altar of the Lord by turning it into a pagan altar, where unclean sacrifices were offered to pagan deities."[80] This would be no different from Matthew referring to Hosea 11:1 (When Israel was a child ... and out of Egypt I called my son). In that case, Matthew did not use Hosea's intended meaning, but carried out an *Inspired Sensus Plenior Application*, by having a whole other meaning, an entirely different meaning for those words, making them applicable to Jesus being called back out of Egypt. It could be that Jesus used Daniel's prophecy about Antiochus Epiphanes, and gave is an *Inspired Sensus Plenior Application*, by having a whole other meaning, a completely different meaning for those words, making them applicable to the Roman armies desolating Jerusalem between 66 and 70 C.E. Then, again, it could be that was what Daniel was pointing to all along, and Jesus used Daniel's words in a grammatical-historical application. Either way, it still comes out the same.

---

[79] Leon Morris, *The Gospel According to Matthew*, The Pillar New Testament Commentary (Grand Rapids, MI; Leicester, England: W.B. Eerdmans; Inter-Varsity Press, 1992), 603.

[80] Larry Chouinard, *Matthew*, The College Press NIV Commentary (Joplin, MO: College Press, 1997), Mt 24:15.

STANDARD OF THE 10TH ROMAN LEGION This Legion attacked and destroyed Jerusalem in the Jewish War (A.D. 70).

During the days of the Maccabees this expression was used to describe the sacrilege of Antiochus IV Epiphanes, the Seleucid king who decreed that an altar to Olympian Zeus and perhaps a statue of himself were to be erected in the temple on 15 Chislev, 167 b.c.: "They erected a desolating sacrilege on the altar of burnt offering. They also built altars in the surrounding towns of Judah." Antiochus further decreed that the Sabbath and other festal observances were to be profaned, that circumcision was to be abolished, and that swine and other unclean animals were to be sacrificed in the temple (cf. 1 Macc. 1:41–50). This was one of the lowest points of Jewish history and was considered by many the primary focus of Daniel's prophecy. Jesus now quotes Daniel directly to clarify that the fulfillment of the "abomination that causes desolation" is yet future.[81]

When Jesus uttered those words of verse 15, the abomination of desolation was yet to appear. Jesus was clearly pointing to the Roman army of 66 C.E., with its distinctive standards, which were idols to the Romans and the empire, but an abomination to the Jews.

Judæa was under the charge of a Roman official, a subordinate of the governor of the Roman province of Syria, who held a relation to that functionary similar to that which the Governor of Bombay holds to the Governor-General at Calcutta. Roman soldiers paraded the streets of Jerusalem; **Roman standards** waved over the fastnesses of the country; Roman tax-gatherers sat at the gate of every town. To the Sanhedrin, the supreme Jewish organ of government, only a shadow of power was still conceded, its presidents, the high priests, being mere puppets of Rome, set up and put down with the utmost caprice. So low had the proud nation

[81] Clinton E. Arnold, *Zondervan Illustrated Bible Backgrounds Commentary: Matthew, Mark, Luke*, vol. 1 (Grand Rapids, MI: Zondervan, 2002), 148.

fallen whose ideal it had ever been to rule the world, and whose patriotism was a religious and national passion as intense and unquenchable as ever burned in any country.[82]

In verse 32 we are told "but the people who know their God will prevail and act effectively," which referred to the Hasmonaeans. A dynamic Jewish leader, Judah Maccabee, of a family known as the Hasmonaeans, led a rebel army that freed the temple from Greek hands. Possibly because of Judah's military ability, he was called Maccabee, meaning "hammer." Maccabee was a "name given to the family of Mattathias, a faithful priest, who led in a revolt (Maccabean War) against the Hellenizing influences of the Seleucid King Antiochus Epiphanes in about 168 B.C.E."[83]

The Hasmonaean Dynasty

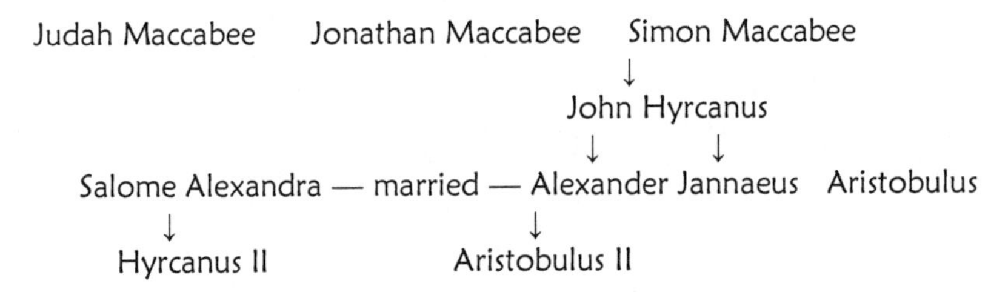

II. Maccabean Revolt

A. Antiochus's Revenge (168–166 B.C.) In the winter of 169/168, the rival brothers Ptolemy VI and Ptolemy VIII agreed to end their dispute and united against their uncle Antiochus IV. Thus, in the spring of 168 Antiochus IV invaded Egypt a second time. He captured Memphis, but when he attempted to subdue Eleusis, a suburb of Alexandria, the Roman general Popillius Laenas gave him an ultimatum from the senate to withdraw immediately from Egypt (cf. Polybius xxix.2.1–4; 27.1–8; Livy xlv.12.1–6; Diodorus xxxi.2; Velleius Paterculus i.10.1f; Appian Syr 66; Justinus xxxiv.3; Dnl. 11:28–30). Antiochus immediately retreated, having learned of Rome's power as its hostage for fourteen years.

Embittered, Antiochus decided to establish Palestine as a buffer state between him and the Roman encroachment (Polybius xxix.27.9; Dnl. 11:30). He destroyed the walls of Jerusalem and refortified the old Davidic city making it the pagan stronghold (Acra). Considering himself

[82] James Stalker, *The Life of Jesus Christ* (Chicago: Henry A. Sumner and Company, 1882), 30–31.

[83] Chad Brand et al., eds., "Maccabees," *Holman Illustrated Bible Dictionary* (Nashville, TN: Holman Bible Publishers, 2003), 1063.

Zeus Epiphanes, he ordered a vigorous hellenization program that would exterminate the Jewish religion. He forbade the Jews to celebrate the sabbath and feasts, to offer the traditional sacrifices, and to perform circumcision, and he ordered the destruction of the copies of the Torah.

The Jews were ordered to offer up unclean sacrifices on idolatrous altars and to eat swine's flesh (2 Macc. 6:18). The climactic act was on 25 Chislev (Dec. 16) 167, when the temple of Jerusalem became the place of worship of the Olympian Zeus. The altar of Zeus was erected on the altar of burnt offering, and swine's flesh was offered on it (Dnl. 11:31f.; 1 Macc. 1:41–64; 2 Macc. 6:1–11).

B. Mattathias (166 B.C.) In every village of Palestine sacrifice was to be offered to the heathen gods under the supervision of imperial representatives. In the village of Modein (27 km, 17 mi, NW of Jerusalem) an aged priest named Mattathias defied the command of Antiochus IV's legate to offer the sacrifice on the heathen altar. When another Jew was about to comply, Mattathias killed him and the legate and destroyed the altar, saying, "Let everyone who is zealous for the law and supports the covenant come out with me" (1 Macc. 2:15–27; Josephus Ant. xii.6.1f [265–272]; cf. Dnl. 11:32–35). Mattathias, his five sons (John, Simon, Judas, Eleazar, and Jonathan) and many other Jews fled to the mountains; this marked the beginning of the Maccabean revolt.

Mattathias and his followers exhorted Jews everywhere to join their struggle against hellenization. They gained the support of the Hasidim, those who were faithful to the Torah. They tore down heathen altars and circumcised children who had been left uncircumcised. After a long life, Mattathias died in 166. He exhorted his sons to continue the struggle and appointed his third son Judas as the commander of the war (1 Macc. 2:42–70; Josephus Ant. xii.6.2–4 [273–286]).

C. Judas Maccabeus (166–160 B.C.)

1. Rededication of the Temple (166–164 B.C.) The selection of Judas to carry on the struggle was the right one, for he proved to be a very capable leader in defeating the Seleucids. In his first year he defeated the Syrian governors Apollonius and Seron (1 Macc. 3:10–26; Josephus Ant. xii.7.1 [287–292]).

Part of Antiochus's inability to put down the Maccabees was caused by the trouble he had in the East, which prevented him from being involved in Judea himself. Instead, he ordered Lysias, regent of the western part of the empire (Syria), to stop the rebellion and to destroy the Jewish race (1 Macc. 3:32–36; Josephus Ant. xii.7.2 [295f]). Lysias sent a large army under the leadership of Ptolemy, Nicanor, and Gorgias.

So confident they were of victory that traders went along to purchase Jewish slaves (1 Macc. 3:38–41). But Judas decisively defeated Gorgias at Emmaus, causing the Syrian soldiers to flee (1 Macc. 4:1–27; Josephus Ant. xii.7.4 [305–312]).

In 164 Lysias made one last attempt against the Jews by personally leading a larger army to attack Jerusalem from the south. Judas, however, completely defeated him in Beth-zur (24 km, 15 mi, S of Jerusalem). Lysias retreated, and Judas marched to Jerusalem and regained all of Jerusalem except the Acra. Having captured the temple mount, he destroyed the altar of the Olympian Zeus, built a new altar, rebuilt the temple, and selected a priest who had remained faithful to Yahweh. Thus on 25 Chislev (Dec. 14) 164, exactly three years after its desecration, the temple was rededicated and the daily sacrifices were restored (1 Macc. 4:36–59; 2 Macc. 10:1–8; Josephus Ant. xii.7.6f [316–326]). This event marked the beginning of the Jewish Feast of Dedication or Lights (Hanukkah). Judas then fortified the Jerusalem walls and the city of Beth-zur. This completed the first phase of the Maccabean struggle. The Maccabees could rejoice, for they had not experienced defeat.

2. Religious Freedom Gained (163 B.C.) Judas's victories made Judah reasonably secure. Two things, however, needed to be accomplished. First, although Judah was reasonably secure, it was felt that all the Jews of Palestine had to be independent from Antiochus's rule. After several campaigns this freedom was won.

Second, the Maccabees wanted to end Syrian control of the Acra in Jerusalem. The Syrian presence was a constant reminder of Antiochus's hellenization program intended to exterminate the Jewish religion. When Judas laid siege to the Acra in the spring or summer of 163, some Syrian soldiers and Hellenistic Jews escaped and went to Antioch for help (1 Macc. 6:18–27).

Antiochus IV died in 163 (Polybius xxxi.9.3f.; Josephus Ant. xii.9.1 [356–59]) and was succeeded by his nine-year-old son Antiochus V Eupator. Just before his death, Antiochus IV had appointed his friend Philip as the regent and guardian over Antiochus V. But Lysias claimed that these privileges had been given to him at an earlier date, and so he crowned Antiochus V (both he and Philip were in Antioch when Antiochus IV died). Because of the troubles in Jerusalem, Lysias with the boy-king went south and defeated Judas at Beth-zechariah (18 km, 11 mi, SW of Jerusalem). There Judas's youngest brother Eleazar was killed.

Lysias then laid siege to Jerusalem (1 Macc. 6:28–54). Judas faced severe food shortages (because it was the sabbatical year) and was about to be defeated. Lysias, however, received the news that Philip was marching from Persia to Syria to claim the boy-king Antiochus V and the kingdom; thus he was anxious to make a peace treaty with Judas. Judas agreed to tear down the walls of Jerusalem, and Lysias guaranteed religious freedom to the Jews (1 Macc. 6:55–63). The Jews, however, were still under the Seleucidian rule.

3. Political Freedom Attempted (162–160 B.C.) Having obtained religious freedom, Judas now wanted political freedom. To counteract his drive, the Seleucids strengthened the Hellenistic elements among the Jews. Lysias, it seems, appointed the high priest Alcimus (Jakim or Jehoakim) who, although of Aaronic descent, was ideologically a Hellenist (cf. 1 Macc. 7:14; 2 Macc. 14:3–7; Josephus Ant. xii.9.7 [384–88]; xx.10.3 [235]) and thus unacceptable to Judas.

Meanwhile in Syria, Demetrius I Soter, nephew of Antiochus IV and cousin of Antiochus V, escaped from Rome (where he had gone as a hostage when Antiochus IV had been released), killed both Lysias and Antiochus V, and assumed the throne. He confirmed Alcimus as high priest (162) of Israel and sent him with an army to Judea under his general Bacchides. The Hasidim accepted Alcimus as the high priest probably, it can be conjectured, because he was of Aaronic descent and because the Syrians (or Seleucids) had guaranteed them freedom of worship. Thus the Hasidim broke from Judas's ranks, but they quickly returned when Alcimus, disregarding his promise not to harm them, slew sixty of them (1 Macc. 7:15–20; Josephus Ant. xii.10.2 [393–97]). Hence Alcimus asked Demetrius for more military help against Judas and his followers, called the HASIDEANS (2 Macc. 14:6). Demetrius sent NICANOR, but he was defeated and killed at Adasa (6 km, 4 mi, N of Jerusalem) on 13 Adar (Mar. 9) 161, (which the Jews celebrate annually as Nicanor's Day); the army fled to Gazara (32 km, 20 mi, W of Adasa) and was destroyed. Alcimus fled to Syria (1 Macc. 7:26–50; Josephus Ant. xii.10.3–5 [398–412]).

Judas sent for help from Rome, but before any could arrive, Demetrius sent Bacchides with Alcimus to avenge Nicanor's death. Because of the might of the Syrian army, many deserted Judas, and in the Battle of Elasa (about 16 km, 10 mi, N of Jerusalem) he was slain (160). His brothers Jonathan and Simon took his body to be buried at Modein (1 Macc. 8:1–9:22; Josephus Ant. xii.10.6–11.2 [413–434]).

D. Jonathan (160–143 B.C.) Judas's death was a great blow to morale. The Hellenists were temporarily in control while Jonathan and his followers were in the wilderness of Tekoa, waging only guerrilla warfare. Bacchides fortified Jerusalem and other Judean cities against possible Maccabean attacks. In May, 159 B.C., Alcimus died, and no successor was chosen. Soon after, Bacchides left his command in Judah and returned to Antioch (157); he went back to Jerusalem at the request of the Hellenists but was defeated at Beth-basi (10 km, 6 mi, S of Jerusalem). He made a peace treaty with Jonathan and then returned to Antioch.

This treaty weakened the Hellenists' position. Jonathan made Michmash (14 km, 9 mi, S of Jerusalem) his headquarters, where he judged the people, punishing the hellenizers (1 Macc. 9:23–27; Josephus Ant. xiii.1.1–6 [1–34]). During the next five years his power increased. In 152 he was further helped by internal struggles for power in Syria. A pretender, Alexander Balas, who claimed to be the son of Antiochus Epiphanes, challenged Demetrius I. Both desired Jonathan's support. Fortunately, Jonathan sided with Alexander Balas, for in 150 Demetrius was slain in a battle against Alexander. Alexander made Jonathan a general, governor, and high priest of Judah and considered him one of his chief friends (1 Macc. 10:22–66; Josephus Ant. xiii.2.3f [46–61]; 4.1f [80–85]). This was certainly a strange alliance, i.e., Alexander Balas, professed son of Antiochus Epiphanes, in league with a Maccabean!

New troubles came in Syria. Demetrius's son, Demetrius II Nicator, challenged Alexander Balas in 147 and finally defeated him in 145. Since Demetrius II was only sixteen and inexperienced, Jonathan took the opportunity to attack the Acra in Jerusalem, where the Hellenistic Jews were still in control. Although Demetrius II opposed the attack, he later conceded to Jonathan by confirming his high-priesthood and granting his request for three districts in southern Samaria. Jonathan was not able to conquer the Acra, however.

In 143 Demetrius II's army rebelled, and Diodotus Trypho (a general of Alexander Balas) claimed the Syrian throne (becoming its first non-Seleucid king) in the name of Alexander Balas's son Antiochus VI. Jonathan took advantage of the situation and sided with Trypho, who in turn made him civil and religious head of the Jews and his brother Simon head of the military. Trypho, however, fearful of Jonathan's success, deceived him, arranged a meeting with him, and subsequently killed him. Jonathan was buried at Modein (1 Macc. 10:67–13:30; Josephus Ant. xiii.4.3–6.6 [86–212]).

Jonathan was succeeded by Simon, the only remaining son of Mattathias. A new phase of the Maccabean rule had emerged. Although generally speaking one does apply the term "Hasmonean" to the whole of the Maccabean family, it is more specifically applied to the high-priestly house from the time of Simon to Rome's intervention in 63 because in that period the Maccabean dream had finally come true, namely, the Israelites had become an independent nation. Hence the political and religious life was headed by one family or dynasty—the Hasmoneans.[84]

Daniel 11:33-35 Updated American Standard Version (UASV)

[33] And those having insight among the people will **impart understanding to the many**; yet they will be made to stumble by sword and by flame, by captivity and by plundering, for some days. [34] Now when they stumble, they will be given a **little help**; and many will join with them by means of smooth speech. [35] And some of those having insight will stumble, in order **to refine, purge and cleanse them** until the time of the end; because it is still to come at the appointed time.

The Jews who believed and knew the Hebrew Scriptures, "imparted understanding to the many," as they also suffered under severe persecution. The vast majority of the Jews, however, would become apostates, falling away or standing off from the truth, while the few Jews committed to the only true God of the Scriptures would receive "little help" from their fellow brothers. Many of the faithful remnant suffered martyrdom. This persecution of God's true followers would carry over into Christianity, or "the time of the end; because it is still to come at the appointed time," that is until the Second Coming of Christ. "The mention of "the end," however, serves as a transition. From verse 36 on, the prophecy leaps the intervening centuries to predict events related to the last generation prior to God's judgment of Gentile power and its rulers—prophecy that has yet to be fulfilled."[85]

---

[84] H. W. Hoehner, "Maccabees," ed. Geoffrey W Bromiley, *The International Standard Bible Encyclopedia*, Revised (Wm. B. Eerdmans, 1979–1988), 198–199.

[85] Walvoord, John. *Daniel* (The John Walvoord Prophecy Commentaries) (Kindle Locations 6307-6309). Moody Publishers.

AMERICA 6 The Kings of the South and the North

Daniel 11:36-45 (the End Times)

Some information from an earlier chapter is worth repeating as repetition for emphasis.

Daniel 8:17, 19, 26 Updated American Standard Version (UASV)

[17] So he came near where I stood. And when he came, I was frightened and fell on my face; but he said to me, "Understand, O son of man, that **the vision is for the time of the end.**" [19] And he said, "Look, I am making known to you what will happen in **the period of the wrath**, for it refers to **the appointed time of the end.** [26] The vision of the evenings and the mornings that has been told is true,[86] but **seal up the vision,**[87] for it refers to **many days from now.**"[88]

"The period of the wrath," has "the basic idea [of] experiencing or expressing intense anger. The word is parallel to *qāṣap*, except that its expression takes a more specific form, especially of denunciation."[89]

Daniel 12:4, 9, 13 Updated American Standard Version (UASV)

[4] But as for you, O Daniel, **conceal these words** and **seal up the book** <u>until</u> **the time of the end**; many shall run to and fro,[90] and **knowledge will increase.**" [9] He said, "Go your way, Daniel, for the words are **shut up** and **sealed until the time of the end.** [13] But go your way till the end; and you shall rest and shall stand in your allotted place at **the end of the days.**"

The "time of wrath," connects it to "time of the end," and says: "It refers certainly to God's time of judgment on Israel at the time of Antiochus Epiphanes; but it also refers to God's future time of judgment during the great tribulation, in the last half of which the little horn of Daniel's first vision will bring even worse affliction" (Wood, Daniel, p. 106).

Campbell adds:

---

[86] Lit *truth*; Heb., *'emet*

[87] I.e., keep the vision secret; Heb., *satar*

[88] Lit *for to days many*; I.e., to the distant future

[89] Leon J. Wood, "568 זַעַם," ed. R. Laird Harris, Gleason L. Archer Jr., and Bruce K. Waltke, *Theological Wordbook of the Old Testament* (Chicago: Moody Press, 1999), 247.

[90] I.e. examine the book thoroughly

> It should also be noted that the expression "time of the end" occurs in Daniel 12:4 where it clearly means the time approaching Christ's Second Coming. The conclusion, then, is that we are to see an Antiochus Epiphanes a dread picture and symbol of Antichrist to come in the end time, or Tribulation" (Campbell, 126).

Kelly, West, Seiss, Pentecost, and Walvoord all support this dual reference approach to our passage. Walvoord says, "The entire chapter is historically filled in Antiochus, but to varying degrees foreshadowing typically the future world ruler who would dominate the situation at the end of the times of the Gentiles (Walvoord, Daniel, p. 196).

Archer, though hesitant, throws his considerable weight with this position as well:

> This interpretation has much to commend it, for Daniel makes clear through the assignment of the symbol of the "little horn" both to Antiochus of Kingdom III and to Antichrist of the latter-day phase of Kingdom IV that they bear to each other the relationship of type-antitype. Insofar as Epiphanes prefigured the determined effort to be made by the Beast to destroy the biblical faith, that prophecy that described the career of Antiochus also pertained to "the time of the end." Every type has great relevance for its antitype. But the future dealings of Antichrist can only be conjectured or surmised. Therefore, our discussion will be confined to the established deeds of Antiochus Epiphanes (Archer, p. 106).[91]

Some Bible scholars rightly understand these references to end times, as an increased understanding of the prophecies in the book of Daniel at that times. "Understandably **Daniel** and his immediate readers could not have comprehended all the details of the prophecies given in this book (cf. v. 8). Not until history continued to unfold would many be able to understand these prophetic revelations. But God indicated that an increased understanding of what Daniel had written would come. People today, looking back over history, can see the significance of much of what Daniel predicted. And in **the time of the end** (cf. v. 9, and note "the end" and "the end of the days" in v. 13) the words of this book that have been sealed (kept intact) will be understood by **many** who will seek to gain **knowledge** from it. This will be in the Tribulation (cf. 11:40, "the time of the end"). Even though Daniel's people may not have fully understood this book's prophecies, the predictions did comfort them. They were assured that God

[91] Anders, Max. *Holman Old Testament Commentary - Daniel* (p. 232). B&H Publishing.

will ultimately deliver Israel from the Gentiles and bring her into His covenanted promises."[92]

Daniel 11:36-37 Updated American Standard Version (UASV)

[36] "Then the king will **do as he pleases**, and he will exalt and magnify himself above every god and will speak astonishing things against the God of gods; and he will prosper until the indignation is finished, for that which is decreed will be done. [37] He will show no regard for the gods of his fathers or for the desire of women, nor will he show regard for any other god; for he will magnify himself above them all.

We are now leaving the era of the Antiochus' and Ptolemies and leaping to "the time of the end" that was just mentioned in verse 35. Many premillennial eschatologists believe that verses 36-45 are referring to the final antichrist prior to the second coming of Jesus Christ and his millennial kingdom. It is, for this reason, we will add chapters in this publication that identifies the antichrist as well. For now, we are going to quote leading eschatologists who see verses 36-45 in this light.

Stephen R. Miller, whom I have quote generously,

> Scholars are in agreement that the vision up to this point has been concerned with events between the time of Cyrus (in which Daniel lived) and the death of Antiochus IV, but with v. 36 this agreement ends. Although there have been other identifications set forth for the "king" of vv. 36–45, there are two principal views today.
>
> Those who adhere to the Maccabean thesis maintain that vv. 36–45 continue to speak of Antiochus IV Epiphanes. However, there are serious problems with this position, not the least of which is the fact that much of the historical data set forth in these verses (even in vv. 36–39) is impossible to harmonize with Antiochus's life. For example, Antiochus did not exalt himself above every god (vv. 36–37), reject "the gods of his fathers," or worship "a god unknown to his fathers" (v. 38); on the contrary, he worshiped the Greek pantheon, even building an altar and

---

[92] J. Dwight Pentecost, "Daniel," in *The Bible Knowledge Commentary: An Exposition of the Scriptures*, ed. J. F. Walvoord and R. B. Zuck, vol. 1 (Wheaton, IL: Victor Books, 1985), 1373.

As to whether the Jews remained God's chosen people after the rejection of Jesus Christ, the Son of God, see this author's CPH Blog article, MODERN ISRAEL IN BIBLE PROPHECY: Are the Natural Jews Today Still God's Chosen People?

https://christianpublishinghouse.co/2017/03/27/modern-israel-in-bible-prophecy-are-the-natural-jews-today-still-gods-chosen-people/

or http://tiny.cc/mdippy

offering sacrifices to Zeus in the Jerusalem temple precincts. Daniel also predicted that this king "will come to his end" in Palestine (v. 45), but it is a matter of historical record that Antiochus IV died at Tabae in Persia.

Exegetical necessity requires that 11:36–45 be applied to someone other than Antiochus IV. The context indicates that the ruler now in view will live in the last days, immediately prior to the coming of the Lord. Verse 40 reveals that this king's activities will take place "at the time of the end" (cf. 10:14), and the "time of distress" mentioned in 12:1 is best understood as the same "distress" (the tribulation) predicted by Jesus Christ in Matt 24:21 as occurring immediately before his second advent (Matt 24:29–31; cf. Rev 7:14). But the clearest indication that this "king" will live in the latter days is that the resurrection of the saints will take place immediately after God delivers his people from this evil individual's power (cf. 12:2). Of course, the resurrection is an eschatological event. Finally, vv. 36–39 seem to introduce this king as if for the first time.[93]

Gleason L. Archer, whom I have quoted at times,

With the conclusion of the preceding pericope at v. 35, the predictive material that incontestably applies to the Hellenistic Empires and the contest between the Seleucids and the Jewish patriots ends. This present section (vv. 36–39) contains some features that hardly apply to Antiochus IV, though most of the details could apply to him as well as to his latter-day antitype, "the beast." Both liberal and conservative scholars agree that all of chapter 11 up to this point contains strikingly accurate predictions of the whole sweep of events from the reign of Cyrus (during which Daniel bought his career to a close) to the unsuccessful effort of Antiochus Epiphanes to stamp out the Jewish faith. But the two schools of thought radically differ in the explanation for this phenomenon. Evangelicals find this pattern of prediction and fulfillment compelling evidence of the divine inspiration and authority of the Hebrew Scriptures, since only God could possibly foreknow the future and see to it that his announced plan would be precisely fulfilled (Archer, The Expositor's Bible Commentary, Vol. 7: Daniel and the Minor Prophets 1985, 143)

John Walvoord, whom I have quoted and referred to often,

[93] Stephen R. Miller, *Daniel*, vol. 18, The New American Commentary (Nashville: Broadman & Holman Publishers, 1994), 304–305.

Beginning in verse 36, Daniel described events that have never been fulfilled historically. Neither Antiochus Epiphanes nor Herod the Great ever sought to "exalt himself and magnify himself above every god." The individual in view is the still-future Antichrist first described in Daniel 7. The expression "the time of the end" (v. 35) marks the sharp break in this prophecy. Up to this point, the prophecy dealing with the Persian and Grecian Empires has been fulfilled minutely and with amazing precision. Now, however, we are in an entirely different situation.[94]

The belief is that verses 36-45 are referring to the final antichrist in the latter part of "the last days," that is, "the time of the end. Therefore, we need to talk about the antichrist briefly here but in-depth in chapters 10-16. We can define the antichrist as anyone, any group, any organization, or any government that is against or instead of Christ, or who mistreat his people. Thus, we are not just looking for one person, one group, one organization, or one power.

Variations of the expression "do as he pleases" are used of God in 4:35, Persia in 8:4, Alexander the Great in 11:3, and Antiochus III in 11:16. A similar expression, "It prospered in everything it did," was used of Antiochus IV in 8:12. Because of his personal charisma, intelligence, evil character, and political power, Antichrist will arrogantly believe that he can function sufficiently well without God. The passage seems to indicate that Antichrist will be an atheist (cf. 2 Thess 2:4; Rev 13:6), although he evidently will use religion to gain his position of power (cf. Rev 17). Baldwin declares: "So thoroughgoing is his egotism that he has no option but to be an atheist."

"Unheard-of things" is a translation of the Hebrew *niplā'ôt* (from *pālā'*, "be surpassing, extraordinary"; noun, *pele'*, "wonder"), which denotes "astonishing, shocking, or unbelievable things." Antichrist will spew out shockingly blasphemous words against Christ (cf. 7:8, 11, 20, 25; 2 Thess 2:4; Rev 13:5–6).

The phrase "the time of wrath" is a translation of one Hebrew word, *za'am*, a term that usually denotes the wrath of God (cf. Isa 10:25; 26:20; 30:27; Mal 1:4), and that is the meaning here. God's wrath will be poured out upon Antichrist and the whole sinful world in the last days during the tribulation period (cf. 12:1; Matt 24:21–22, 29–31; Rev 6–19). When that period is over, this tyrant's activities will cease. Though Antichrist will be judged, he himself is part of God's judgment upon the

[94] Walvoord, John. *Daniel* (The John Walvoord Prophecy Commentaries) (Kindle Locations 6319-6324). Moody Publishers.

wicked (cf. 2 Thess 2:12), for those who reject the truth will believe his lies and follow him to their doom (cf. Rev 16:13–16). When the evil leader has accomplished his purpose, judgment will fall upon him (cf. 7:11, 26; 2 Thess. 2:8; Rev 19:20). Even Antichrist's activities and the tribulation are permitted by the sovereign God to accomplish his purposes.[95]

Regarding the king of the north, the angel added, says "Then the king will do as he pleases, and he will exalt and magnify himself above every god **[refusing to acknowledge the sovereignty of God Almighty]** and will speak astonishing things against the God of gods; and he will prosper until the indignation is finished, for that which is decreed will be done. He will show no regard for the gods of his fathers or for the desire of women, nor will he show regard for any other god; for he will magnify himself above them all."

Fulfilling these prophetic words, the king of the north "will show no regard for the gods of his fathers," such as the liberal progressive world that we are experiencing today with their communistic attitudes that promote outright atheism. Thus, the king of the north has made a god of himself, 'magnifying himself over everyone.' 'Showing no regard for the desire of women.' Commentators are getting bogged down in trying to identify who these women are. However, it might be best to think of how women were viewed in Bible times, as subservient to pagan husbands and subordinate to Jewish and Christian husbands. Might we look at it as the king of the north 'showing no regard for these women, namely, lands or powers that are subservient and subordinate to the king of the north, "for he will magnify himself above them all." Verse 37 "concludes by again emphasizing the atheistic nature of Antichrist, "Nor will he regard any god, but will exalt himself above them all" (cf. 2 Thess. 2:4). This deluded tyrant will even demand that the earth's inhabitants worship him rather than their deities (cf. Rev 13:12, 14–15)."[96]

Daniel 11:38 Updated American Standard Version (UASV)

[38] But instead he will give glory to the god of fortresses; to a god that his fathers did not know he will give glory by means of gold and silver and precious stones and desirable things.

Going on with the prophecy, the angel said, "he [king of the north] will give glory to the god of fortresses," that is, the king of the north will place his trust in the power of the military. He believes that he can save

---

[95] Stephen R. Miller, *Daniel*, vol. 18, The New American Commentary (Nashville: Broadman & Holman Publishers, 1994), 306–307.

[96] IBID, 307–308.

himself and control the world through his "god" of military prowess, sacrificing great wealth, specifically, "gold and silver and precious stones and desirable things," on the "god" of military power.

Daniel Walvoord points this out for us,

> Examining all other passages relating to the end time, it becomes evident that the sole confidence of a final world ruler is in military power, personified as "the god of war," or "god of fortresses." In other words, he is a complete materialist in contrast to all previous religions and all previous men who claim divine qualities. This is blasphemy to the ultimate, the exaltation of human power and attainment. He is Satan's masterpiece, a human being who is Satan's substitute for Jesus Christ, hence properly identified as the Antichrist. (Walvoord 2012)

Daniel 11:39 Updated American Standard Version (UASV)

[39] He will act effectively against the most fortified strongholds, along with a foreign god; he will give great honor to those who acknowledge him and will cause them to rule over the many, and he will distribute land for a price.

The king of the north is placing all of his trust his militaristic "foreign god," acting most "effectively," proving that he is the most formidable military power in "the last days." (2 Tim. 3:1) The king of the north "will give great honor to those who acknowledge him," namely, lands or powers that are subservient and subordinate to the king of the north, as verse 37 stated, "he will magnify himself above them all." The king of the north will reward those who support his worldview with political, financial, and even at times military support.

It is now time to identify more specifically but not absolutely who the **king of the north** is. **Remember**, we can define the antichrist as **any**one, **any** group, **any** organization, or **any** government that is *against* or *instead of Christ*, or who mistreat his people. Thus, we are not just looking for one person, one group, one organization, or one power. In 'the time of the end," the latter part of the "last days," we are looking for a **composite power** or **kingdom** (government) made up of various powers or kingdoms. This author would suggest Russia, North Korea, Iran, as well as radical Islam apocalyptic ideology, and especially the socialistic, liberal-progressive worldview of many countries and the press (media) throughout the world. This composite power is a definite threat to Christ and Christianity. For eight years, the composite king of the north, antichrist, had its greatest ally in President Obama, who put the world at risk with his ideologies. He is an antichrist in that he went to war with true conservative Christianity in favor of Islam. Obama was trying to destroy the king of the south from within by weakening the United States of America military, as well as her Judeo-Christian moral values.

Daniel 11:40 Updated American Standard Version (UASV)

[40] "At the time of the end, the king of the south will attack him, but the king of the north will rush upon him like a whirlwind, with chariots and horsemen, and with many ships; and he will come into countries and will overflow and pass through.

In these "last days" or "time of the end," the **king of the south** for this author is the United States of America and any ally powers. Have we seen the king of the south "attack" the king of the north during "the time of the end"? (Daniel 12:4, 9) In a specific sense, we are really not in the "time of the end" as of yet because that is a brief period, the great tribulation, just before the second coming of Christ. However, there is little doubt that the election of Donald J. Trump as president of the United States has put the king of the south in an attack mode like never before in recent history. Trump is carrying out the office in a far more conservative worldview than anyone had suspected he would. He is restoring the king of the south to its glory as the protector of the world and true Christianity. The king of the north has responded to the Trump presidency like a "whirlwind" both 'militarily' and in message. From day one, Trump has been under attack from every quarter of the world, especially the liberal progressive media.

Daniel 11:41 Updated American Standard Version (UASV)

[41] And he will come into the beautiful land and many will fall victim, but these will escape from his power: Edom and Moab and the foremost of the sons of Ammon.

"He **[the antichrist Obama]** will come into the beautiful land [spiritual domain of Christ's disciples] and many will fall victim [persecution of genuine Christians], but these will escape from his power [harming but by no means stopping their activity, as Trump is elected]."

Daniel 11:42-43 Updated American Standard Version (UASV)

[42] And he will stretch out his hand against countries and the land of Egypt will not escape. [43] And he will rule over the hidden treasures of gold and silver and over all the desirable things of Egypt; and the Libyans and the Ethiopians will be at his steps.

The king of the south, the United States and allies, "Egypt," has not had complete success against the king of the north because there was an antichrist, Obama, weakening her from within. For example, the king of the south was losing a ten-year war against radical Islam and was having her military gutted, as the world viewed the king of the south as weak and despondent. How are we to understand the reference to "the Libyans and the Ethiopians will be at his steps." The "Libyans and the Ethiopians" were neighbors of the ancient king of the south, Egypt; however, today they can refer to nations or powers follow in step with the composite king of the north. The battle between the king of the south and the king of the north is entering the latter part of the last days.

Daniel 11:44-45 Updated American Standard Version (UASV)

[44] But reports out of the east and out of the north will disturb him, and he will go out in a great rage to annihilate and to devote many to destruction. [45] And he shall pitch his palatial tents between the sea and the glorious holy mountain. Yet he shall come to his end, with none to help him.

In time, the composite king of the north will embark on his final campaign against the king of the south, and in a great rage [he will] annihilate and … devote many to destruction." It is impossible to know the specific action that the composite king of the north will take. Nevertheless, motivated by "reports out of the east and out of the north [that] will disturb him," the composite king of the north will carry out a campaign of some sort "in a great rage to annihilate and to devote many to destruction." We can infer the campaign is directed at the king of the south and her allies but what "reports" will be the catalyst that will "disturb" the composite king of the north that prompt such an attack is unknowable at this point.

AMERICA 7 Babylon the Great, the Beast, the Seven Kings, and the Eighth King of Revelation

Revelation 17:1-18 (the Last Days)

Revelation 17:1-2 Updated American Standard Version (UASV)

17 Then one of the seven angels who had the seven bowls came and said to me, "Come, I will show you the judgment of the great prostitute who is seated on many waters, [2] with whom the kings of the earth committed acts of immorality, and those who dwell on the earth were made drunk with the wine of her immorality."

Who is this "great prostitute"? We need to note that this prostitute is 'committing acts of immorality with the kings of the earth, meaning she is not another governmental power. "And the kings of the earth, who committed sexual immorality and mourn wail over her when they see the smoke of her burning" (Rev. 18:9-10), also suggesting she is not a political power of any sort. Additionally, "the merchants, who became rich from her, will stand far off in fear of her torment, weeping and mourning," mean that she is not big business either. However, we see that the 'nations were deceived by great prostitute's sorcery.' This suggests some religious aspect, namely, all false religions, with the apostate churches of Christendom taking the lead in the time of the end. Adding support to this is the fact that "Prostitution frequently symbolizes idolatry or religious apostasy (cf. Jer. 3:6–9; Ezek. 16:30ff.; 20:30; Hos. 4:15; 5:3; 6:10; 9:1). Nineveh (Nah. 3:1, 4), Tyre (Is. 23:17), and even Jerusalem (Is. 1:21)."[97] "With the information that this prostitute **sits on many waters**, John may begin to think that she is, in fact, another symbolic figure. The original Babylon lay on the Euphrates River and had devised an elaborate system of irrigation canals (Jer. 51:13). Later in the chapter, these waters are interpreted globally—they are all the peoples and nations of the whole world (v. 15)."[98] "John mentioned Babylon already in 14:8, where he wrote that an angel cried, 'Fallen, fallen is Babylon the Great, which made all the nations drink the wrathful wine of her fornication.' Worldly Babylon should be seen as a universal force of evil that influences the multitudes of humanity to such an

---

[97] MacArthur, John. The MacArthur Bible Commentary (Kindle Locations 67538-67539). Thomas Nelson.

[98] Kendell H. Easley, *Revelation*, vol. 12, Holman New Testament Commentary (Nashville, TN: Broadman & Holman Publishers, 1998), 305.

extent that the people are desensitized. Babylon is "the archetypal source of every idolatrous manifestation in time and space.'"[99]

Revelation 17:3 Updated American Standard Version (UASV)

[3] And he carried me away in the Spirit into a wilderness, and I saw a woman sitting on a scarlet beast that was full of blasphemous names, and it had seven heads and ten horns.

There was an earlier pronouncement of judgment against ancient Babylon that was described as being "against the wilderness of the sea." (Isaiah 21:1, 9) The city of ancient Babylon lay on both sides of the Euphrates River. It had a double system of walls, which surrounded Babylon, making it seemingly making it invincible. So, the warning to ancient Babylon was that regardless of it walls and it watery defenses, it was going to become lifeless and desolate. Here in Revelation, John is being carried away in his vision to a wilderness to see Babylon the Great and the fate she too was to suffer. She too was going to become desolate and a waste regardless of her being "seated on many waters (all the peoples and nations of the whole world)." (Rev. 18:19, 22, 23) The great prostitute is not alone!

The great prostitute's "position atop the beast is quite fitting to picture the influence of the religious power over the secular leader. The scarlet beast is the same one who emerged out of the sea in 13:1. The earlier passage does not give his color, but it does note his seven heads and ten horns and names of blasphemy."[100] The antichrist(s) (13:1, 4; 14:9; 16:10) is made up of false religion (apostate churches of Christendom) and governments, political powers, which control the world. (v. 16) In Scripture, scarlet is often the color of luxury, splendor, and royalty. Rather than having blasphemous names, like the beast of Revelation 13, on its seven heads only, it is "full of blasphemous names," because of seeing itself as being divine (cf. 13:1; Dan. 7:25; 11:36; 2 Thess. 2:4). The seven heads and ten horns picture the level of the political Antichrist's control. "The relationship between the harlot and the beast has existed throughout human history but will reach its ultimate closeness in the days just before Christ returns. She controls him, but she also is dependent on him as the friction between the two later in chapter 17 will show (17:16)."[101]

---

[99] Simon J. Kistemaker and William Hendriksen, *Exposition of the Book of Revelation*, vol. 20, New Testament Commentary (Grand Rapids: Baker Book House, 1953–2001), 463.

[100] Robert L. Thomas, *Revelation 8-22: An Exegetical Commentary* (Chicago: Moody Publishers, 1995), 285.

[101] IBID., 286.

Revelation 17:4 Updated American Standard Version (UASV)

4 The woman was clothed in purple and scarlet, and she was adorned with gold and precious stones and pearls, and she had in her hand a golden cup that was full of detestable things and the unclean things of her sexual immorality.[102]

If someone in the days of the apostle John were wearing both purple and scarlet at the same time, this would suggest great wealth, which can be contrasted with the white garments of moral purity that are worn by the followers of the Lamb. (Rev. 7:9; 19:14; See 1 Tim. 2:9-10) The gold, precious stones and pearls show the brash but wasteful and excessive grandeur of a wealthy whore. Just consider all of the magnificent buildings, rare statues and priceless paintings, incalculable icons, and other religious things, as well as infinite amounts of property and cash, that the apostate churches of Christendom have amassed. The "golden cup that was full of detestable things" may appear splendid on the outside, but its contents are detestable, unclean. (Compare Matt. 23:25-26.) This symbolic golden cup contains all the filthy practices and lies that this great prostitute uses in her seduction of the nations, as she brings them under her spell. Then, there is "he unclean things of her sexual immorality," which is pictorial of her sick adulterous relationship with the political leaders and businesses of the world.

Revelation 17:5 Updated American Standard Version (UASV)

5 And on her forehead a name was written, a mystery: "Babylon the great, the mother of prostitutes and of the detestable things of the earth."

Robert L. Thomas writes,

> *Mystērion* in the NT is usually a mystery to be revealed. So here the true character and identity of the woman, previously kept concealed, are now objects of clear revelation (Hailey). The word implies a new revelation, not something to be kept hidden. In this case it is the exposing of what is evil about Babylon (Lenski). Subsequent revelation will show her to be a great city (17:18), but also a vast system of idolatry through the centuries that the great city represents (Bullinger). The system had its beginning on the plains of Shinar through the work of Nimrod and will reach its pinnacle there just before the second advent (Bullinger, Seiss). Reports of Babylon's present utter desolation and impossible restoration are radically overstated.

---

[102] **Sexual Immorality:** (Heb. *zanah*; Gr. *porneia*) A general term for immoral sexual acts of any kind: such as adultery, prostitution, sexual relations between people not married to each other, homosexuality, and bestiality. – Num. 25:1; Deut. 22:21; Matt. 5:32; 1 Cor. 5:1.

The other question about the syntactical role of *mystērion*, whether it is in apposition to ὄνομα (*onoma*, "name") or part of the inscription on the woman's head is resolvable through a comparison with 14:8 and 18:2. The woman's name is "Babylon the Great," not "Mystery Babylon the Great" (Smith, Walvoord). This along with the fact that *mystērion* seems to have a parenthetical independence here brings a decision favoring the appositional relationship. This gives the sense, "a name written, which is a mystery" (Johnson).

"Babylon the great, the mother of harlots and of the abominations of the earth" (Βαβυλὼν ἡ μεγάλη, ἡ μήτηρ τῶν πορνῶν καὶ τῶν βδελυγμάτων τῆς γῆς [*Babylōn hē megalē, hē mētēr tōn pornōn kai tōn bdelygmatōn tēs gēs*]) is the name that constitutes the mystery. Babylon is a theme in Scripture beginning in Gen. 10:9–10 with its first mention and continuing into these closing chapters of the last book of the Bible. It was a city where false religion began (Gen. 11:1–9) that has continually plagued Israel, the church, and the world (Walvoord). It will once again become the world's leading city religiously as well as commercially and politically as the end draws near. Her role as "the mother of harlots and of the abominations of the earth" makes her the progenitress of everything anti-Christian. This includes all false religions, not just those that are Christian in name only, but also everything that is pagan and idolatrous under Satan's control (Seiss). The Genesis 11 passage tells where it all began, with the building of a tower that became a forerunner of the world's idolatrous practices throughout history (Seiss, Walvoord). So the metropolis that functions as headquarters for the beast's empire has a long reputation for its anti-God stance. It is a city, but it is also a vast religious system that stands for everything God does not tolerate.[103]

Revelation 17:6 Updated American Standard Version (UASV)

[6] And I saw that the woman was drunk with the blood of the holy ones and with the blood of the witnesses of Jesus. Well, on seeing her I was greatly amazed. [7] And the angel said to me: "Why is it that you were amazed? I will tell you the mystery of the woman and of the wild beast that is carrying her and that has the seven heads and the ten horns.

The woman is the great prostitute of false religion headed by the apostate churches of Christendom, who has long been "drunk with the blood [persecution] of the holy ones [true genuine Christians] and with the blood of the witnesses of Jesus." The history of the abuses of the apostate churches of Christendom in spilling the blood of true Christians who

[103] Robert L. Thomas, *Revelation 8-22: An Exegetical Commentary* (Chicago: Moody Publishers, 1995), 289–290.

attempt to maintain a true faith in Jesus Christ is there for all to see, and will only worsen as we close out "the last days" in "the time of the end." The antichrist apostate churches will spill an innumerable amount of blood of Christian martyrs as will also be true of the martyrs who refuse to worship the beast during the great tribulation.

Why was the apostle John "greatly amazed"? "It may have been the sight of such unrestrained wickedness in the true nature of the woman and God's permitting her to exist (Kiddle). It may have been his inability to grasp the symbolic meaning of what he saw. It may have been the contrast between the splendidly attired woman and beast on the one hand and a city in ruins that he had expected to see (Swete, Ladd). It could have been some combination of these, but whatever it was, it was different from the marveling of the earth-dwellers over the beast in 13:3, because he was not about to become a follower of the beast."[104]

Revelation 17:8 Updated American Standard Version (UASV)

[8] "The beast that you saw was, and is not, and is about to come up out of the abyss and go to destruction. And those who dwell on the earth, whose names have not been written in the scroll of life from the founding of the world, will be amazed when they see how the wild beast that was, and is not, and is to come.

Abyss: (Gr. *abussos*) It is a very deep place, which is rendered "the bottomless pit" in some versions (KJV). This is found the NT and refers to a place or condition, where Satan and his demons will be confined for a thousand years. (Rev. 20:1-3) Abaddon rules over the abyss (Rev. 9:11) The beast is of Satan's design and will rise from the abyss in the last days. (Rev. 11:7) The beast will go off into destruction. (Rev 17:8) It is used at times to refer to the grave as well. – Lu 8:31; Rom. 10:7; Rev. 20:3.

Book of Life: (Gr. *biblos tēs zōēs*) In biblical times, cities had a register of names for the citizens living there. (See Ps. 69:28; Isa. 4:3) God, figuratively speaking, has been writing names in the "book of life" "from the foundation of the world." (Rev. 17:8) Jesus Christ talked about Abel as living "from the foundation of the world," this would suggest that we are talking about the world of ransomable humankind after the fall. (Lu 11:48-51) Clearly, Abel was the first person to have his name written in the "book of life." The individuals who have their names written in the "book of Life" do not mean they are predestined to eternal life. This is evident from the fact that they can be 'blotted out' of the "book of life." (Ex 32:32-33; Rev. 3:5) Jesus ransom sacrifice alone gets one written in the "book of life," if they accept the Son of God. However, it is remaining faithful to God that

[104] IBID, 291.

keeps them from being 'blotted' out of the "book of life." (Phil. 2:12; Heb. 10:26-27; Jam. 2:14-26) It is only by remaining faithful until the end that one can be retained permanently in the "book of life."–Matt. 214:13; Phil. 4:3; Rev. 20:15.

Revelation 17:9-11 Updated American Standard Version (UASV)

[9] Here is the mind which has wisdom. The seven heads are seven mountains on which the woman sits, [10] and they are seven kings; five have fallen **[Egypt, Assyrian, Babylon, Medo-Persia, and Greece]**, one is **[Rome]**, the other has not yet come **[United States]**; and when he comes, he must remain a little while. [11] And the beast that was, and is not, is also himself an eighth, and is of the seven, and he is going to destruction.

We can conclude that the first wild beast from the sea (vss. 1-10) and the second wild beast from the earth (vss. 11-18) of Revelation 13 represent two governmental powers. The first wild beast "the dragon **[Satan, Rev. 12:3, 9]** gave it his power and his throne and great authority." The second wild beast "exercises all the authority of the first beast on his behalf and compels the earth and those who live on it to worship the first beast." Therefore, these beasts or governmental powers are against Christ. Consequently, they are antichrists.

We must not overreact to this, believing that everyone within the government is somehow a tool, being possessed and used by Satan or his demons. We must realize that God uses the human governments for his own purposes as well. We have seen in the United States of late, what other countries have long known, without the law enforcement, a part of the government, there would be anarchy. Moreover, without the military might of the United States government, the world would be overrun by evil, such as Islam. If there were not legislatures, we would have no laws, which give structure to our human society. Some leaders and governments throughout human history have been used by Satan to try to stop pure worship, but others have protected the rights of its citizens, which include the freedom of worship. (Romans 13:3, 4; Ezra 7:11-27; Acts 13:7) Nevertheless, because of satanic influence and human imperfection, no human society has ever, nor will they ever bring true peace and security.

Because of Satan's influence over human governments, while Christians are to be in subjection to superior authorities (Rom 13:1), this is only as long as they do not ask anything that is in opposition to God's will and purpose. For example, if the government said, "no more evangelizing about the Bible," we would obey God rather than man. – Acts 5:29.

Thomas writes, "The best solution is that the seven kings represent seven literal Gentile kingdoms that follow one another in succession (Walvoord). In Dan. 7:17, 23 kings and kingdoms are interchangeable, showing that a king can stand for the kingdom ruled by that king (Swete, Lee). The seven kingdoms are the seven that dominate world scene throughout human history: Egypt (or Neo-Babylonia, Gen. 10:8–11), Assyria, Babylon, Persia, Greece, Rome, and the future kingdom of the beast (Seiss, Hailey)."[105]

Revelation 17:12-14 Updated American Standard Version (UASV)

[12] The ten horns which you saw are ten kings who have not yet received a kingdom, but they receive authority as kings with the beast for one hour. [13] These are of one mind,[106] and they hand over their power and authority to the beast. [14] They will make war on the Lamb, and the Lamb will conquer them, for he is Lord of lords and King of kings, and those with him are called and chosen and faithful."

The ten horns represent all the political powers that presently hold power on the world scene, which also support the image of the beast. Walvoord writes, "The final stage of this world empire has a nucleus of ten kings apparently joined in a confederacy represented by the ten horns. In contrast to the seven heads of the beast, these kings do not rule in succession but simultaneously at the end time." He goes on to say, "The ten horns' rule as kings is subject to the beast, and their time in power is brief. They are a phase of the transmission of power from the various kingdoms to that of the beast itself."[107]

Revelation 17:15-17 Updated American Standard Version (UASV)

[15] And he said to me, "The waters that you saw, where the prostitute is seated, are peoples and crowds and nations and tongues.[108] [16] And the ten horns that you saw and the beast, these will hate the prostitute and will make her desolate and naked, and they will eat her flesh and will burn her up with fire. [17] For God has put it into their hearts to carry out his purpose by being of one mind and handing over their royal power to the beast, until the words of God are fulfilled.

Ancient Babylon heavily relied on her watery defenses, Babylon the Great today also heavily relies on her many "peoples and crowds and nations and tongues." Kendell H. Easley says, "Surprise. We expected the final Antichrist and his federated powers to hate the Lamb, but we could

---

[105] Robert L. Thomas, *Revelation 8-22: An Exegetical Commentary* (Chicago: Moody Publishers, 1995), 297.

[106] Or *purpose*

[107] Walvoord, John. Revelation (The John Walvoord Prophecy Commentaries) (Kindle Locations 4227-4228). Moody Publishers.

[108] Or *languages*

not anticipate that **the beast and the ten horns will hate the prostitute** [world religions with apostate Christendom taking the lead]. This reflects, however, an observation readily verified from history: evil often turns on itself, carrying the seeds of its own defeat. The twentieth century witnessed a striking example: Russian communism, which arose with such promise at the beginning of the century, caved in on itself by the end of the century. Treachery and treason seem always to find a place in world power politics. Whether the three actions are sequential or simultaneous descriptions of the seventh bowl judgment hardly matters. First, they will **bring her to ruin and leave** the woman once decked out in scarlet and rich apparel **naked**, an ironic punishment for a wealthy harlot. Second, **they will eat her flesh**—just as the wicked Jezebel, queen in Samaria, was literally devoured by dogs (1 Kgs. 21:23), a fitting fate for someone who trusted a seven-headed beast. Third, they **will burn her with fire**. This describes suitably the destruction of a wicked city, but was also the punishment of certain whores in the Old Testament (Lev. 21:9)."[109]

Revelation 17:18 Updated American Standard Version (UASV)

[18] And the woman whom you saw means the great city that has a kingdom over the kings of the earth."

In short, antichrist that Satan used to influence the world, false religion of every sort, especially the apostate churches of Christendom will have control over the earth in the latter part of the last days, the time of the end.

---

[109] Kendell H. Easley, *Revelation*, vol. 12, Holman New Testament Commentary (Nashville, TN: Broadman & Holman Publishers, 1998), 313–314.

AMERICA 8 Donald Trump Takes Oath of Office for President of the United States, what Does This Mean for Christians?

> In January 2016, prominent evangelical Jerry Falwell Jr compared Trump to Christ, claiming the billionaire property tycoon lived "a life of loving and helping others, as Jesus taught". "You inspire us all," televangelist Pat Robertson told Trump in February 2016. Franklin Graham, son of renowned evangelist Billy Graham, even suggested that "it was the hand of God" that helped Trump defeat Hillary Clinton.[110]

Some Christians have claimed that the United States is found in Bible prophecy as the King of the South in Daniel, one of the seven kings of Revelation 17, or that Donald Trump was elected at the hand of God. Are these interpretations correct? Yes and no. Rather than just blurt out the answer in a very brief manner, let us reason together as we work our way to the answer.

One thing that we will learn from this Andrews' books is this; there are a few things that will build us up spiritually and maintain our strength in these **last days**. Our relationship with fellow Christians, our regular attendance at Christian meetings, and our sharing our faith with others, will strengthen us, make us steadfast. These are provisions of God that will help us to "be strong in the Lord and in the strength of his might." (Eph. 6:10) Max Anders comments, saying, "Paul introduces his final subject by urging the Ephesian believers to **be strong in the Lord**. When it comes to spiritual warfare, we cannot be sufficiently strong by ourselves. If we are going to have adequate strength for the spiritual battles of life, it must be the Lord's strength. Only he has the **mighty power** sufficient to win spiritual battles against the demonic enemy."[111] As we **grow in knowledge and understanding**, our chief desire will be to share our faith.

While Jesus was referring to our giving to the poor, we learn an important message from his words, "your Father who sees in secret will reward you." (Matt. 6:4) He is well aware of any difficult times that befall us. Even though God's "throne is in heaven; his own eyes see, his watchful

---

[110] Many white evangelicals stand by Trump because they are ... January 01, 2018

https://www.newstatesman.com/world/2017/12/many-white-evangelicals-stand-trump-because-they-are-more-white-evangelical

[111] Max Anders, *Galatians-Colossians*, vol. 8, Holman New Testament Commentary (Nashville, TN: Broadman & Holman Publishers, 1999), 190.

eyes examine the sons of men." (Ps. 11:4) We know that God never has to sleep, so he is ever watchful, having loving interest in the welfare of his people. God "will command his angels concerning you to guard you in all your ways. On their hands they will bear you up, lest you strike your foot against a stone." (Ps. 91:11-12) Steven Lawson writes, "In part, this sovereign guardianship will be carried out by his **angels** whom the Lord will **command** and commission to **guard you in all your ways**. Satan quoted these verses to Christ in his temptation and shrewdly omitted this last phrase, "in all your ways" (Matt. 4:6; Luke 4:10–11). This divine protection extends only to the place of trusting and obeying God. The angels **will lift you up in their hands, so that you will not strike your foot against a stone** (Ps. 34:7)."[112]

Remember the precious promise that God's eyes "run to and fro throughout the whole earth, to give strong support to **those whose heart is complete toward him**." (2 Chron. 16:9) God is "is the everlasting God, the Creator of the ends of the earth. He does not faint or grow weary; his understanding is unsearchable. He gives power to the tired one, and full might to those lacking strength." (Isa. 40:28-29) Isaiah then promises that those who place their hope in God, they "will regain power; they will soar on wings like eagles; they will run and not grow weary; they will walk and not tire out." (Isa. 40:31) Contentment and peace belong to those, who accept that the Father's power is always available to them, knowing that God is always interested in their best interests. We need to believe that "we know that **all things work together for good** for those who love God, for those who are called according to his purpose." – Romans 8:28.

We need to understand Roman's 8:28 better as it is often misused. Many read into (**eis**egesis) Paul's words that God causes everything to happen both good or bad. This is certainly one reason that the subject of biblical prophecy is very misunderstood, as well as suffering and evil. It is true that nothing happens outside of God's plan for our good. God is responsible for everything, but not always **directly**. If he started the human race, and we end up with what we now have, in essence, he is responsible. Just as parents, who have a child are similarly responsible for the child committing murder 21 years into his life because they procreated and gave birth to the child. The mother and father are **indirectly** responsible. King David commits adultery with Bathsheba and has her husband Uriah killed to cover things up, and impregnates Bathsheba, but the adulterine child, who remains nameless, died. Is God responsible for the death of that child? We can answer yes and no to that question. He is responsible in two ways: **(1)** He created humankind so there would have been no affair,

---

[112] Steven Lawson. *Holman Old Testament Commentary – Psalms 76-150* (Kindle Locations 2561-2564). B&H Publishing Group.

murder, adulterine child if he had not. **(2)** He did not step in and save the child when he had the power to do so. However, he is not **directly** responsible, because he did not make King David and Bathsheba commit the acts that led to the child being born, nor did he bring an illness on the adulterine child, he just did not move in to protect the child, in a time that had a high rate of infant deaths.

God is **indirectly** responsible for **all** things and **directly** responsible for **some** things. When we attribute things to God we need to qualify (i.e., explain) them. Without explaining the **directly** or **indirectly** part of God being responsible, we would be saying God brought about Vlad Dracula, Joseph Stalin, and Adolf Hitler for our good. God is **indirectly** responsible for all events in human history because he allowed sin to enter the world, as opposed to just destroying Satan, Adam, and Eve and starting over. God is directly responsible for many human events because he directly stepped in miraculously and used a group, person, organization, or country to carry out his will and purposes.

God is **indirectly** responsible for Joseph Stalin and Adolf Hitler. God is **directly** responsible for Babylon conquering Jerusalem. God is directly responsible for helping William Tyndale bring us the first printed English translation of the Bible. We can only know afterward (sometimes) if God is directly or indirectly responsible, and then, it is still an educated guess. Overly attributing everything to God without explaining whether he is directly or indirectly responsible is why unbelievers sometimes see Christians as illogical and irrational. A four-year-old child was rescued from a surging river by a priest in 1894. If the child were rescued in the same manner today, the media would quote Christian leaders as saying God used the priest to save the child. However, only afterward do we know that this is not true. Why? Because that four-year-old child, who nearly drowned in that river in 1894 was Adolf Hitler. Hitler being saved by the priest can be **indirectly** attributed to God not **directly**.

The reason people think that God does not care about us is the words of some religious leaders, which have made them, feel this way. When tragedy strikes, what do some pastors and Bible scholars often say? When 9/11 took place, with thousands dying in the twin towers of New York City, many ministers said: "It was God's will. God must have had some good reason for doing this." When religious leaders make such comments or similar ones, they are actually blaming God for the bad things that happened. Yet, the disciple James wrote, "Let no one say when he is tempted, 'I am being tempted by God,' for God cannot be tempted with evil, and he himself tempts no one." (James 1:13) God never **directly** causes what is bad. Indeed, "far be it from God that he should do wickedness, and from the Almighty that he should do wrong." (Job 34:10 God has **allowed** sin, old age, wickedness, suffering, and death to enter humanity after the rebellion by Satan, Adam, and Eve. He did not **cause** Satan to rebel, Eve to eat of the forbidden tree, or Adam to join that rebellion but God had allowed them to exercise the free will that he gave them. God has allowed the United States to exist and carry on as it has. More on this in a moment.

God has allowed wickedness and suffering, old age and death as an object lesson for his creation. What has this object lesson proven? God does not cause evil and suffering. (Rom. 9:14) The fact that God has allowed evil, pain, and suffering have shown that independence from God has not brought about a better world. (Jer. 8:5-6, 9) God's permission of evil, pain, and suffering has also proved that Satan has not been able to turn all humans away from God. (Ex. 9:16; 1 Sam. 12:22; Heb. 12:1) The fact that God has permitted evil, pain, and suffering to continue has provided proof that only God, the Creator, has the capability and the right to rule over humankind for their eternal blessing and happiness. (Eccl. 8:9) Satan has been the god of this world since the sin in Eden (over 6,000 years), and how has that worked out for man, and what has been the result of man's course of independence from God and his rule? – Matthew 4:8-9; John 16:11; 2 Corinthians 4:3-4; 1 John 5:19; Psalm 127:1.

United States in Bible Prophecy?

1 Timothy 2:1-2 Updated American Standard Version (UASV)

2 First of all, then, **I urge** that entreaties and **prayers**, petitions and thanksgivings, **be made on behalf of** all men, [2] **for kings and all who are in high positions**, that **we may lead a peaceful and quiet life**, godly and dignified in every way.

Some would argue that President Donald Trump is no Christian at all and that he is an immoral man in the extreme. We will allow God to judge Donald Trump in his own time. The only conservativism that we need to worry about is conservative Christianity. Conservative Christians should not have voted for Trump because he is a true conservative or because he is a faithful Christian because those things are irrelevant in the scheme of things.

Paul told Timothy that we are to pray for leaders. Why? Paul answers, "that we may lead a peaceful and quiet life, godly and dignified in every way." (1 Tim. 2:1-2) **In other words**, we pray for and vote for the leader that is going to make decisions that will allow us the freedom to carry out our ministry quietly and in peace.

How Do True Conservative Christians View Voting?

While Trump may or may not be a conservative, genuine, Christian by any means (Matt 7:17-18, 21-23), he is adamant about proposing conservative justices on the US Supreme Court, which can protect Christians freedom for decades to come. Christians will not be forced to share in the sins of the world (i.e., make a cake as a bakery for homosexual weddings), they can act on their conscience. Trump is also very serious about protecting America and the rest of the world from Islamic terrorism and Islam's agenda of undermining our Christian nation(s). Trump is also serious about dealing with the illegal immigrants that are costing the nation and being used only for Democratic votes.

However, more importantly, President Trump is rebuilding what Present Obama tore down. President Obama has the **worldview** that the United States was too big and too powerful and had abused its power by victimizing and taking from weaker nations. Therefore, under Obama's twisted reasoning, if the United States was weakened, the other countries could be strengthened, which would then make the world a fairer place, namely, a social justice mentality. President Obama weakened the united states military crippling them from fulfilling one Bible principle. He also very much weakened the moral fabric of the United States by implementing liberal progressive values in place of biblical Judeo-Christian values. The election of Donald J. Trump halted this implemented liberal progressive worldview from taking us down the path that many European countries had long known. This author will now say that in one year Trump has shown himself willing to fulfill Paul's words in two places with Scripture. Again, Paul told Timothy that we are to pray for leaders, so "that we may lead a peaceful and quiet life, godly and dignified in every way." (1 Tim. 2:1-2) However, President Trump, against all the odds has been carrying out another aspect of God's Word.

Romans 13:1 Updated American Standard Version (UASV)

13 Let every soul[113] be in subjection to the governing authorities. For **there is no authority except by God**, and those that exist have been **placed[114] by God.**

Does this verse mean that God has miraculously set up and established every governmental authority since the beginning of man? No, not at all. God is indirectly allowed governments to form, meaning that they serve a purpose by their presence. Many governments make some effort to make

---

[113] Or *person*

[114] Or *established, instituted*

laws that protect their public. Some governments abuse their power in the extreme, like Adolf Hitler. Obama abused his power in that he willfully contributed to the United States abandoning their biblical Judeo-Christian values and shift toward the liberal progressive worldview. He also willfully weakened the United States ability to protect the world from existing threats. Governmental authorities exist because God has allowed them to exist. In some cases, some leaders use their power to protect religious freedom and promote a biblical worldview. The United States has protected the world for over a century from wicked nations and other threats, spilling much of their people's blood and treasures. The world has largely been ungrateful. However, this peace that we have had since World War II, has allowed Christian to carry out their evangelism work in relative freedom. – Matthew 24:14; 28:19-20; Acts 1:8.

Trump is finding himself under attack from the liberal, progressive, socialist media, democratic politicians, Hollywood and so many other segments of society. Why? Because Obama was about building a socialist nation that hated itself and loved other countries more. Now, Trump is rolling that back and making America first. This does not mean that we ignore other countries. Rather it means that we put American conservative values first. It bears repeating as to why we support whichever politician that will give us religious freedom and protect us from enemies. Paul answers, "that we may lead a peaceful and quiet life, godly and dignified in every way." (1 Tim. 2:1-2) In other words, we pray for and vote for the leader that is going to make decisions that will allow us the freedom to carry out our ministry quietly and in peace. If you are spiritually awake and see the battle that is going on, you need to vote Trump into a second term.

We have, but one leader, Jesus Christ, and the United States has been a great tool to protect Christianity for centuries and can do so up unto the great tribulation. We do not know what the future holds in detail, but we do know that a great tribulation is on the horizon and things are going to go from bad to worse. – Matthew 24:21-28; 2 Timothy 3:1-7.

Therefore, let us carry out our ministry because the time is short, and we can use this period of peace wisely. We need to find a way for true Christians to unite under one God, becoming one in doctrine, word, and deed. We need to proclaim the Word of God, teach and make disciples. (Matt 24:14; 28;19; Ac 1:8) Not all so-called Christians are going to survive Christ's return. (Matt 7:21-23, 1 John 2:15-17) Jesus asked, "when I return will I really find the faith." (Lu 18:8) Not at this point and time with our 49,000 different Christian denominations all swearing they are the truth and the way even though they are all divided. Even churches within the same denominations are divided because of autonomy. Christ's second coming will happen in one of two ways.

ONE: Jesus chooses true Christians out of all of these denominations, and the false Christians will hear the words, "'I never knew you; depart from me, you workers of lawlessness.'" (Matt. 7:23)

TWO: Before the end comes one true form of Christianity will develop and all true Christians will see the light and migrate in the name of uniting under the one God. (Ex. 3:12; 19:17; Deut. 4:35; 4:39; Josh. 22:34; 2 Sam. 7:28; 1 Ki 8:60)

For the Christians that voted for Donald Trump and now believe he is not living up to his word, you need to step back and see the big picture. President Trump is battling Satan's world powers from the oval office, and he cannot do it alone. He needs to be voted in again so that he can restore some of what Obama tore down. Imagine yourself trying to alter a country that was turned upside down from within and you have most other countries against you, the liberal media 24/7 attacking you, liberal Hollywood campaigning against you, big business donating money to your enemies, your own conservative party attacking you, you have hundreds of holdovers from liberal progressive Obama's White House throughout the government, no one truly supporting you, how would you implement your campaign promises? He is not a dictator, nor does he have the power to implement many of his promises on his own. He is doing the best job he can under these trying circumstances. We need the extra four years from 2020 to 2024 to undo all the damage Obama has caused. Replace Trump with another lifetime conservative in 2020 will only return the United States to the status quo of politicians doing what they do.[115]

---

[115] Recommended Reading

THE CULTURE WAR: How the West Lost Its Greatness & Was Weakened From Within by Hanne Nabintu Herland

http://www.christianpublishers.org/apps/webstore/products/show/7558051

AMERICA 9 What are the Characteristics of the Antichrist?

If one were to ask different Christians what they believe about the Antichrist, there would be different views on the subject. "Dispensationalists look for a future Roman ruler who will appear during the tribulation and will rule over the earth. Those in the Amillennialist School interpret the term symbolically."[116] It is more than these two choices, though, as some feel the Antichrist is one person while others feel that it is a group of people, who are in opposition to Christ while others feel it is anyone that is "anti" Christ." Powerful people of the past have been labeled the Antichrist, such as the Roman Emperor Nero, Adolf Hitler, the German philosopher Friedrich Nietzsche, and more recently, radical Islam.[117] However, others are looking for a powerful world leader to come, or that is here already but has not stepped out of the shadows, who will rule the world. For these ones, they point to Revelation chapter 13 as referring to the Antichrist,

What About Revelation Chapter 13

Revelation 13:18 Updated American Standard Version (UASV)

[18] Here is wisdom. Let the one who has understanding calculate the number of the beast, for it is the number of a man [the antichrist], and his number is six hundred and sixty-six [666].[118]

Let us start with the number 666. Notice first, we are not told the significance of the number six hundred and sixty-six. However, we are told here who will ascertain the importance of that number, the "one who has understanding." We do know some things. We know that "man" (Gk., *anthrōpos*), often signifies the whole of mankind, i.e., humanity. We also know that the number six in the Bible, one less than seven (perfect) can denote imperfection. We also know that when something is mentioned three times, it is a way of intensifying what is being said. Therefore, six hundred and sixty-six (666) could be signifying gross human imperfection. This would very much refer to ones that are alienated from God, which would put some in opposition to Christ.

---

[116] http://biblia.com/books/hlmnillbbldict/Page.p_75

[117] The Islamic Antichrist: The Shocking Truth about the Real Nature of the Beast by Richardson, Joel (Jul 28, 2009)

[118] One early MS reads 616

Revelation Chapter 13: In order for this chapter of Revelation alone to apply, the antichrist must just be one person, and we will soon discover that this just is not the case. Let us look at Revelation 13:2, "And the beast that I saw was like a leopard; its feet were like a bear's, and its mouth was like a lion's mouth. And to it the dragon gave his power and his throne and great authority." What do these features denote?

> The body parts of this brute are a composite of three of the four creatures of Daniel 7:1–6, but in reverse order: body of **a leopard**, feet of **a bear**, and mouth of **a lion. In** Daniel's vision, these represented historical empires that opposed Judah, such as Babylon and Persia. Here they are all combined into one monster—raw political-military power.
>
> The Christians of John's day immediately grasped that the form of the monster current in their day was imperial Rome. Where did Rome's power come from? **The dragon gave the beast his power and his throne and great authority**. Although God has ordained that government be used for good (Rom. 13:1–7), clearly the devil has mastered the art of twisting what God means for good and turning it to evil.[119]

Revelation 13:1 Updated American Standard Version (UASV)

[1] And the dragon stood on the sand of the sea. Then I saw a beast coming up out of the sea, having ten horns and seven heads, and on his horns were ten diadems, and on his heads were blasphemous names.

What or who do these seven heads represent? The seven heads are seven world empires throughout Bible history that have had some impact on God's people, five of which were before John's day: Egypt Assyria, Babylon, Medo-Persia, and Greece. The sixth of those world empires was in existence during John's day, Rome, with the seventh world empire, yet to come. Look at John's reference again in the same book.

Revelation 17:9-10 Updated American Standard Version (UASV)

[9] Here is the mind which has wisdom. The seven heads are seven mountains on which the woman sits, [10] and they are seven kings; five have fallen [Egypt, Assyrian, Babylon, Medo-Persia, and Greece], one is [Rome], the other has not yet come [?]; and when he comes, he must remain a little while.

We can conclude that the first wild beast from the sea (vss. 1-10) and the second wild beast from the earth (vss. 11-18) of Revelation 13 represent

---

[119] Kendell H. Easley, *Revelation, vol. 12, Holman New Testament Commentary* (Nashville, TN: Broadman & Holman Publishers, 1998), 227.

two governmental powers. The first wild beast "the dragon **[Satan, Rev. 12:3, 9]** gave it his power and his throne and great authority." The second wild beast "exercises all the authority of the first beast on his behalf and compels the earth and those who live on it to worship the first beast." Therefore, these beasts or governmental powers are against Christ. Consequently, they are antichrists.

Antichrist Defined and Explained

We can now define the antichrist as anyone, any group, any organization, or any government that is *against* or *instead of* Christ, or who mistreat his people. Thus, we are not just looking for one person, one group, one organization, or one power.

The Bible does not refer to just one antichrist. There has been an innumerable number of antichrists since the apostle John wrote his letters at the end of the first century.

1 John 2:18 Updated American Standard Version (UASV)

18 Little children, it is the last hour [John is the last of the 12 apostles and is almost a hundred, close to death]; and just as you heard that antichrist is coming, even now many antichrists have arisen; whereby we know that it is the last hour [of John's protection (the apostolic period), as he dies shortly thereafter].

As is spelled out within the text, "the last hour," John was referring to the apostolic period of the twelve apostles. At the time of this writing, about 98 C.E., all of the other apostles are dead, and John is close to being one hundred years old. The apostolic period was a time when the twelve apostles could protect the Christian congregation from the upcoming great apostasy that Jesus and the New Testament writers warned was coming. New Testament textual scholar Philip Comfort comments on this,

> Once the final, authorized publication was released and distributed to the churches, I think it unlikely that any substantive changes would have occurred during the lifetime of the apostles or second-generation coworkers. By "substantive," I mean a change that would alter Christian doctrine or falsify an apostolic account. The primary reason is that the writers (or their immediate successors) were alive at the time and therefore could challenge any significant, unauthorized alterations. As long as eyewitnesses such as John or Peter were alive, who would dare change any of the Gospel accounts in any significant manner? Any one among the Twelve could have testified against any falsification. And there was also a group of 72 other disciples

(Luke 10:1) who could do the same. Furthermore, according to 1 Corinthians 15:6, Jesus had at least five hundred followers by the time he had finished his ministry, and these people witnessed Jesus in resurrection. Most of these people were still alive (Paul said) in AD 57/58 (the date of composition for 1 Corinthians); it stands to reason that several lived for the next few decades—until the turn of the century and even beyond.[120]

2 John 1:7 Updated American Standard Version (UASV)

[7] For many deceivers have gone out into the world, even those who do not confess the coming of Jesus Christ in the flesh. This is the deceiver and the antichrist.

We also notice that John says there are "many antichrists." John refers to these collectively as "the antichrist" here in 2 John 1:7. Should Christians be looking for some future time, to identify some specific antichrist?

1 John 4:3 Updated American Standard Version (UASV)

[3] and every spirit that does not confess Jesus is not from God; this is the spirit of the antichrist, of which you have heard that it is coming, and now it is in the world already.

First John was written in the last years of the first century, about 98 C.E., and yet John says that there were antichrists already in the world during his day. It is the signs of antichrists in John's day, which let him, know it was the last hour. What characteristics do the antichrists have?

1 John 2:22 Updated American Standard Version (UASV)

[22] Who is the liar but the one who denies that Jesus is the Christ? This is the antichrist, even the one who denies the Father and the Son.

Clearly, any who deny that Jesus is the Messiah or Christ, the anointed one, the unique Son of God is the antichrist.

1 John 2:18-19 Updated American Standard Version (UASV)

[18] Little children, it is the last hour; and just as you heard that antichrist is coming, even now many antichrists have arisen; whereby we know that it is the last hour. [19] They went out from us, but they were not of us; for if they had been of us, they would have continued with us; but they went out, so that they would be revealed that they all are not of us.

Apostates are any who stand off from the truth, who also go a step further by attacking their former brothers of the faith. In the above, we see

---

[120] Philip Comfort, *Encountering the Manuscripts: An Introduction to New Testament Paleography & Textual Criticism* (Nashville, TN: Broadman & Holman, 2005), 255–256.

John is talking about apostates being among the antichrists, as he specifically said in verse 18 that 'even now there are many antichrists,' followed by verse 19 that says, "they went out from us." Those who went out from them were ones, who had abandoned the first-century Christian congregation. This would then also include "the man of lawlessness" also known as the "the lawless one," or "son of destruction" described by Paul. (2 Thess. 2:3, 8) In addition, it would also include "false teachers among you, who will secretly bring in destructive heresies, even denying the Master who bought them." (2 Pet. 2:1) See Identifying the Man of Lawlessness in later chapter.

John 15:20-21 Updated American Standard Version (UASV)

[20] Remember the word that I said to you: 'A servant is not greater than his master.' If they **persecuted me**, they **will also persecute you**. If they kept my word, they will keep yours also. [21] But all these things they will do to you on account of my name, because they do not know the one who sent me.

Psalm 2:2 Updated American Standard Version (UASV)

[2] The kings of the earth take their stand,
and the rulers take counsel together,
against Jehovah and against his anointed one [Messiah or Christ] , saying,

Matthew 24:23-26 Update American Standard Version (UASV)

[23] Then if any man says to you, 'Look, here is the Christ!' or 'There he is!' do not believe it. [24] For **false Christs** and false prophets will arise and will show great signs and wonders, so as to mislead, if possible, even the chosen ones.[121] [25] Behold, I have told you in advance. [26] So if they say to you, 'Behold, he is in the wilderness,' do not go out, or, 'Behold, he is in the inner rooms,' do not believe it.

Jesus' prophecy about the end of the Jewish age **of his day** and the end of wicked humanity **in our day**, reads, "See that no one leads you astray. For many will come in my name, saying, 'I am the Christ,' and they will **lead many <u>astray</u>**." (Matt 24:4-5) Here in our current verses, Jesus tells us who specifically is being "led astray," "For false Christs [Gr., *pseudochristoi*] and false prophets will arise and will show great signs and wonders, so as to mislead, if possible, even <u>the chosen ones</u>." Any who falsely claim to be Christ (anointed one or Messiah), or claim to be a special representative of Christ, are included in the "antichrist" [Gr., *antichristos*],

[121] Or *the elect*

which as we have already seen is mentioned five times by the apostle John. – 1 John 2:18, 22; 4:3; 2 John 1:7.

There were false Christs and false prophets that came on the scene before 70 C.E., and the destruction of the Jewish age. Jewish historian Flavius Josephus confirms this as he writes that before the Romans ever attacked, false Messiahs prompted rebellion. We have Menahem ben Judah, who claimed to be the Jewish Messiah and is mentioned by Josephus. Then, there is Theudas, who claimed to be the Messiah a Jewish rebel of the 1st century C.E., who between 44 and 46 CE, led his followers in a short-lived revolt. However, as is self-evident, they showed themselves to be false, charlatans, as they did not deliver the Jewish people from the Roman armies. After the destruction of Jerusalem, up unto this day, the Jews[122] have not put faith in Jesus Christ, the Son of God, but have rather continued their search for a Messiah in the flesh.

Conversely, both Jewish and non-Jewish Christians have evidenced their faith in Jesus Christ, as they have continued to look at the end of Satan's rule over the earth, the end of wicked humankind, the return of Jesus Christ and his millennial reign. There have been many notable people in the 18th to the 21st century, who has been claimed to be the reincarnation or incarnation of Jesus or the Second Coming of Christ. Either they have made these claims, or their followers have made the claim. To mention just a couple, Jim Jones (1931–1978), founder of Peoples Temple, this started as a branch of a mainstream Protestant group before becoming a cult. Then, we have Marshall Applewhite (1931–1997), an American, who posted a famous message declaring, "I, Jesus, Son of God," whose Heaven's Gate cult committed mass suicide on March 26, 1997. Wayne Bent (1941–), AKA Michael Travesser of the Lord Our Righteousness Church. He claimed, "I am the embodiment of God. I am divinity and humanity combined."

If any reader does not believe that they can fall victim to charismatic persons, they are deceiving themselves. Millions of Christians have fallen victim to such ones, and they have not even had the satanic power of 'showing great signs and wonders,' which will be the result before humanities "great tribulation." Then, we have Christians that pick up these end times books, going around speaking of how much truth are within them, when the author(s) has gone beyond what the Word of God says. Finally, there are Pentecostals and Charismatic Christians that number over 500 million, a quarter of the world's two billion Christians. This author sees the religious leaders of these groups as the false Christs, antichrists, false prophets that will be the catalyst to the major false Christs, antichrists, false

---

[122] This is not to say that no individual Jewish persons have not converted to Christianity, as hundreds of thousands have in the last two millennium.

prophets before the great tribulation. **Excessive** emotionalism within Christianity brings about a blind desire for the return of Christ, opening many up to a situation in which religious leaders offer biblical passages that incorrectly match a return of Christ, e.g. signs of the times, a charismatic person, world events, bad proof-texting, and the like.

Thus, the antichrist is any person, group, organization, or power.

(1) The antichrist denies that Jesus is the Christ,

(2) The antichrist denies the Father and the Son,

(3) Some of the antichrists have abandoned the Christian faith, and after that work in opposition to Christ,

(4) The antichrist is anti-Christian

AMERICA 10 How Can We Identify the Antichrist?

1 John 2:18 Updated American Standard Version (UASV)

[18] Little children, it is the last hour; and just as you heard that **antichrist is coming**, even now **many antichrists** have arisen; whereby we know that it is the last hour.

If we were sitting by the radio, and the newscaster came on to warn us about an escaped murderer from the county jail, we would listen intensely as they described what he looked like. We would be very cautious until we heard he had been captured.

As Christians, we have received a very similar warning about the Antichrist being on the loose, and we want to listen intently as the Bible tells us about how we can identify him, her, or it. John writes, "Every spirit that does not confess Jesus is not from God; this is the spirit of the antichrist, of which you have heard that it is coming, and now it is in the world already." (UASV) Was the Antichrist in the world only in the tomb of the apostle John, or is the Antichrist present now, or is the Antichrist coming at a future time?

In chapter 1, we discovered that it is John alone, who uses the term "Antichrist," of which he does five times. From those five times, we gather this entity is "against" (i.e., denies Christ) or "instead of" (i.e., false Christs) Jesus Christ. The Bible gives us clear insight into the Antichrist, but as we saw in the introduction, interpreters have run amuck into speculation.

Misidentifying the Antichrist

The greatest misidentification has been the interpretation that the Antichrist is just one particular person. Moreover, there have been many who have been suggested as contenders. Early on, it was thought that Roman Emperor Nero was the Antichrist. He was definitely antichristian, which is, in essence, an antichrist. Jesus said, "If they persecuted me, they would also persecute you." (John 15:20) More recently, it was suggested that Adolf Hitler was the Antichrist. Again, Hitler was certainly antichristian. Many have pointed to Revelation 13 in reference to the Antichrist, but they are not so in the sense that many might think. Yes, these beasts or governmental powers of Revelation 13 are against Christ. Consequently, they are antichrists, as we saw in chapter 1. However, some suggest that the mark of the beat, 666, will be the mark of the Antichrist. Yes, while chapter 1 helped us appreciate what 666 might stand for, it does not fit the misidentification of the Antichrist being but one person. It does fit the biblical truth that there are many antichrists, i.e., many humans in opposition to Christ, by way of their gross human imperfection.

Who Make Up the Antichrist?

When Jesus came to the earth, he had to face many enemies; Herod, who tried to have Jesus killed as a child, Satan who followed him into the wilderness to tempt him, the Jewish religious leaders, and eventually the Roman government by way of Pontius Pilate. Even though Jesus returned to heaven, and is now untouchable, he still has many enemies. The apostle John stated,

1 John 2:22 Updated American Standard Version (ASV)

[22] Who is the liar but the one who denies that Jesus is the Christ? This is the antichrist, even the one who denies the Father and the Son.

The Bible speaks of apostasy, which is one who stands off from what is true. Thus, we would refer to one of these as an apostate. Michael Fink writes, "In 2 Thess. 2:3 Paul addressed those who had been deceived into believing that the day of the Lord had already come. He taught that an apostasy would precede the day of the Lord. The Spirit had explicitly revealed this falling away from the faith (1 Tim. 4:1). Such apostasy in the latter times will involve doctrinal deception, moral insensitivity, and ethical departures from God's truth." (Brand, Draper and Archie 2003, 87) These are ones come in many shades of doctrinal deceit. They reject clear teachings of Scripture and spread false teachings about the Father and the Son. Therefore, they are a part of the antichrist. Jesus forewarned his disciples, and by implication us,

Luke 21:12 Updated American Standard Version (UASV)

[12] But before **all these things**, they will lay their hands on you and will persecute you, delivering you to the synagogues and prisons, bringing you before kings and governors for My name's sake.

"All these things" is referring to the events of 21:7-11, which is a reference to the destruction of Jerusalem in 70 C.E.[123] Thus, "Before international warfare and natural chaos come, the church will face persecution, Jesus continued. Belief in Christ and his name will be cause enough for you to be put in jail and punished by the government. Jewish religious leaders will join force with the government to make this happen." (Buter 2000, 351) This happened to the first century Christians, but by implication, if the world hated them because of bearing the name of Christ,

---

[123] See Acts 5:36; 21:38

how much more so would this not be the case in end times. Are Christians not suffering persecution in this liberal-progressive world that is not emerging? Yes, listen to the principle as Paul laid it out,

2 Timothy 3:12 Updated American Standard Version (UASV)

[12] Indeed, all who desire to live a godly life in Christ Jesus will be persecuted,

Those ones that are of gross human imperfection, 666, because they are alienated from God by heart and mind, are the cause of such mistreatment. In other words, they are working "against" Christ, making them a part of the antichrist. Jesus himself said, "He who is not with me is against me." Those who are antichrists have one outcome in the end.

The Destruction of Antichrist

Psalm 5:6 Updated American Standard Version (UASV)

[6] You destroy those who speak lies;
Jehovah abhors the bloodthirsty and deceitful man.

The apostle John wrote,

2 John 1:7 Updated American Standard Version (UASV)

[7] For many deceivers have gone out into the world, even those who do not confess the coming of Jesus Christ in the flesh. This is the deceiver and the antichrist.

Those who are lying and deceiving, the antichrists, the Father by way of the Son will bring destruction upon them. As we move through these last days, true Christians should be well prepared not to allow anti-Christian trickery treachery, and pressure to cause them to have a spiritual shipwreck. The apostle John warns us,

2 John 1:8 Updated American Standard Version (UASV)

[8] Watch yourselves, that you do not lose what we have worked for, but that you may receive a full reward.

The Antichrist is Further Identified

Christians not only have to battle the Agnostic and atheist, but they must also contend with liberal Bible scholars, and even some moderates, who use higher criticism in their interpretation. It is here that we should also expound a little more on the "criticism" portion of the term "higher criticism" and "textual criticism." It might be more helpful if we talk for a moment about biblical criticism. It is divided into two branches: lower criticism and higher criticism. Lower criticism, also known as textual criticism, is an investigation of manuscripts by those, who are known as textual scholars, seeking to establish the original reading, which is no longer available. Higher criticism, also known as literary criticism takes that original text that has been established by textual criticism, looking for any sources that may lie behind it.

Lower criticism (i.e., textual criticism), has been the bedrock of scholarship over the last 500 years, which has given us a master text, i.e., a critical text, which is a 99.95 percent reflection of the original published Greek New Testament. It has done nothing but contribute to the furtherance of Bible scholarship, removing interpolations, correcting scribal errors, and giving us a critical text, allowing us to produce better translations of the New and Old Testaments.

In contrast, **higher criticism** (i.e., literary criticism) has unlocked the floodgates of pseudo-scholarly works whose consequence has been to weaken, challenge and undercut Christian's confidence in the Scriptures. In an effort to determine the origin of each book, its author, its location where it was written, and how much can be attributed to the traditional author, the sources behind a Bible book, higher criticism has destroyed the trustworthiness of the Bible, picking it apart until there is little left. Fortunately, some conservative scholars[124] have **undermined** these higher critics for their illogical, unreasonable, lack of common sense that they have had as they have attempted their dissecting of God's Word. Many of higher criticism do not believe in literal antichrists, but rather see it as merely a concept of good versus evil, and to these critics, the idea of a literal antichrist is nothing more than a myth.

Matthew 24:23-26 Updated American Standard Version (UASV)

[23] Then if anyone says to you, 'Look, here is the Christ!' or 'There he is!' do not believe it. [24] For false Christs and false prophets will arise and will show great signs and wonders, so as to mislead, if possible, even the chosen ones. [25] Behold, I have told you beforehand. [26] So if they say to you, 'Behold, He is in the wilderness,' do not go out, or, 'Behold, He is in the inner rooms,' do not believe it.

So that false Christs and false prophets may not fool the chosen ones of God or those who are truly Christian, Jesus gave us the warning found here in Matthew. Those who are claiming that they are Christ himself, the return of Christ, are the false Christs. On the other hand, false prophets are those that claim that God reveals the truth to them, and them alone.

---

[124] Such scholars as Robert L. Thomas, Norman L. Geisler, Gleason L. Archer, F. David Farnell, and Joseph M. Holden, et al. have fought for decades, to educate us about the dangers of higher criticism.

It is right before and during the Great Tribulation when we will hear reports that Christ has returned. There will be both false Christs and prophets, who will be used by Satan to carry out great signs and miracles, a so-called evident demonstration of their real credentials as the Christ or a prophet of Christ. These false ones will present such a showy display that even true Christians will fall for their deception. We need to understand because one may have the ability to perform miracles; this does not mean the miracles are from God. – Matthew 7:21-23.

We have seen that Christians are easily swayed into mere charismatic personalities. How much more so would they be deceived by a charismatic person, who can also perform miracles and signs. Millions of Christians flock to mega-churches and televangelists, such as Joel Osteen, Benny Hinn, Paul and Jan Crouch, Pat Robinson, Jimmy Swaggart, Ted Haggard, Jim and Tammy Baker, and Joyce Meyer. Moreover, tens of millions will be the first to buy a book about end times, the last days, the prophecy of the Great Tribulation and Armageddon, such as *The Harbinger: The Ancient Mystery That Holds the Secret of America's Future*. These Christians will come to church with books likes these under their arms, swearing up and down that every word is so true, convincing others to buy into the lie.

Write a book about the last days, and it becomes a New York Times Bestselling book. Be a Bible scholar who puts ten years of research into a book on the historical reliability of Jesus' resurrection, and he will sell a few thousand books. These writers of the end times, last days, Great Tribulation and Armageddon are a foretaste of what is to come. These authors come across in their books as though they have been given information directly from God, a special insight, which allows them to disclose these so-called mysterious secrets. If tens of millions of Christians drink down these books and the televangelist, as if they are quenching their thirst, there is little doubt that Jesus' warning will do them any good.

2 Thessalonians 2:3, 7, 9 English Standard Version (ESV)

[3] Let no one deceive you in any way. For that day will not come, unless the rebellion comes first, and the man of lawlessness is revealed, the son of destruction, [7] For the mystery of lawlessness is already at work. Only he who now restrains it will do so until he is out of the way. [9] The coming of the lawless one is by the activity of Satan with all power and false signs and wonders,

Antichrist Equals Anti ("Instead of or "against") Christ

Matthew 16:16 Updated American Standard Version (UASV)

[16] Simon Peter answered, "You are the Christ, the Son of the living God."

The Christ [Heb. Messiah, anointed one] that Peter spoke of and was/is being opposed; he is the one spoken of by the prophets. Who was born in Bethlehem around 1 B.C.E., who began his ministry in 29 C.E., who gave his life as a ransom for many in 33 C.E., and who was resurrected on the third day, and ascended back to heaven 40 days after his resurrection?

Looking a little deeper into the term, "Antichrist," it seems that it has two meanings. It does have the meaning of "anti," "against," "opposed to," but the preposition also carries the meaning "instead of." Thus, we are looking for ones or groups that are "against" Jesus Christ or his disciples. However, we are also looking for ones who are "instead of" Christ, a false or pseudo-Christ. As we have seen from the two previous chapters, many believe that the antichrist is one individual person, who is still yet to come. However, we have also seen that antichrist applies to all persons who claim to be the one and only representative or Christ or coming in place of Christ, as well as all persons, groups or organizations that are *opposed* to Christ. Again, Jesus said, "He who is not with me is against me" (Matt 12:30) On this verse Stuart K. Weber writes, "Jesus eliminated the possibility of anyone remaining "neutral" toward him. Anyone who was not seeking to live for Jesus was, by default, Jesus enemy." (Weber 2000, 177)

Hebrews 5:13-14 Updated American Standard Version (UASV)

[13] For everyone who partakes of milk is unacquainted with the word of righteousness, for he is an infant. [14] But solid food belongs to the mature, to those who through practice have their discernment trained to distinguish between good and evil.

The milk metaphor is easy for every generation because we all know that a babe grows into physical maturity by the milk that he consumes. So too, the spiritual babe grows into maturity by taking in the metaphorical milk of elementary Bible doctrine. Once they have reached maturity, they can then take in "solid food," deeper Bible truths. Paul tells us at 1 Corinthians 13:11, "When I was a child, I spoke like a child, I thought like a child, I reasoned like a child. When I became a man, I gave up childish ways." These Hebrew Christians needed to get off the elementary Bible doctrines ("milk") and move on to the deeper biblical truths of "solid food."

If we are to appreciate and apply the Bible in our lives, we must first fully understand it. We must know what the author of a Bible book meant by the words that he used, as should have been understood by his original intended audience. Then, we will be able to attach the significance that it has on our lives. If we are unaware of the correct way of interpreting the Scriptures, grammatical-historical interpretation, then we are going to be one of those who Peter spoke of as, 'the ignorant and unstable, who twist the Scriptures to their own destruction.' Tens of millions of Christians unknowingly share an incorrect understanding of Scripture every day, because they are not aware of the rules and principles of interpretation, while others may be aware of some, yet fail to apply them correctly.

The Antichrist and Religions

The Scriptures are very clear as to who Jesus was/is, and those who claim that he was merely a human in history, rejecting his divinity, are antichrists. All, who willfully manipulate Scriptures, to get it to say what they want it to say, are guilty of theological bias and is the antichrist. Devotees of Oriental religions, atheists, deists[125] or agnostics, are antichrists.

John 1:14 (NASB)	**Galatians 4:4** (NASB)
[14] And the Word became flesh, and dwelt among us, and we saw His glory, glory as of the only begotten from the Father, full of grace and truth.	[4] But when the fullness of the time came, God sent forth His Son, born of a woman, born under the Law,

Anyone who denies the value of Jesus' ransom sacrifice is an antichrist. John the Baptist said of Jesus, "Behold, the Lamb of God, who takes away the sin of the world!" (John 1:29) Jesus said of himself, "the Son of Man came ... to give his life as a ransom for many." (Matt 20:28) The apostle John wrote, "The blood of Jesus his Son cleanses us from all sin." (1 John 1:7) The apostle Peter said of Jesus, "but with the precious blood of Christ, like that of a lamb without blemish or spot." (1 Pet. 1:19) The apostle Paul wrote, "God shows his love for us in that while we were still sinners, Christ died for us. Since, therefore, we have now been justified by his blood, much more shall we be saved by him from the wrath of God." (Rom. 5:8-9) Isaiah, prophesied,

Isaiah 53:12 Updated American Standard Version (UASV)

[12] Therefore I will divide him a portion with the many,
and he shall divide the spoil with the strong,
because he poured out his soul to death
and was numbered with the transgressors;
yet he bore the sin of many,
and makes intercession for the transgressors.

---

[125] Deism is a belief in God based on reason rather than revelation and involving the view, which God has set the universe in motion but does not interfere with how it runs.

yet he bore the sin of many,
  and makes intercession for the transgressors.

Whether we wish to accept it or not, a number of religious leaders, from a number of Christian denominations reject the atoning work of Christ. Some even believe the teaching of the atonement is offensive to their moral senses. They say that the death of Jesus Christ was not needed for human salvation.

They even say that Scripture does not teach that Christians receive a righteous standing with God because of Jesus' death. These ones would be antichrists, as atonement is a biblical "doctrine that God has reconciled sinners to Himself through the sacrificial work of Jesus Christ." (Brand, Draper and Archie 2003, 142)

Acts 20:28-30 Revised Standard Version (RSV)

[28] Take heed to yourselves and to all the flock, in which the Holy Spirit has made you overseers, to care for the church of God which he obtained with the blood of his own Son. [29] I know that after my departure fierce wolves will come in among you, not sparing the flock; [30] and **from among your own selves** will arise men **speaking perverse things**, to **draw away the disciples after them.**

Yes, Jesus was warning of the coming danger, of ones who were out to steal those who are his disciples. They too are his enemy, trying to take his disciples for them. Jesus repeats his warning twice, "by their fruit you will recognize them." (Matt. 7:16, 20) The distinguishing marker is good versus bad (literally worthless, rotten) fruit.

The main good fruit is mentioned in verse 21, only those, who are doing the will of the Father, are producing good fruit. Another fruit is the God's Word itself. As Jesus said, so it is, "If you continue in my word you are truly my disciples, and you will know the truth, and the truth will set you free." (John 8:31-32) Yes, genuine Christians "must worship in spirit and truth." – John 4:24

How do we "worship in spirit and truth"? We worship in spirit when a heart filled with faith and love motivates our life course, our walking with God. This means that we are completely devoted to pure worship as it is revealed within Scripture. In addition, to worship in spirit means that we allow our lives to be guided by the Spirit inspired Word of God. Through Bible study, prayer and worship, as well as application of God's Word, our spirit, new personality must be in harmony with God's Spirit. We worship in truth by coming to an accurate knowledge of the Word of God, and following its revealed truths, not man. We need to reject the false teachings that has infiltrated into the Way (Ac 9:2; 19:9), and the Truth (3 John 1:4).

If this means that we discover our form of Christianity is not in harmony with the spirit and truth of God, we must choose another course. This means that if we have had a mistaken view of the antichrist all along, we must now humbly accept the truth as Scripture has clearly stated.

Yes, those, who standoff from the Truth and the Way, would not be seeking their own disciples, but rather they would be seeking, "to draw away the disciples after them." i.e., the disciples of Christ. Jesus was well aware that the easiest way to defeat any group is to divide them, and so was Satan, who had been watching humanity for over 4,000 years, and especially the Israelites (Isaac and Ishmael / Jacob and Esau / Israel and Judah), as "Satan disguises himself as an angel of light. So it is no surprise if his servants, also, disguise themselves as servants of righteousness."—2 Corinthians 11:14-15

The apostle Peter also spoke of these things about **64 C.E.**, "there will be false teachers among you, who will secretly bring in destructive heresies . . . in their greed they will exploit you with false words.." (2 Pet. 2:1, 3) These abandoned the faithful words, became false teachers, rising within the Christian congregation, sharing their corrupting influence, intending to hide, disguise, or mislead.

These dire warnings by Jesus and the New Testament authors had their beginnings in the first century C.E. Yes, the false teachers, causing division, began small, but burst forth on the scene in the second century. Paul wrote,

2 Thessalonians 2:3-4 Updated American Standard Version (UASV)

[3] Let no one deceive[126] you in any way, for it will not come unless the apostasy[127] comes first, and the man of lawlessness is revealed, the son of destruction, [4] who opposes and exalts himself against every so-called god or object of worship, so that he takes his seat in the temple of God, showing himself as being God.

"[Paul says it] Is Already at Work."

About **51 C.E.**, some 18-years after Jesus' death, resurrection and ascension, division was already starting to creep into the faith, "the mystery of lawlessness is already at work." (2 Thess. 2:7) Yes, the power of **the man of lawlessness** was already present, which is the power of Satan, the god of

[126] Or *seduce*

[127] **Apostasy:** (Gr. *apostasia*) The term literally means "to stand away from" and is used to refer to ones who 'stand away from the truth.' It is abandonment, a rebellion, an apostasy, a refusal to accept or acknowledge true worship. In Scripture, this is used primarily concerning the one who rises up in defiance of the only true God and his people, working in opposition to the truth.–Ac 21:21; 2 Thess. 2:3.

this world (2 Cor. 4:3-4), and his tens of millions of demons, are hard at work behind the scenes.

There were even some divisions beginning as early as **49 C.E.**, when the elders wrote a letter to the Gentile believers, saying,

> Since we have heard that some persons have gone out from us and troubled you with words, unsettling your minds, although we gave them no instructions (Ac 15:24)

Here we see that some *within* the Christian congregtion was being very vocal about their opposition to the direction the faith was heading. Here, it was over whether the Gentiles needed to be circumcised, suggesting that they needed to be obedient to the Mosaic Law. – Acts 15:1, 5.

As the years progressed throughout the first-century, this divisive "talk [would] spread like gangrene." (2 Tim. 2:17, **c. 65 C.E.**) About **51 C.E.**, They had some in Thessalonica, at worst, going ahead of, or at best, misunderstanding Paul, and wrongly stating by word and a bogus letter "that the day of the Lord has come." (2 Thess. 2:1-2) In Corinth, about **55 C.E.**, "some of [were saying] that there is no resurrection of the dead. (1 Cor. 15:12) About **65 C.E.**, some were "saying that the resurrection has already happened. They [were] upsetting the faith of some." (2 Tim 2:16-18)

Throughout the next three decades, no inspired books were written. However, by the time the apostle John writes his three letters in 96-98 C.E., he tells us "Now many antichrists have come. Therefore we know that it is the last hour." (1 John 2:18) Again, these are ones, "who denies that Jesus is the Christ" and ones who not confess "Jesus Christ has come in the flesh is from God." (1 John 2:22; 4:2-3)

From 33 C.E. to 100 C.E., the apostles served Christ as a restraint against "the apostasy" that was coming. Paul stated at 2 Thessalonians 2:7, "For the mystery of lawlessness is already at work. Only he [Apostle by Christ] who now restrains it [the apostasy] will do so until he **[apostles]** is out of the way." 2 Thessalonians 2:3 said, "Let no one deceive you in any way **[misinterpretation or false teachers of Paul's first letter]**. For that day **[presence, parousia (second coming) of Christ]** will not come, unless the apostasy comes first, and the man of lawlessness **[likely one person, or maybe an organization / movement, empowered by Satan]** is revealed, the son of destruction."

Again, we must keep in mind that the meaning of any given text is what the author meant by the words that he used, as should have been understood by his audience, and had some relevance/meaning for his audience. The rebellion [apostasy] began slowly in the first century and would break forth after the death of the last apostle, i.e., John. As historian, Ariel Durant informed us earlier, by 187 C.E., there were 20 varieties of Christianity, and by 384 C.E., there were 80 varieties of Christianity. Christianity would become one again, a universal religion, i.e., Catholicism. Today, we have over 41,000 varieties of Christianity.

Outline of Christian Divisions

Start of Apostasy - 2nd Century

Roman Catholic Church

- 4th Century (Constantine)
- 5th Century Coptic
  - Jacobite
- 1054 C.E. Eastern Orthodox
  - Russian
  - Greek
  - Romanian and others
- 16th Century Reformation
  - Lutheran
  - German
  - Swedish
  - American and others
  - Anglican
  - Episcopal
  - Methodist
  - Salvation Army
  - Baptist
  - Pentecostal
  - Congregational
  - Calvinism
  - Presbyterian
  - Reformed Churches

Pre-Reformation

- **Bishop Agobard** of Lyons, France (779-840), was against image worship, churches dedicated to saints and church liturgy that was contrary to Scripture.

- **Bishop Claudius** (d. between 827 and 839 C.E.)

- **Archdeacon Bérenger**, or Berengarius, of Tours, France (11th century C.E.), excommunicated as a heretic in 1050

- **Peter of Bruys** (1117-c. 1131), left the church because he disagreed with infant baptism, transubstantiation, prayers for the dead, worship of the cross and the need for church buildings.

- **Henry of Lausanne** (died imprisoned around 1148), spoke out against church liturgy, the corrupt clergy and the religious hierarchy.

- **Peter Waldo** (c. 1140–c. 1218) and the Waldenses, rejected purgatory, Masses for the dead, papal pardons and indulgences, and the worship of Mary and the saints.

- **John Wycliffe** (c. 1330-1384) preached against corruption in the monastic orders, papal taxation, the doctrine of transubstantiation (doctrine that the bread and wine of Communion become, in substance, but not appearance, the body and blood of Jesus Christ at consecration), the confession, and church involvement in temporal affairs.

- **Jan Hus** (c. 1369-1415) preached against the corruption of the Roman Church and stressed the importance of reading the Bible. This swiftly fetched the anger of the hierarchy upon him. In 1403, the church leaders ordered him to stop preaching the antipapal notions of Wycliffe, whose books they had openly burned. Hus, nevertheless, went on to pen some of the most hurtful impeachments against the Church and their practices, such as the sale of indulgences. He was condemned and excommunicated in 1410.

Reformation

- **Girolamo Savonarola** (1452-98) was of the San Marcos monastery in Florence, Italy, spoke out against the corruption in the Church.

- **Martin Luther** (1483-1546) was a monk-scholar, was also a doctor of theology and a professor of Biblical studies at the University of Wittenberg. He took issue with papal indulgences, power, purgatory, plenary remission of all penalties of the pope, among many other issues.

• **Ulrich Zwingli** (1484-1531) was a Catholic priest, who agreed with Luther in many doctrinal areas, in addition to the removal of all vestiges of the Roman Church: images, crucifixes, clerical garb, and even liturgical music. However, he disagreed with Luther's literal interpretation of the Eucharist, or Mass (Communion), as he said it "must be taken figuratively or metaphorically; 'This is my body,' means, 'The bread signifies my body,' or 'is a figure of my body.'" This one issues caused the them to part ways.

• **Anabaptists** (i.e., rejected infant baptism, so rebaptized adults, *ana* meaning "again" in Greek), **Mennonites** (Dutch Reformer Menno Simons), and **Hutterites** (Tyrolean Jacob Hutter), felt that the Reformers did not go far enough in rejecting the failings of the Catholic Church.

• **John Calvin** (1509-64) published *Institutes of the Christian Religion*, in which he summarized the ideas of the early church fathers and medieval theologians, as well as those of Luther and Zwingli. His theological views would take too much space. John Calvin had Michael Servetus burned to death as a heretic. Calvin defended his actions in these words: "When the papists are so harsh and violent in defense of their superstitions that they rage cruelly to shed innocent blood, are not Christian magistrates shamed to show themselves less ardent in defense of the sure truth?" Calvin's religious extremism and personal hatred made him unwilling to see and understand the radicalness of his judgments and choked out and Christian principles.

• **William Tyndale** (1494-1536) had to flee from England, published his New Testament in 1526, and completed most of the Old Testament after his betrayal and arrest, in a dungeon. He would be strangled at the stake, and his body was burned. The 1611 King James Version was actually 97 percent Tyndale's translation. He denounced the practice of prayer to saints. He taught justification by faith, the return of Christ, and mortality of the soul.

• **Jacobus Arminius** (1560-1609), graduated from Holland's Leiden University, after which he spent six years in Switzerland, studying theology under Théodore de Bèze, the successor to Protestant Reformer John Calvin. Rather than support Calvinism, he went against it, especially the doctrine of predestination, which was at the core of Calvinism.

Catholicism Summary

Roman Catholicism has tainted itself with its history of immorality and bloodshed, as well as its pagan-tainted religious ideas and practices. The centuries-long oppression, torture, rape, pillage, and murder of tens of millions of men, women, and children cannot come from true Christianity. They were the biggest offenders of the apostasy that Paul said had to come before the return of Christ.

Protestantism Summary

The Reformation gave us a return to the Bible in the common person's languages, which the Catholic Church had locked up in the dead language of Latin for 500-years. The Reformers brought the common folk freedom from papal authority but also from many erroneous Bible doctrines and dogmas that had gone on for a thousand years. However, the Protestant denominations have found themselves so fragmented and divided; one can only wonder where the truth and the Way are to be found. All 41,000 plus denominations that call themselves Christian cannot be just different roads leading to the same place.

Over eighty percent of Protestant Christianity is liberal-progressive as to their biblical and social beliefs, which began in earnest in the late 18th century up until the present. This covers too much area for a summary, but to mention just a few, they treat the Bible as being from man, not inspired and fully inerrant. They prefer to explain away the Bible accounts of miracles as myths, legends, or folk tales. They do not believe in the historicity of Bible characters such as Adam and Job. They say that Moses did not write the first five books of the Bible but that they were written by several authors from the tenth to the fifth centuries B.C.E., and were compiled thereafter. They say Isaiah did not author the book bearing his name in the early eighth century B.C.E., but that two or three authors penned it, centuries later.

In addition, they claim that Daniel did not pen his book in the sixth century B.C.E., but rather it was written in the second-century B.C.E. They claim that the Bible is full of errors, mistakes, and contradictions, as to the history, science, and geography. They claim that the antichrist is merely good versus evil, and is not to be taken literally. Higher criticism has opened Pandora's Box to an overflow of pseudo-scholarly works whose result has been to weaken, challenge and destabilize people's assurance in the trustworthiness of the Bible. Who needs enemies like agnostics and atheists, when we have liberal Bible scholars? We have not even delved into their unbiblical views of social justice, gay marriage, homosexual priests, women in the pulpits and far more.

Some may ask what about the remaining twenty percent of Christian denominations. Most of those are moderate in beliefs, which cast doubt on the trustworthiness of the Scriptures, and give fodder to the liberal-progressive denominations. These are fence-riders, who have abandoned the Truth and the Way of true, pure worship within Christianity. Before delving into the so-called conservative parts of Christianity, let us look at the charismatics.

We have charismatic Christianity, the fastest growing segment, which emphasizes the work of the Holy Spirit, spiritual gifts, and modern-day miracles, speaking in tongues[128] and miraculous healing, even snake handling in some areas. All of this is unbiblical and based on emotionalism.

Those who believe that charismatic Christianity is false Christianity, persons such as this author, are said to be overly critical. Supporters of Charismatic Christianity say we "should be focusing on the fact that while many in the church continue to abandon our Christian faith, the Pentecostal/Charismatic community continues to offer the church a legitimate growth mechanism."[129]

I would respond that a denomination founded on, grounded in unbiblical beliefs is not true Christianity, and are the false teachers and prophets that Jesus and the New Testament writers warned us were coming in the last days.

Therefore, charismatic Christianity is no Christianity at all, and all who are being brought in, are being obscured from finding the path of true Christianity. Further Catholicism brought in almost the whole world from 500 to 1500 C.E. Based on the same false, illogical reasoning from above; this would supposedly be a sign of their being true Christianity.

So-called conservative Christianity is so small that it barely receives any press. In fact, most of the press that conservative Christianity does receive, they are attacks from liberalism and atheism. Honestly, we should not confuse radical Christianity, such as the Westboro Baptist Church,[130] with truly conservative, fundamentalist Christianity. However, even here within conservative Christianity, we find differences doctrinally, and yes, even in the so-called salvation doctrines.

Are all of the 41,000 different varieties of Christianity just different roads leading to the same place? Are all of the various conservative churches the Truth and the Way? The answer is no, as far as this writer is concerned.

---

[128] http://www.christianpublishers.org/speaking-in-tongues-truth

[129] http://tiny.cc/j5d7mx

[130] www.godhatesfags.com/

We need to return to the question that Jesus asked, "When the Son of Man comes, will he find faith on earth?" (Lu 18:8) Jesus would not find faith on earth, not at the level that one might expect, not at present.

The Antichrist and Politics

As we just saw, much of the antichrist movement is made up of those alienated from God in their gross human imperfection, and religion. Well, here we will discover that governments and politicians can be antichrists as well. We begin with the obvious, communist and socialist governments are liberal-progressive both politically and religiously. They seek to displace any hope for God's kingdom and have its citizens place all their hope in human governments. Any government that oppresses Jesus' disciples are in essence in opposition to him. If they are persecuting, oppressing, and opposing Christians, they too are antichrists. – Matthew 25:31–46; Acts 9:5

The position of being an antichrist is not limited to communist countries, as it applies to Islamic countries, even **individual politicians** within a democratic constitutional monarchy (UK, Canada, Australia), and, yes, the federal republic of the United States. This would also apply to the United Nations, who is no friend to Christianity. Many view the United Nations as the world's only true hope for peace and security, which hope alone, belongs to Jesus Christ. – 1 Thessalonians 5:3

This author is a great advocate of the United States of America, which has served as the protector and police officer of the world. If it were not for the United States, many evil empires, e.g., German, Russian or Islam, would be ruling the world, and we would be living in far worse times.

Romans 13:1, 3 Updated American Standard Version (UASV)

1 Let every soul[131] be in subjection to the governing authorities. For there is no authority except by God, and those that exist have been placed[132] by God. 3 For rulers are not a cause of fear, not to the good deed, but to the bad. Do you want to be free of fear of the authority? Keep doing good, and you will have praise from it;

The United States has played a very large role in this manner. It has protected the world from evil and has relieved the pains of many. If genocide is taking place, it is the United States first to respond. If a country is invaded, it is the United States first on the scene. If there is a natural disaster, it is the United States first on the scene. Notice the words of Paul,

---

[131] Or *person*

[132] Or *established, instituted*

1 Timothy 2:1-3 Updated American Standard Version (UASV)

2 First of all, then, I urge that entreaties and prayers, petitions and thanksgivings, be made on behalf of all men, [2] for kings and all who are in high positions, that we may lead a peaceful and quiet life, godly and dignified in every way. [3] This is good, and it is acceptable in the sight of God our Savior,

Yes, we are even to pray for political leaders and governments. Why? Paul gives us the answer quite plainly, "that we may lead a peaceful and quiet life." We pray that government will not enact any laws that will infringe on our religious freedoms, and even that they will enact some that will expand or religious freedoms. If we can pray for such, why can we not act on behalf of our prayers by voting for the conservative politician over against the liberal one, because he or she is likely to be of the same mind? This is, of course, a conscience decision that each Christian must make for themselves.

However, we do not want to go beyond Scripture. We do not wish to see the United States as the entity that will be used to bring in true peace and security because it is not. Only Jesus Christ and his kingdom will do so. Further, we do not want to see the United States as an arm of God's kingdom; it is not an extension of God's kingdom. We have noticed in the last six years of the Obama presidency[133] that the country has swung liberal-progressive, and has failed in its role as the protector and police officer to the world. This should wake us up to the fact that it is nothing more than a human government, ran by imperfect humans, and within a moment, it can be converted into just the opposite of why we had appreciated it. This is not to say that, we cannot vote for persons, who may get the United States back to its former greatness. In chapter 4, we will delve even more into a detailed picture of this antichrist spirit or mentality. This is **not** to take away from **the fact** that the antichrist is **literally** a person, groups, organizations, and governments.

[133] If one were to Google antichrist, Obama would be very prominent as a choice. Is he the antichrist? **Not** in the way one might think, i.e., the one, long awaited antichrist that Satan uses. However, he is the antichrist in the sense that he does nothing for Christianity, but rather seems to work in opposition to them. Thus, he is the antichrist like any other person that is not for Christ, but is against Christ, by way of his disciples.

AMERICA 11 The Antichrist Uncovered

Jesus was quite clear as to how the world would treat Christians,

Matthew 24:9-11 Updated American Standard Version (UASV)

[9] "Then they will deliver you up to tribulation, and will kill you, and you will be hated by all nations because of my name. [10] And then many will fall away,[134] will betray[135] one another, and will hate one another. [11] And many false prophets will arise and will lead many astray.

Christians are hated because of Jesus' name, which makes any such ones antichrists, "against" Christ. Some of these false prophets were actually former Christians. However, these Christians John says, "went out from us, but they were not of us; for if they had been of us, they would have continued with us." –1 John 2:18, 19.

As we have seen from the beginning of this publication, there is no one antichrist, but many individuals from the time of Jesus first coming in the first century, up unto his return in the future. Being that some of these antichrists are also false prophets, they are in the business of deceiving true Christians. How do they go about this business of deceiving?

The Antichrist and False Teachings

As we have learned apostasy is standing off from the truth, and any engaging in such are antichrists. The apostle Paul warned Timothy,

2 Timothy 2:15-18 Updated American Standard Version (UASV)

[15] Do your best to present yourself to God as one approved, a workman who does not need to be ashamed, rightly handling[136] the word of truth. [16] But avoid empty speeches that violate what is holy, for they will lead to more and more ungodliness, [17] and their word will spread like gangrene; Hymenaeus and Philetus are among them. [18] men who have gone astray from the truth saying that the resurrection has already taken place, and they upset the faith of some.

On these verses, Knute Larson writes,

---

[134] Lit *be caused to stumble*

[135] Or *hand over*

[136] Or *accurately handling* the word of truth; *correctly teaching* the word of truth

2:15. Timothy, by contrast, must do his best to **present [himself] to God as one approved, a workman who does not need to be ashamed.** Timothy, and all who follow Christ, are to consecrate themselves to God, working diligently for his approval. The teacher whom God approves has no need of shame in his presence.

God bestows his approval on the one who exhibits truth, love, and godliness in daily living, and who **correctly handles the word of truth.** The false teachers were mishandling God's words, using them for their own benefit. Timothy was commissioned to handle the words of God correctly. All preaching should present the truth clearly, cutting through erroneous ideas or inaccurate opinions.

The pastor or teacher must acquaint himself thoroughly with Scripture. He should familiarize himself with historical information and the context of the passage, especially when trying to reach back through the centuries to gain an accurate understanding of God's revelation.

2:16. Paul again issued a warning: **Avoid godless chatter.** Paul was not referring to backyard chats or little conversation groups that met over tea. The phrase "godless chatter" describes the empty babbling of false teachers. Their doctrines may have been quite organized and intricate, but Paul labeled them "chatter" because they were without substance.

In addition, their teachings did not promote the life and practices which God approves. Paul declared that those who indulged in such chatter would **become more and more ungodly**. In vivid contrast to God's truth, which results in godliness, the false teachings degenerate into greater ungodliness.

2:17–18. But these false teachers and their philosophies were not pitiful little people to be ignored. They were causing great harm to those whom they influenced: **Their teaching will spread like gangrene.** Just as the teaching they followed was rotten, so its foul and corrupt nature infected more aid more people. In contrast, truth is always life producing, creating wholeness and health. Paul gave two examples of leaders who abandoned the faith and whose spurious teachings brought destructive results: **Hymenaeus and Philetus, who have wandered away from the truth.**

Other than this mention by Paul, these two men pass unknown in history. But because their names were known to Timothy, they were probably leaders within the Ephesian church. Yet, they wandered away. This describes a slow drifting from the truth. These men did not make a dramatic break from the Christian faith and run after strange philosophies. They slowly shifted their thinking, toyed with new ideas, held to what they liked and discarded what was unappealing. After a time, they had denied the faith.

Paul highlighted one main point of their false teaching: **they say that the resurrection has already taken place**. This supposition, rampant among the false teachers, taught that the fullness of salvation had come. Consequently, there was no future bodily resurrection, for the true resurrection was spiritual. This led to the practice of discounting anything connected with physical life making daily obligations and concerns for holy living irrelevant. Spiritualizing the resurrection diminished the sacrifice of Christ, removed the necessity of enduring hardship, and promoted immoral living. In this way, **they destroy the faith of some**. (Larson 2000, 287)

Deceptively, Hymenaeus and Philetus taught that the resurrection had already come, and it was merely a symbolic one, meaning that Christians had only been resurrected in a spiritual sense. This is somewhat true on two fronts: (1) When one becomes a Christian; he moves over from death to life (John 5:24; 1 John 3:14), and (2) it is the Christian God made alive even though he was dead in trespasses and sins. (1 Pet 4:3-6; Eph. 2:1-5, See ASV) In these verses what is meant? Christians were one dead spiritually, but after accepting Christ, and having forsaken the practice of sin; they have passed over from death to life in that the condemnation to death that all humans face is lifted, and they have the hope of eternal life. Nevertheless, what Hymenaeus and Philetus taught went beyond this truth, into their denying Jesus promise of a literal resurrection of the dead under the kingdom of God. – John 5:28-29.

Less than one hundred years after Hymenaeus and Philetus, we have a group called the Gnostics,[137] who developed the idea of a purely symbolic resurrection. They believed that one could acquire knowledge Greek, *gnosis*) in a mystical way. Gnostics fused biblical truths with Greek philosophy and Oriental mysticism. For example, they taught that all physical matter was evil, which, would mean that Jesus did not come in the flesh; otherwise, he would have been evil. Thus, they claimed that it only appeared as though Jesus came in the flesh. In other words, it only seemed as though he had a human body, which is known as Docetism, an early heresy that claimed that Jesus Christ was not a real person. As we have repeatedly shown, in the above, this is one of the most direct signs that the

[137] Gnosticism was an early Christian religious movement teaching that salvation comes by learning esoteric spiritual truths that free humanity from the material world, believed in this movement to be evil.

apostle John warned against, which made one who professed such an antichrist. – 1 John 4:2-3; 2 John 7.

The Antichrist Rejects God's Kingdom

The antichrist has another issue, and it is with Jesus' role as the king of God's kingdom, which will rule over the earth. (Dan. 2:44-45; 7:13-14; Rev. 5:10; 11:15) There are some, who do not take this literally any more than they take the antichrist literally. For some, the kingdom is in the mind or heart. – Luke 17:21, See KJV, ASV, and TEV.[138]

The Catholic Encyclopedia (1910) said under "Kingdom of God":

> The 'kingdom' means not so much a goal to be attained or a place . . . **it is rather a tone <u>of mind</u>** (Luke, xviii,20-21), it stands for an influence which must permeate **<u>men's minds</u>** if they would be one with Him and attain to His ideals.[139]

The Southern Baptist Convention of 1925 put it this way:

> The Kingdom of God is **the reign of God in the heart and life** of the individual in every human relationship, and in every form and institution of organized human society. The chief means for promoting the Kingdom of God on earth are preaching the gospel of Christ, and teaching the principles of righteousness contained therein. The Kingdom of God will be complete when every thought and will of man shall be brought into captivity to the will of Christ. And it is the duty of all Christ's people to pray and labor continually that his Kingdom may come and his will be done on earth as it is done in heaven.[140]

The Southern Baptist Convention of 1963 and 2000 put it this way:

> The Kingdom of God includes both His general sovereignty over the universe and His particular kingship over men who willfully acknowledge Him as King. Particularly the Kingdom is

---

[138] A poor rendering, "the kingdom of God is within you," should rather be rendered, "the kingdom of God is in your midst." See NASB, ESV, RSV, HCSB, and LEB The context is Jesus speaking to the unrighteous Pharisees (vs 20), so he would not be saying the Kingdom was in them, but rather that because the king himself was talking to them, it was in their midst.

[139] http://www.catholic.com/encyclopedia/kingdom-of-god

[140] http://www.sbc.net/bfm2000/bfmcomparison.asp

the realm of salvation into which men enter by trustful, childlike commitment to Jesus Christ. Christians ought to pray and to labor that the Kingdom may come and God's will be done on earth. The full consummation of the Kingdom awaits the return of Jesus Christ and the end of this age.

What does Jesus and the Bible say about the kingdom of God? Jesus said, "My kingdom is not of this world."[141] (John 18:36) Jesus also said, "The ruler of this world [Satan] is coming. He has no claim on me" (John 14:30) Indeed, Paul tells us, at present, "The god of this world [Satan] has blinded the minds of the unbelievers." (2 Cor. 4:4) Now, we can appreciate why Jesus will be removing all present-day governments, becoming the sole ruler over the earth. (Ps. 2:2, 6-9; Rev. 19:11-21) When Christians recite the Lord's Prayer, this is what they are actually praying for, "Thy kingdom come. Thy will be done in earth." – Matthew 6:10, KJV.

Should the kingdom of God be viewed as a real government? Isaiah 9:6-7 says, "For to us a child is born, to us a son is given; and the government shall be upon his shoulder, and his name shall be called Wonderful Counselor, Mighty God, Everlasting Father, Prince of Peace. Of the increase of his government and of peace there will be no end ..." (ASV, RSV, ESV, NASB, and HCSB) It does have a king, Jesus Christ. (Dan 7:13-14; Mark 14:61-62) Jesus will have co-rulers under him, and they will rule over the earth. (Rev 5:9-10; 20:4; 22:5; Matt 19:28) The word "government" means "a group of people who have the power to make and enforce laws for a country or area." Well, will not Jesus and his co-rulers have power and authority (Matt 28:18), to enforce the will and purposes of the Father over the earth? Whether one sees it as a government or a kingdom, these are synonymous as to its purpose.

The Antichrist Misleads

The antichrist not only misleads Christians into rejecting biblical truths as to doctrine but also in the case of morality as well. Paul warned, "For the time is coming when people will not endure sound teaching, but having

---

[141] 18:36 **My kingdom is not of this world.** By this phrase, Jesus meant that His kingdom is not connected to earthly political and national entities, nor does it have its origin in the evil world system that is in rebellion against God. If His kingdom was of this world, He would have fought. The kingships of this world preserve themselves by fighting with force. Messiah's kingdom does not originate in the efforts of man but with the Son of Man forcefully and decisively conquering sin in the lives of His people and, some day, conquering the evil world system at His Second Coming when He establishes the earthly form of His kingdom. His kingdom was no threat to the national identity of Israel or the political and military identity of Rome. It exists in the spiritual dimension until the end of the age (Rev. 11:15). MacArthur, John (2005-05-09). *The MacArthur Bible Commentary* (Kindle Locations 48413-48415). Thomas Nelson. Kindle Edition.

itching ears they will accumulate for themselves teachers to suit their own passions."[142] (2 Tim. 4:3) To the Corinthians, Paul writes,

2 Corinthians 11:13-15 Updated American Standard Version (UASV)

[13] For such men are **false** apostles, **deceitful** workers, **disguising** themselves as apostles of Christ. [14] And no wonder, for even Satan disguises himself as an angel of light. [15] Therefore it is not a great thing if his servants also disguise themselves as servants of righteousness, **whose end will be according to their deeds.**

Peter writes,

2 Peter 2:1-3 Updated American Standard Version (UASV)

2 But **false prophets** also arose among the people, just as there will also be **false teachers** among you, who will secretly introduce destructive heresies, even **denying the Master** who bought them, bringing swift destruction upon themselves. [2] Many will follow their acts of shameless conduct,[143] and because of them the way of **the truth will be spoken of abusively**; [3] and in their greed they will exploit you with false words; their judgment from long ago is not idle, and their destruction is not asleep.

He also went on to write,

2 Peter 2:12-15 Updated American Standard Version (UASV)

[12] But these, like unreasoning animals, born as creatures of instinct to be captured and destroyed, blaspheming about matters of which **they are ignorant**, in their destruction will also be destroyed, [13] suffering wrong as the wage for their wrongdoing. They count it pleasure to revel in the daytime. They are blots and blemishes, reveling in their deceptions, while they feast with you. [14] having eyes[144] full of adultery that never cease from

---

[142] Professing Christians and nominal believers in the church follow their own desires and flock to preachers who offer them God's blessings apart from His forgiveness, and His salvation apart from their repentance. They have an itch to be entertained by teachings that will produce pleasant sensations and leave them with good feelings about themselves. Their goal is that men preach "according to their own desires." Under those conditions, people will dictate what men preach, rather than God dictating it by His Word. MacArthur, John (2005-05-09). *The MacArthur Bible Commentary* (Kindle Locations 60857-60860). Thomas Nelson. Kindle Edition.

[143] Or *their sensuality; their licentious ways; their brazen conduct*

[144] **Eye:** (Heb. *ʿă·yin*; Gr. *ophthalmos*) Both the Hebrew and the Greek can refer to the organ of sight. (Matt. 9:29; 20:34) Illustratively, the eye is an important way of communicating with the mind, which influences our emotion and actions. When Satan tempted Eve, he motivated her through what she saw with her eyes. Eve had seen this tree many times now "it was a delight to the eyes." (Gen 3:6) Satan also tempted Jesus with the things seen by the eyes. (Lu 4:5-7) The apostle John spoke of "the lust of the eyes" as being "from the world." (1 John 2:16-17) The Bible uses the "eyes" to express emotions, like "haughty

sin, enticing unstable souls, having a heart trained in greed, accursed children; [15] forsaking the right way, they have gone astray, having followed the way of Balaam, the son of Beor, who loved the wages of unrighteousness;

False religious leaders, antichrists, abandon Bible principles,

Leviticus 18:22 Updated American Standard Version (UASV)

[22] You shall not lie with a male as you lie down with a woman;[145] it is an abomination.

Romans 1:26-27 Updated American Standard Version (UASV)

[26] For this reason God gave them over to degrading passions; for their women exchanged natural relations[146] for those that are contrary to nature, [27] and the men likewise gave up natural relations with women and were violently inflamed in their lust toward one another, males with males committing the shameless deed, and receiving in themselves the due penalty for their error.

1 Corinthians 6:9-10 Updated American Standard Version (UASV)

[9] Or do you not know that the unrighteous will not inherit the kingdom of God? Do not be deceived; neither fornicators, nor idolaters, nor adulterers, nor men of passive homosexual acts, nor men of active homosexual acts,[147] [10] nor thieves, nor greedy persons, nor drunkards, nor revilers, nor swindlers, will inherit the kingdom of God.

---

eyes" (Pro. 6:17), "alluring eyes" (Pro. 6:25) "eyes full of adultery" (2 Pet. 2:14), "whose eye is evil [a selfish man]" (Pro. 23:6) or "an evil eye [a greedy man]" (Pro. 28:22). It can also refer to understanding. – Lu 19:42; Eph. 1:18.

[145] Homosexuality – Genes or learned?

https://christianpublishinghouse.co/2016/10/14/homosexuality-genes-or-learned/

Avoiding Homosexuality and Controlling Same-Sex Attraction?

https://christianpublishinghouse.co/2016/10/14/avoiding-homosexuality-and-controlling-same-sex-attraction/

The Bible's Viewpoint of Homosexuality

https://christianpublishinghouse.co/2016/10/14/the-bibles-viewpoint-of-homosexuality/

Explaining the Bible's View of Homosexuality

https://christianpublishinghouse.co/2016/10/14/explaining-the-bibles-view-of-homosexuality/

[146] Or *natural sexual relations*; Lit *natural use*

[147] The two Greek terms refer to passive men partners and active men partners in consensual homosexual acts

Hebrews 13:4 Updated American Standard Version (UASV)

[4] Let marriage be honorable among all, and let the marriage bed be without defilement, for God will judge sexually immoral people[148] and adulterers.

Jude 1:7 Updated American Standard Version (UASV)

[7] just as Sodom and Gomorrah and the surrounding cities, which likewise indulged in sexual immorality and pursued unnatural desire, serve as an example by undergoing a punishment of eternal fire.

Christians Must Exercise Discernment

Based on all that we have covered in this publication, it is best that we heed the advice of the apostle John, the one who tells us of the antichrist. He writes, "My dear friends, do not believe all who claim to have the Spirit, but test them to find out if the spirit they have comes from God. For many false prophets have gone out everywhere." — 1 John 4:1, GNT

We should follow the example set by the Bereans,

Acts 17:10-11 Updated American Standard Version (UASV)

[10] The brothers immediately sent Paul and Silas away by night to Berea, and when they arrived, they went into the synagogue of the Jews. [11] Now these were more noble-minded than those in Thessalonica, who received the word with all eagerness,[149] **examining the Scriptures daily to see whether these things were so.**

We pray with Paul,

Philippians 1:9 Updated American Standard Version (UASV)

[9] And this I pray, that your love may abound yet more and more in accurate knowledge[150] and all discernment;[151]

It is as Jesus said,

---

[148] **Sexual Immorality:** (Heb. *zanah*; Gr. *porneia*) A general term for immoral sexual acts of any kind: such as adultery, prostitution, sexual relations between people not married to each other, homosexuality, and bestiality. – Num. 25:1; Deut. 22:21; Matt. 5:32; 1 Cor. 5:1

[149] Or with all *readiness of mind*. The Greek word *prothumias* means that one is eager, ready, mentally prepared to engage in some activity.

[150] *Epignosis* is a strengthened or intensified form of *gnosis* (*epi*, meaning "additional"), meaning, "true," "real," "full," "complete" or "accurate," depending upon the context. Paul and Peter alone use *epignosis*.

[151] Or insight, experience (Gr, *aisthesei*)

John 8:32 Updated American Standard Version (UASV)

[32] and you will know the truth, and the truth will set you free."

What the Bible Really Says About the Antichrist

1 John 2:18 Updated American Standard Version (UASV)

[18] Children, it is the last hour; and just as you heard that antichrist is coming, even now **many antichrists** have appeared; from this we know that it is the last hour.

1 John 2:22 Updated American Standard Version (UASV)

[22] Who is the liar but the one who denies that Jesus is the Christ? This is the antichrist, the one who **denies the Father and the Son**.

1 John 4:3 Updated American Standard Version (UASV)

[3] and every spirit that **does not confess Jesus** is not from God; this is the *spirit* of the antichrist, of which you have heard that it is coming, and now it is already in the world.

2 John 1:7 Updated American Standard Version (UASV)

[7] For many **deceivers** have gone out into the world, those who do not acknowledge Jesus **Christ** ***as*** **coming in the flesh**. This is the **deceiver** and the antichrist.

A Deceiver Who Deceives

Lastly, simply know that the antichrist is anyone, group or organization that denies the Father and the Son, Jesus came in the flesh, who oppose Jesus or his kingdom, and his disciples. Also, it is any that deny God's Word as being inspired and fully inerrant, waters down biblical truths, to appease man. It is any that claim they alone speak for Christ, are his representation here on earth, or that they are Christ.

AMERICA 12 Identifying the Man of Lawlessness

2 Thessalonians 2:8 Updated American Standard Version (UASV)

[8] Then the lawless one will be revealed, whom the Lord Jesus will do away with by the spirit of his mouth, and wipe out by the appearance of his presence,

When we think of the past year, in the news media, we have witnessed atrocious cases of lawlessness around the world. We have seen hundreds of young ones killed in gang violence here in the United States. We have witnessed videos of the Islamic terrorist group known as ISIS, where hundreds of women and children have been raped and murdered, Christians have been beheaded and burned alive. However, there has been a far more treacherous lawless element that has been at work behind the scenes, truly going unnoticed for many centuries. In the Bible, it is called, "the man of lawlessness."

It is imperative that we identify this man of lawlessness. Why? Because his objective is to undermine the righteous standing of every genuine Christian and cost them their hope of everlasting life. How does the man of lawlessness accomplish such a task? He does so by getting Christians to abandon the truth for the lie. Jesus said, "true worshipers will worship the Father in spirit and truth." (John 4:23) It is the man of lawlessness' mission to get us away from our pure worship. He is in opposition to God and His purposes and is adamantly opposed to his dedicated worshippers. If any of us is so bold as to believe we are above being misled, we are just the ones he is looking for, as "pride goes before destruction, and a haughty spirit before a fall." – Proverbs 16:18, ESV.

2 Thessalonians 2:3 Updated American Standard Version (UASV)

[3] Let no one deceive[152] you in any way, for it [the Lord's day of destruction of ungodly men] will not come unless the apostasy[153] comes first, and the man of lawlessness is revealed, the son of destruction,

Paul prophesied that an apostasy would develop and before that apostasy would be brought to an end the man of lawlessness would come. In fact, in verse 7 Paul stated, "For the mystery of lawlessness is already at work ..." Notice that, just like the antichrist, in te first century, this man of lawlessness was already making himself known.

---

[152] Or *seduce*

[153] Namely, to stand off from the truth, i.e., to not only fall away from the faith, but to then turn on the faith, rebellion.

Origin of the Lawless Man

2 Thessalonians 2:9-10 Updated American Standard Version (UASV)

[9] but the one whose coming is in accordance with the activity of Satan, with all power and signs and false wonders, [10] and with every unrighteous deception[154] for those who are perishing, because they did not receive the love of the truth so as to be saved.

We see here that it is Satan, who originated this lawless man. Satan, the father of the lie, is also the one who has and who will continue to sustain the lawless one. In addition, just as Satan is an enemy of God and his people, so too, this man of lawlessness.

2 Thessalonians 2:8 Updated American Standard Version (UASV)

[8] Then the lawless one will be revealed, whom the Lord Jesus will do away with by the spirit of his mouth, and wipe out by the appearance of his presence,

This man of lawlessness has but one future, i.e., destruction, along with anyone who goes along with him.

2 Thessalonians 1:6-9 Updated American Standard Version (UASV)

[6] since indeed God considers it just to repay with affliction those who afflict you, [7] and to give relief to you who are afflicted along with us when the Lord Jesus will be revealed from heaven with His mighty angels in flaming fire, [8] in flaming fire, inflicting vengeance on those who do not know God and on those who do not obey the gospel of our Lord Jesus. [9] These ones will pay the penalty of eternal destruction, from before the Lord[155] and from the glory of his strength,

Paul gives further information in helping his readers to identify this man of lawlessness.

2 Thessalonians 2:4 Updated American Standard Version (UASV)

the son of destruction, [4] who opposes and exalts himself against every so-called god or object of worship, so that he takes his seat in the temple of God, showing himself as being God.

Here we see that Satan will raise up this lawless man, making him a false object of reverence, who will even place himself above God. On this Knute Larson writes, "This man will oppose everything connected with the divine–not only Christianity but anything that has to do with theism. This

---

[154] Lit *seduction*

[155] Lit *from before the face of the Lord*

man will wage war against everything that hints at religion, faith, or spirituality. He will try to eradicate worship of any kind: prayers, songs, gatherings, and shrines."

He goes on saying, "The man of sin will set himself up **in God's temple**, or more literally, put himself into God's seat in the inner sanctuary of the temple, **proclaiming himself to be God**. This will be more than a taking over of some building. The man of sin will understand the implications and claims that attend taking his seat in the sanctuary of God. He will anoint himself as divine. He will usurp the rightful place of God and declare himself as the one to be worshiped." (Larson 2000, 106)

This lawless one is a hypocrite, a false teacher claiming to be Christian, who "takes his seat in the temple of God," namely, what such false teachers claim to be that temple.

Identifying the Lawless Man

Just like the antichrist, we have to ask, are we looking for a single individual? Was Paul speaking of just one person, who would be this man of lawlessness? No, for if he were just one person, he would have to be able to go without dying. Paul had stated that the man of lawlessness was "already at work" in Paul's day, and would be at work up unto the Lord's day of the destruction of ungodly men, that is, beyond the day of the penning of this book, which would make the lawless one almost 2,000 years old. Apparently, no ordinary man has lived that long. Therefore, the expression man of lawlessness must be composite, standing for a body or class of people.

Who are these ones that have been "at work" since Paul's day and are still "at work" in our day? Clearly, they are a body of arrogant, proud, self-important, self-righteous, ambitious leaders within false Christianity, who over the centuries have had great power within Satan's world, placing themselves above God and his Word. This author has written extensively about the fact that 41,000 different Christian denominations call themselves the truth and the way. Consider the fact that, they all have ministers, clergy, priests, elders, pastors, yet each conflicting with the others in some aspect of doctrine or practice. Many are actually in opposition to God's law, personality, standards, ways, and will, so, in effect, they are in opposition to God himself. (See Mark 3:24; Romans 16:17; 1 Corinthians 1:10) Many of these denominations do not keep hold of what the Bible really teaches. They have violated the principle of what Paul spoke of, 'not going beyond what is written.' (1 Cor. 4:6, ESV) In principle, the words of Jesus to the Jewish religious leaders of his day, wherein there were many different sects of Judaism, has much to offer us. He said, "And why do you break the commandment of God for the sake of your tradition?" (Matt 15:3, ESV) He went on to say, "in vain do they worship me, teaching as doctrines the commandments of men." (15:9) Lastly, Jesus said, "they are blind guides. And if the blind lead the blind, both will fall into a pit." – Matthew 15:14.

So, again, this man of lawlessness is a composite person. The false religious leaders within Christianity, who are being used by Satan whether they are aware of it or not. Of these lawless ones, be it the Pope, Cardinals, Bishops, preachers, ministers, elders, or pastors, they will share in the destruction of the man of lawlessness, for their sins. Worse still, those within the churches, who make up the flocks of these false religious leaders of Christendom, will also share in the Lord's day of the destruction of ungodly men. King David wrote, "I do not sit with men of falsehood, nor do I consort with hypocrites." (Psa. 26:4, ESV) If one of God's holy ones are in one of these false denominations that call themselves Christian, God will offer them deliverance. The Palmist also wrote, "Hate evil, you who love the Lord, Who preserves the souls of His godly ones; He delivers them from the hand of the wicked." (Psa. 97:10, NASB) Jesus spoke of those who believed they were on the correct path, but, in fact, they were not. Jesus said,

Matthew 7:21-23 Updated American Standard Version (UASV)

[21] "Not everyone who says to me, 'Lord, Lord,' will enter the kingdom of heaven, but the one who does the will of my Father who is in heaven. [22] On that day many will say to me, 'Lord, Lord, did we not prophesy in your name, and cast out demons in your name, and do many mighty works in your name?' [23] And then I will declare to them, 'I never knew you; depart from me, you who practice lawlessness.'

Learning a Lesson from the Apostle Paul

The actual way to God was through the Israelite nation for over 1,500 years. When Jesus arrived he began what would become known as Christianity, his followers being called Christian.

Matthew 9:16-17 Updated American Standard Version (UASV)

[16] But no one puts a patch of unshrunk cloth on an old garment; for the patch pulls away from the garment, and the tear becomes worse. [17] Nor do they put new wine into old wineskins. If they do, then the wineskins burst and the wine spills out and the wineskins are ruined. But they do put new wine into new wineskins, and both are preserved."

Jesus was making a point to the disciples of John the Baptist that no one should expect the followers of Jesus Christ to try to retain the old practices of Judaism, such as a ritualistic fasting. A Christian can fast if he chooses to do so, but there are no obligations to do so. Jesus did not come to patch up the old ways of worship by way of Judaism, which would be set aside on the day of Jesus' ransom sacrifice. Christianity is not to conform to the old way of worship, to the form Jewish religious system, with the traditions of men.

As Jesus said, Christianity was not going to be a new patch on an old garment or a new wine in an old wineskin. Any Christian or so-called Jewish Christian, who tries to suggest the mixing of the two are nothing more than false prophets. – Matthew 24:11.

We can define antichrist as anyone, any group, any organization, or any government that is *against* or *instead of* Christ, or who mistreat his people. Thus, we are not just looking for one person, one group, one organization, or one power. The Bible does not refer to just one antichrist. The greatest misidentification has been the interpretation that the Antichrist and the man of lawlessness is just one particular person.

Our Point Begins with Paul

Paul, who as we know was known as Saul before becoming the apostle Paul. Nevertheless, the objective way of believing certain Bible doctrines as being the truth is as follows. The biblical view of the doctrine __________ is __________, and it is the truth, unless, enough evidence comes along to say otherwise. If we grow in knowledge and understanding, our conclusions based on previous knowledge may need to be revised. For increased knowledge can require adjustments in one's thinking. We must remember the Apostle Paul studied under the renowned Pharisee Gamaliel, who was the grandson of Hillel, the Elder (110 B.C.E.[156] – 10 C.E.), the founder of one of the two schools within Judaism. Paul describes himself as "circumcised on the eighth day, of the people of Israel, of the tribe of Benjamin, a Hebrew of Hebrews; as to the law, a Pharisee; as to zeal, a persecutor of the church; as to righteousness under the law, blameless." (Phil 3:5-6) He also states, "But whatever gain I had, I counted as loss for the sake of Christ. Indeed, I count everything as loss because of the surpassing worth of knowing Christ Jesus my Lord. For his sake I have suffered the loss of all things and count them as rubbish, in order that I may gain Christ" (Phil. 3:7-8) Thus, we know that the Israelites were God's chosen people and the only way to God for some 1,500 years.

However, Jesus brought a new way, Christianity. Saul/Paul was slow to accept this because he could not see Jesus Christ as the long-awaited

---

[156] B.C.E. years ran down toward zero, although the Romans had no zero, and C.E. years ran up from zero. (100, 10, 3, 2, 1 ◀B.C.E. | C.E.▶ 1, 2, 3, 10, and 100)

Messiah. Nevertheless, after Jesus visited Paul on the road to Damascus and Ananias, a Christian disciple of Damascus, visited Paul, he saw the Old Testament Scriptures pointing to the Messiah accurately, he was able to humble himself and accept a different belief, i.e., Christianity was the truth and the way.

To believe without enough support, to believe in the face of contrary evidence is irrational. Therefore, we must humbly examine the facts behind what we believe, to establish the truth continually. Just as the apostle Paul exhorted the Christians at Corinth to "examine yourselves, to see whether you are in the faith. Test yourselves" (2 Cor. 13:5); we could say the very same thing about our beliefs. We could say, 'examine our beliefs, to see whether they are the truth, test our beliefs.'

Now, this is not to suggest that our beliefs are to be ever changing, but that they should be able to stand up to scrutiny when they are challenged by something we have heard or read. However, this refinement of our beliefs should not be confused with allowing unfounded, damaging doubts to grow in our hearts and minds, doubts that can destroy our confidently established beliefs and our relationship with our heavenly Father. **Unfounded doubt** is defined as something that is not supported by any evidence or a minuscule amount of evidence, to cause uncertainty of belief or opinion that often interferes with our decision-making skills.

Our Point Ends with Us

We need to dig deeper into biblical truths, not as a sign of unfounded doubt but to make sure what we believe is so. If we think that we can survive off the basic Bible knowledge that we acquired in the beginning and the simple snacks we receive at each Christian meeting, we are sadly mistaken because our spiritual health will deteriorate. It would be similar to our believing that we could maintain our physical health by only eating here and there.

Acts 17:10-11 Updated American Standard Version (UASV)

Paul and Silas in Berea

[10] The brothers immediately sent Paul and Silas away by night to Berea, and when they arrived, they went into the synagogue of the Jews. [11] Now these were more noble-minded than those in Thessalonica, for they received the word with great eagerness, examining the Scriptures daily to see whether these things were so.

Note that they **(1)** "received the word with all eagerness," and then went about **(2)** "examining the Scriptures daily to see if these things were so." If the apostle Paul was to be examined to see if what he said was so, surely uninspired commentators must be examined as well.

1 Timothy 1:13 Updated American Standard Version (UASV)

[13] although formerly I [Saul/Paul] was a blasphemer, and a persecutor, and a violent man. But I was shown mercy because I had **acted unknowingly** with a lack of trust,

Suppose we **do not** realize that our particular Christian denomination or our Christian leader is a false teacher. Does our failing to reject it necessarily free us of further responsibility in the matter? If God continues to send us holy ones who attempt to share biblical truths be it by book, magazines, the internet, or even in person and we ignore such ones, we are sharing in the sins of others, which is a sin in and of itself. – 2 John 1:9-11.

Romans 10:2-3 Updated American Standard Version (UASV)

[2] For I [Saul/Paul] bear them witness that they [the Jews] have a zeal for God, but not according to accurate knowledge.[157] [3] For, being ignorant of the righteousness of God, and seeking to establish their own, they did not submit to God's righteousness.[158]

What has been demonstrated here thus far? Just because one is very active in their Christian denomination or church, this activity does not guarantee that they are receiving God's approval or that they are doctrinally correct. See Jesus words below for those who believed that they were in an approved relationship. It takes real heart and character to accept that one may be on the wrong path when it comes to long-held biblical beliefs. It takes an act of humility to accept that we may need to make an adjustment in our view of a certain doctrine. Jesus words from above bear repeating.

Matthew 7:21-23 Updated American Standard Version (UASV)

[21] "Not everyone who says to me, 'Lord, Lord,' will enter the kingdom of heaven, but the one who does the will of my Father who is in heaven. [22] On that day many will say to me, 'Lord, Lord, did we not prophesy in

---

[157] *Epignosis* is a strengthened or intensified form of *gnosis* (*epi*, meaning "additional"), meaning, "true," "real," "full," "complete" or "accurate," depending upon the context. Paul and Peter alone use *epignosis*.

[158] **10:3 ignorant of God's righteousness.** Ignorant both of God's inherent righteousness revealed in the law and the rest of the OT (which should have shown the Jews their own unrighteousness) and of the righteousness which comes from Him on the basis of faith (see note on 1:17). **their own righteousness.** Based on their conformity to God's law and often to the less demanding standards of their own traditions (Mark 7:1–13). MacArthur, John (2005-05-09). *The MacArthur Bible Commentary* (Kindle Locations 52230-52233). Thomas Nelson. Kindle Edition.

your name, and cast out demons in your name, and do many mighty works in your name?' [23] And then I will declare to them, 'I never knew you; depart from me, you who practice lawlessness.'

It was Saul/Paul's zeal and his conscience that was pricked to defend what he thought was the truth, and yet he openly admitted that his was over-zealous, that his zeal was misdirected, because of ignorance. This should cause us to pause and reflect. The presence of false teachers in the Christian congregation from the first century onward means that one cannot just accept naively that they are getting the truth. It would be foolish to assume such.

1 Thessalonians 5:21 Updated American Standard Version (UASV)

[21] But examine everything carefully; hold fast to that which is good;

The Greek word *dokimazete* rendered simply as "test" in the English Standard Version or the Holman Christian Standard Bible denotes a careful examination of "everything." If one is to make a careful examination of everything, it will require that they are not just passively going along, but rather, one should be buying out the time, to have an accurate understanding of God's Word, by doing an in-depth study of what they believe to be true.

Certainly, if what Paul had to say about the Scriptures was under examination, no one else is above having their beliefs examined. The Jews of Berea did not just accept what Paul was saying about the death and resurrection of Jesus, as being so. Moreover, Paul commended them for their due diligence. (See 17:3) This was no brief or superficial examination of the Scriptures either; they met **daily** to **examine** the Scriptures. For the above reasons, it is only through living by faith and accurate knowledge that we can receive God's favor.

Pride and Haughtiness Is an Identifying Marker

The man of lawlessness throughout history has evidenced such pride, arrogance, and haughtiness that they have controlled world leaders. They have used the pretext of God's Word and Bible doctrines, they have controlled the masses, as well as an intermediary between the world leaders and God. For centuries, these false Christs have crowned and dethroned kings and emperors. In many ways, their words and deeds have been similar to those of the Jewish religious leaders of Jesus' day, "We have no king but Caesar." (John 19:15, ESV) However, Jesus words were far different, "My kingdom is not of this world." – John 18:36.

To place themselves above God's people, these false religious leaders, these men of lawlessness have adopted different clothing, which is usually black, and in some cases a white color around the neck. Keep in mind; others dress in $5,000 suits while their flocks are fleeced. Jesus and his disciples did no such thing. In fact, when Jesus was being arrested, Judas had to kiss him because he could not be distinguished from the others with him. Moreover, they have bestowed upon themselves titles such as "Father," "Holy Father," "Reverend," "Most Reverend," "His Excellency," and "His Eminence," when Jesus said, "call no man your father on earth, for you have one Father, who is in heaven." (Matt. 23:9) Remember, these ones are wolves in sheep's clothing.

In Matthew Chapter 7, Jesus started out by talking about two paths and false teachers. False teachers imply false teachings. Again, what did Jesus say he would say to those who thought they were doing the right thing or thought they were teaching the right thing but were not? 'I never knew you; depart from me, you workers of lawlessness.' (Matt. 7:23)

We have false teachers, who are difficult to recognize, as they appear as innocent as sheep. Recognizing them can only be accomplished by recognizing their fruit (words and deeds), as well as knowing the true will of the Father. Does it not then seem prudent on our behalf that we should apply,

2 Thessalonians 2:10 Updated American Standard Version (UASV)

[10] and with all wicked deception for those who are perishing, because they did not receive the love of the truth so as to be saved.

2 Corinthians 13:5 Updated American Standard Version (UASV)

[5] Examine yourselves, to see whether you are in the faith. Test yourselves. Or do you not realize this about yourselves, that Jesus Christ is in you?—unless indeed you fail to meet the test!

Yes, the ones, who are deceived by these false teachers, will perish because refused to be receptive to the truth. Therefore, we need to be in a constant mode of examining ourselves, as well as our beliefs, to see whether we are really in the truth. We would be wise if we heed the insight from Paul to the Corinthians,

2 Corinthians 11:13-15 Updated American Standard Version (UASV)

[13] For such men are false apostles, deceitful workers, disguising themselves as apostles of Christ. [14] And no wonder, for even Satan disguises himself as an angel of light. [15] Therefore it is not a great thing if his servants also disguise themselves as servants of righteousness, whose end will be according to their deeds.

Rejection of the Truth Is an Identifying Marker

The apostle Paul said that this man of lawlessness was going to grow with apostasy (rejection of the truth). Actually, the first sign Paul gave as to the identity of this lawless class is that "the day of the Lord [i.e., the day of judgment and destruction of ungodly men] ... will not come unless the apostasy comes first." (2 Thess. 2:2-3) What exactly did Paul mean by "apostasy"? He meant to stand off from the truth, i.e., to not only fall away from the faith but to then turn on the faith, rebellion. On this apostasy, Knute Larson writes,

> Before that great day comes, Paul declared, the **rebellion** must occur. The word used here is *apostasia*, or apostasy. Before the day of the Lord, there will be a great denial, a deliberate turning away by those who profess to belong to Christ. It will be a rebellion. Having once allied themselves with Christ, they will abandon him. Within the recognized church there will come a time when people will forsake their faith. Throughout history there have been defections from the faith. But the apostasy about which he wrote to the Thessalonians would be of greater magnitude and would signal the coming of the end. (Larson 2000, 106)

The Great Apostasy

2 Thessalonians 2:1a, 3 Updated American Standard Version (UASV)

[1] Now we request you, brothers, with regard to the presence of our Lord Jesus Christ ... [3] Let no one deceive[159] you in any way, for it will not come **unless the apostasy comes first**, and the man of lawlessness is revealed, the son of destruction,

On this text, New Testament scholar Jon A. Weatherly writes, "Following the warning about deception, the rest of the verse in the Greek text is an anacoluthon, a subordinate clause with no clause to complete it. Literally, the text reads, 'Because unless the rebellion comes first and the man of lawlessness is revealed.' Translators must supply the clause introduced with 'because' (ὅτι, *hoti*), which can be clearly inferred from v. 2. Since the question concerns the coming of the day of the Lord, Paul

[159] Or *seduce*

apparently expects the reader to conclude that the day is preceded by the rebellion and revelation of the man of lawlessness."[160] (Weatherly 1996)

The apostle Paul says to the Ephesian elders; there is but "one Lord, one faith, one baptism." (Eph. 4:5) Paul penned those words about 60 C.E., and he was informing them that there was but one Christian faith. Yet, today we see more varieties of Christian faith than we care to count, all claiming that they are the truth and the way. Whenever a brave soul dares to be truthful and bring up that there are doctrinal differences, different doctrinal position, and different standards of conduct, he is shouted down as an alarmist. They claim that most of these denominations are the same on the essential doctrines, i.e., the salvation doctrines. Well, this actually is not true and is an attempt at hiding the truth, because even the salvation doctrines have anywhere from three to five different interpretations. Regardless, we must concern ourselves with a crucial question from Jesus Christ, "when the Son of Man comes, will he find faith on earth?" (Lu 18:8) This is a whole other discussion. We concern ourselves with how these divisions came about in the first place.

As has already been stated, but bears repeating, the blame lies with Satan. He attempted to have Jesus killed as a baby; he tempted Jesus in the wilderness after his baptism, and he attempted persecution right from the start. Peter wrote, "Be sober-minded; be watchful. Your adversary the devil prowls around like a roaring lion, seeking someone to devour." (1 Pet. 5:8) Initially, the persecution to this young Christian body came from Jewish religious leaders, and then from the Roman Empire itself. With "all authority in heaven" (Matt. 28:20) Jesus watched on, as the Holy Spirit guided and directed them, this infancy Christian congregation endured the best that Satan and his henchman had to offer. (See Rev. 1:9; 2:3, 19) As we know from Scripture, Satan is not one to give up, so he devised a new plan, divide and conquer. Yes, he would cause divisions within the Christian congregation. Satan broke out the ultimate weapon – **the apostasy.**[161] We need not believe that all of a sudden, the apostasy came into the Christian congregation. No, Jesus was watching from heaven, and he made sure that he warned them while he was here on earth of what was to come and he made the young Christian congregation aware of what was coming and when it was getting started. – Colossians 1:18.

---

[160] Jon A. Weatherly, *1 & 2 Thessalonians*, The College Press NIV Commentary (Joplin, MO: College Press Pub. Co., 1996), 2 Th 2:3.

[161] In the Greek New Testament, the noun "apostasy" (Gr., *apostasia*) has the sense of "desertion, abandonment or rebellion." (Acts 21:21, ftn.) There it predominantly is alluding to abandonment; a drawing away from or abandoning of pure worship.

"[Jesus] Be Aware of False Prophets ...

[Peter] There Will Be False Teachers Among You"

Matthew 7:15 Updated American Standard Version (UASV)

[15] "Beware of the false prophets, who come to you in sheep's clothing, but inwardly are ravenous wolves."

Jesus was well aware of what Satan would try to accomplish step-by-step, and that divisions through those from within were on the list. New Testament scholar Stuart K. Weber says, "Jesus had an important reason for inserting the wolf metaphor (Acts 20:27–31)–to alert his listeners to the danger of a false prophet. If the false prophets were thought of as a source of bad fruit, then the disciples might think it was enough simply to recognize and ignore the false prophet, refusing to consume his bad fruit, and awaiting God's judgment on him. But the wolf metaphor attributes a more active and malicious motive to the false prophet. He is actually an enemy of the sheep, and, if not confronted, will get his way by destroying the sheep." (Weber 2000, 101)

Weber mentions Acts 20:28-30, where Paul, about **56 C.E.**, warned the Ephesian elders,

Acts 20:28-30 Updated American Standard Version (UASV)

[28] Pay careful attention to yourselves and to all the flock, in which the Holy Spirit has made you overseers, to care for the congregation of God, which he obtained with the blood of his own Son. [29] I know that after my departure fierce wolves will come in among you, not sparing the flock; [30] and **from among your own selves** men will arise, **speaking twisted things**, to **draw away the disciples after them.**

Yes, these, who stand off from the truth and the way, would not be seeking their own disciples, but rather they would be seeking, "to draw away the disciples [Jesus' disciples] after them." Jesus was well aware that the easiest way to defeat any group is to divide them, and so was Satan, who had been watching humanity for over 4,000 years, and especially the Israelites (Isaac and Ishmael / Jacob and Esau / Israel and Judah), as "Satan disguises himself as an angel of light. So it is no surprise if his servants, also, disguise themselves as servants of righteousness." – 2 Corinthians 11:14-15.

There was even some divisions beginning as early as **49 C.E.**, when the elders wrote a letter to the Gentile believers, saying,

Acts 15:24 Updated American Standard Version (UASV)

[24] Since we have heard that some went out from among us and troubled you with words, unsettling your souls,[162] although we gave them no instructions,

Here we see that some *within* [those who were Christians but had left the faith], were being very vocal about their opposition to the direction the faith was heading. Here, it was over whether the Gentiles needed to be circumcised, suggesting that they needed to be obedient to the Mosaic Law. – Acts 15:1, 5.

"[Paul says it] Is Already at Work"

About **51 C.E.**, some 18-years after Jesus' death, resurrection and ascension, division was already starting to creep into the faith, "the mystery of lawlessness **is already at work**." (2 Thess. 2:7) Yes, the power of **the man of lawlessness** was already present, which is the power of Satan, the god of this world (2 Cor. 4:3-4), and his tens of millions of demons, are hard at work behind the scenes.

The apostle Peter also spoke of these things about **64 C.E.**, "there will be false teachers among you, who will secretly bring in destructive heresies ... in their greed they will exploit you with false words.." (2 Pet. 2:1, 3) These abandoned the faithful words, became false teachers, rising within the Christian congregation, sharing their corrupting influence, intending to hide, disguise, or mislead.

These dire warnings by Jesus and the New Testament Authors had their beginnings in the first century C.E. Yes, they began small, but burst forth on the scene in the second century.

As the years progressed throughout the first-century, this divisive "talk [would] spread like gangrene." (2 Tim. 2:17, **c. 65 C.E.**) About **51 C.E.**, They had some in Thessalonica, at worst, going ahead of, or at best, misunderstanding Paul, and wrongly stating by word and a bogus letter "that the day of the Lord has come." (2 Thess. 2:1-2) In Corinth, about **55 C.E.**, "some of [were saying] that there is no resurrection of the dead. (1 Cor. 15:12) About **65 C.E.**, some were "saying that the resurrection has already happened. They [were] upsetting the faith of some." – 2 Timothy 2:16-18.

Throughout the next three decades, **no** inspired books were written. However, by the time of the apostle John's letter writing days of 96-98 C.E., he tells us "Now many antichrists have come. Therefore we know that it is the last hour." (1 John 2:18) These are ones, "who denies that Jesus is

[162] This means that some, who left the Christian faith and were not trying to subvert (undermine) the faith of others.

the Christ" and ones who not confess "Jesus Christ has come in the flesh is from God." – 1 John 2:22; 4:2-3.

From 33 C.E. to 100 C.E., the apostles served Christ as a restraint against "the apostasy" that was coming. Paul stated at 2 Thessalonians 2:7, "For the mystery of lawlessness is already at work; but only until the one who is right now acting as a restraint [Jesus' apostles] is out of the way." 2 Thessalonians 2:3 said, "Let no one deceive you in any way [misinterpretation or false teachers of Paul's first letter], for it will not come unless the apostasy comes first, and the man of lawlessness [composite person, or maybe an organization / movement, empowered by Satan] is revealed, the son of destruction."

So, again, how did this apostasy, this rebellion, grow out of the first-century Christian congregation? Repeating Paul's words to Thessalonica about "the thing that acts as a restraint" on the lawless one. We have already said that it was the apostles, who acted as this restraining force. It was the presence of the apostles, with the powerful gift of the Holy Spirit, which held off the apostasy in its full force. (Acts 2:1-4; 1 Cor. 12:28) Nevertheless, when the last apostle John died in about 100 C.E., this restraint was removed. Again, we look at an example, from the words of New Testament textual scholar, Philip W. Comfort,

> Once the final, authorized publication was released and distributed to the churches, I think it unlikely that any substantive changes would have occurred during the lifetime of the apostles or second-generation coworkers. By "substantive," I mean a change that would alter Christian doctrine or falsify an apostolic account. The primary reason is that the writers (or their immediate successors) were alive at the time and therefore could challenge any significant, unauthorized alterations. As long as eyewitnesses such as John or Peter were alive, who would dare change any of the Gospel accounts in any significant manner? Any one among the Twelve could have testified against any falsification. And there was also a group of 72 other disciples (Luke 10:1) who could do the same. Furthermore, according to 1 Corinthians 15:6, Jesus had at least five hundred followers by the time he had finished his ministry, and these people witnessed Jesus in resurrection. Most of these people were still alive (Paul said) in AD 57/58 (the date of composition for 1 Corinthians); it stands to reason that several lived for the next few decades—until the turn of the century and even beyond.[163]

---

[163] Philip Comfort, *Encountering the Manuscripts: An Introduction to New Testament Paleography & Textual Criticism* (Nashville, TN: Broadman & Holman, 2005), 255–256.

We must keep in mind that the meaning of any given text is what the author meant by the words that he used, as should have been understood by his audience, and had some relevance/meaning for his audience. The rebellion [apostasy] began slowly in the first century and would break forth after the death of the last apostle, i.e., John. As the historian, Ariel Durant informed us earlier, by 187 C.E., there were 20 varieties of Christianity, and by 384 C.E., there were 80 varieties of Christianity. Christianity would become one again, a universal religion, i.e., Catholicism.

Gnostic Belief

Marcion (85-c.160) was a semi-Gnostic, who believed that the teachings of Jesus were irreconcilable with the actions of the God of the Old Testament. He viewed the God of the Old Testament, Jehovah, to be vicious, violent and cruel, an oppressor who gave out material rewards to those worshiping him. In contrast, Marcion described the New Testament God, Jesus Christ, as a perfect God, the God of unadulterated love and compassion, of kindness and quick to forgive.

Montanus (late second century) was a "prophet" from Asia Minor, who believed that their revelation came directly from the Holy Spirit, which superseded the authority of Jesus, Paul, Peter, John, James, anyone really. They believed in the imminent return of Christ and the setting up of the New Jerusalem in Pepuza. He was more concerned about Christian conduct than he was Christian doctrine, wanting to get back to the Christian values of the first century. However, he took this to the extreme, just as John Calvin would some 1,300 years later in the 16th century. Montanism was a movement focused around prophecy, especially the founder's views, being seen as the light for their time. They believed that the apostle and prophets had the power to forgive sin.

Valentinus (c.100-c.160) was a Greek poet, who founded his school in Rome and most prominent early Christian gnostic theologian. He claimed that though Jesus' heavenly (spiritual) body was of Mary, he was not actually born from her. This belief came about because Gnostics viewed all matter as evil. Therefore, if Jesus had really been a real human person with a physical body, he would have been evil. Another form of Gnosticism was Docetism, which claimed that Jesus Christ was not a real person, i.e., it was mere appearance and illusion, which would have included his death and resurrection.

Manes (c. 216-274) was the prophet and the founder of Manichaeism, a gnostic religion. He sought to combine elements of Christianity, Buddhism, and Zoroastrianism, based on a rigid dualism of good and evil, locked in an eternal struggle. He believed that salvation is possible through education, self-denial, fasting and chastity. He also believed that he was an "apostle of Jesus Christ," (Ramsey 2006, 272) although, strictly speaking, his religion was not a movement of Christian Gnosticism in the earlier approach.

Beginning with the Council of Nicaea in 325 C.E., Emperor Constantine legalized Christianity in an attempt at reunited the empire. He thoroughly understood that religious division was a threat to the continuation of the Roman Empire. However, it was Emperor Theodosius I (347 – 395 C.E.), who banned paganism and imposed Christianity as the State religion of the Roman Empire. The Roman Catholic Church can trace its existence back to the council of Nicaea in 325 C.E. at best. Protestantism had its beginnings in the Reformation of the 16th century. However, there were dissensions in within Catholicism for a thousand years. Another identifying marker was the unscriptural clergy class that would develop over the coming centuries after the Council of Nicaea. This relegated the Christians to a second-class status. This is the way, the apostate; man of lawlessness slowly took the reins of power. It was Constantine the Great, who legalized Christianity, but it was Theodosius I (d. 395 C.E.), who made Christianity a state religion. For centuries there was the Holy Roman Empire (5th to the 15th century C.E.),[164] which was anything but holy. As schisms and rifts took place, Christianity fragmented into tens of thousands of denominations. An example of such glorification by the man of lawlessness, setting oneself up over God is that of the papacy of Rome.

Lucio Ferraris in his *Ecclesiastical Dictionary*, which was used as a standard for Roman Catholic divinity, offers its readers the following on papal power, "The pope is of such dignity and highness, that he is not simply man, but, as it were, God, and the vicar of God. Ferraris goes on, "The pope is father of fathers; since he possesses the primacy over all, is truly greater than all, and the greatest of all. He is called most holy because he is presumed to be such ... Hence the pope is crowned with the triple crown as king of heaven, of earth and of hell ... he is also above angels and is their superior ... He is of such great dignity and power that he occupies one and the same tribunal with Christ; so that whatever the pope does, seems to proceed from the mouth of God." Ferraris in his Ecclesiastical Dictionary goes on saying, "God on earth, the only prince of the faithful of Christ, the greatest king of all kings, possessing the plentitude of power, to whom the government of the earthly and heavenly kingdom is [entrusted]. (Elliott 1941, 157)

Let us consider the humble words of Peter, who said to the Roman army officer Cornelius, who "fell down at his feet and worshiped him," "Stand up, . . . I am only a man after all"! (Acts 10:25-26, the Catholic Jerusalem Bible) Then there is the humility of an angel when the apostle John bowed down in a worshipful attitude before him. The angel said,

---

[164] The precise term "Holy Roman Empire" was not used until the 13th century.

"You must not do that! I am a fellow servant with you and your brothers the prophets, and with those who keep the words of this book. Worship God." – Revelation 22:8-9, ESV.

While we have covered Catholicism and the pope, the question that many might have is, 'have the Protestant denominations faired any better?' The answer is actually a mixed review in that "yes" in a small way and "no" in a major way. One of the major contributions of the Protestant Reformation was that these men gave us the Bible in our common languages, be it French, German, English, etc. Another benefit was the abandonment of many of the false doctrines of the Catholic Church, such as transubstantiation, Mary as the mother of God, apostolic succession, among so many others. The third greatest contribution was the search for biblical truths. However, we must note that many of the excellent reasons for rebelling against the Catholic Church were short-lived, as the fragmentation of denominations grew even faster after the Reformation. Most Protestant denominations have no reliable way of interpreting the Scriptures. Most use historical-critical methods of interpretation, which is subject and allows the reader to determine the meaning while few denominations use the historical-grammatical method, which is objective and the meaning is drawn from what the author meant. Several books have been written on this issue alone.

Much of Protestantism has failed to affirm Scripture as inspired, fully inerrant and authoritative. In addition, many denominations have abandoned the Word of God by leaving the literal translation philosophy for an interpretive translation known as the dynamic or functional equivalent.[165] These ones would argue that the Bible is full of errors, contradiction, myths, and legends. Many would argue that Moses is not the author of the first five book but rather several authors penned the book from the 10th and 5th centuries B.C.E. Many would argue that there are three authors, who penned the book, which we know as Isaiah, and none is the Isiah of the 8th-century B.C.E. They claim that Daniel did not write the book bearing his name, as it was written centuries later. Many more similar points could be made. As has been stated, the Protestant denominations cannot preserve any unity in their doctrinal views. Protestantism has failed to have any cohesion or to carry out the one commission that Jesus Christ gave: to proclaim the Gospel, teach Bible doctrines and to make disciples. They have failed to evangelize in their own communities. They have failed to teach the Bible to their own flock, as over ninety percent of churchgoers are biblically illiterate.

---

[165] Do We Still Need a Literal Bible? Discover the Truth about Literal Bibles Authored by Don Wilkins

http://www.christianpublishers.org/apps/webstore/products/show/4676433

New Testament textual scholar Daniel B. Wallace writes, "In Protestantism, one really doesn't know what he or she will experience from church to church. Even churches of the same denomination are widely divergent. Some have a rock-solid proclamation of the Word, while others play games and woo sinners to join their ranks without even the slightest suggestion that they should repent of anything. Too many Protestant churches look like social clubs where the offense of the gospel has been diluted to feel-good psycho-theology. And the problem is only getting worse with mega-churches with their mini-theology. This ought not to be."[166]

Is this evaluation or appraisal of Catholicism and Protestantism too strong? Before we answer that, let it be said, Catholicism is a part of the composite body of the man of lawlessness, so there is no help that Titanic of a religious organization from going down, but we can help those within, to find their way to the correct path, which leads to life. Besides, the vast majority of Protestantism is also a part of that body or composite of the man of lawlessness. Again, we cannot save the huge organization from going under, but we can pull members off their ship before it goes down in destruction with the ungodly men. However, I do believe God is using Protestantism in the sense that the true church will be identifiable before the end comes and those loving the truth will be able to make the choice to follow God or follow traditions.

If we are to identify whether our church or our denomination is a part of the man of lawlessness, we must apply the rule that Jesus gave for identifying false prophets. He said,

Matthew 7:15-16 Updated American Standard Version (UASV)

[15] "Beware of the false prophets, who come to you in sheep's clothing, but inwardly are ravenous wolves. [16] You will recognize them by their fruits. They do not gather grapes from thorn bushes, or figs from thistles, do they? [17] So every good tree bears good fruit, but the bad tree bears bad fruit.

We have spoken of the fruitage in the above. In the next chapter, we will look more at these fruitages. We will talk more about the fate of the man of lawlessness and for those sharing in his sins. Moreover, we will consider what the responsibilities of true Christians are as to this lawless one.

---

[166] The Problem With Protestant Ecclesiology — Fr. John Peck, http://frjohnpeck.com/the-problem-with-protestant-ecclesiology/ (accessed January 03, 2016).

AMERICA 13 Destruction of the Man of Lawlessness

Matthew 7:19-20 Updated American Standard Version (UASV)

[19] Every tree that does not bear good fruit is cut down and thrown into the fire. [20] So then, you will recognize them by their fruits.

As we learned from the previous chapter, the apostle Paul had said that the man of lawlessness was "already at work" in his day, in which he was referring to a body or composite of individuals who would go out from the Christian congregation, as they apostatized [attacking] true Christianity. In addition, they worked to take disciples away from true Christian as opposed to going out and making their own, This rebellion against true Christian would grow exponentially after the death of the last apostle, John in 100 C.E. These lawless ones went beyond the Scriptures doctrinally and in their practices. – 2 Thessalonians 2:3, 7; Acts 20:29-30; 2 Timothy 3:16-17; 4:3-4.

In time, this lawless body would become Catholicism. Two steps made this possible: Roman Constantine the Great (272 – 327 C.E.) legalizing Christianity and Theodosius I (347 – 395 C.E.), who made paganism illegal and made Christianity the state religion. Over the centuries, church leadership continued to place themselves above the churchgoers. This was just as Paul had foretold would take place with this lawless one, "who opposes and exalts himself against every so-called god or object of worship, so that he takes his seat in the temple of God, showing himself as being God." – 2 Thessalonians 2:4.

What will eventually happen to this man of lawlessness? The apostle Paul answers, "Then the lawless one will be revealed, whom the Lord Jesus will do away with by the spirit of his mouth, and wipe out by the appearance of his presence." (2 Thess. 2:8) This means that this false Christianity will be with us unto the second coming of Christ.[167] Jesus Christ will come with his angelic army to carry out a destruction of the ungodly men. (2 Thess. 1:6-9; Rev. 19:11-21) This destruction of the man of lawlessness and any who share in his sin is a direct result of their having dishonored the Father and the Son, as they abandoned the faith and true worship, taking tens of millions with them. Jesus offered these Christians help in identifying the correct path, as well as realizing they were not doing the will of the Father.

---

[167] *The SECOND COMING of CHRIST: Basic Bible Doctrines of the Christian Faith* by Edward D. Andrews

http://www.christianpublishers.org/apps/webstore/products/show/5383701

Using Discernment

Discernment is keenly selective judgment. In other words, we have the ability to judge well, and our ability to determine is finely tuned and able to sense minor differences, distinctions, or details, to obtain spiritual direction and understanding. A Christian, who has both knowledge and *discernment*, can make decisions that if Jesus were in our place, and in our imperfect human condition, he would have made the exact same decision. One way that we can use *discernment* is in our sharing of the biblical truths with others who possess different worldviews and backgrounds, to save some. The apostle Paul said,

1 Corinthians 9:19-23 Updated American Standard Version (UASV)

[19] For though I am free from all men, I have made myself a slave to all, so that I may gain more. [20] And so to the Jews I became as a Jew, that I might gain Jews; to those under the law I became as under the law, though I myself am not under the law, that I might gain those under the law. [21] To those without law I became as without law, although I am not without law toward God but under the law toward Christ, that I might gain those without law. [22] To the weak I became weak, that I might gain the weak. I have become all things to all men, that I might by all means save some. [23] But I do all things for the sake of the gospel, that I may become a fellow partaker of it.

Keep in mind that, even though Paul said, "I became as," so that he might become all things to all men, so as to save them, he never became anything that would be contrary to God's will and purposes. A bad example of this would be the modern day Christian heavy metal bands, who by all appearances, are just like the worldly ones. Such bands are nine parts world to one part Christian. Can we imagine young Timothy, Paul's student and traveling companion, being a member of Stryper, Vengeance Rising, Deliverance, Believer, Tourniquet and P.O.D?

Much of modern day Christianity, has become like the world in their misguided attempt to evangelize the world. They are nine parts world to one part Christian. This so-called evangelism is an excuse for loose conduct, i.e., an excuse to be worldly under the guise of 'saving some.' While we are using an extreme hyperbolic example here of being like the world, to save some out of the world, which is complete foolishness, there are many other minor to major examples within modern day Christianity.

Jesus used hyperbole, which is to over exaggerate to emphasize a point, but sadly, in our day, we do not need to over exaggerate because our example found in these so-called Christian metal bands is a reality.

The man of lawlessness is a false teacher. He is twisting the Scriptures, which seem correct, but are not, so as to mislead. What these lawless ones do is offer texts that are true; then, providing texts that are not being interpreted correctly, so we have a mixture of truth and lie.

John 17:16 Updated American Standard Version (UASV)

[16] They are not of the world, even as I am not of the world.

Romans 12:2 English Standard Version (ESV)

2 And do not be conformed to this world, but be transformed by the renewing of your mind, so that you may prove what the will of God is, that which is good and acceptable[168] and perfect.

12:2 do not be conformed. "Conformed" refers to assuming an outward expression that does not reflect what is really inside, a kind of masquerade or act. The word's intent implies that Paul's readers were already allowing this to happen and they must stop. this world. Better translated, "age," which refers to the system of beliefs, values—or the spirit of the age—at any time current in the world. This sum of contemporary thinking and values forms the moral atmosphere of our world and is always dominated by Satan (cf. 2 Cor. 4:4). transformed. The Greek word, from which the English word "metamorphosis" comes, connotes a change in outward appearance. Matthew uses the same word to describe the Transfiguration of Jesus (Matt. 17:2). Just as Christ, briefly and in a limited way, displayed outwardly His inner, divine nature and glory at the Transfiguration, Christians should outwardly manifest their inner, redeemed natures, not once, however, but daily (cf. 2 Cor. 3:18; Eph. 5:18). renewing of your mind. That kind of transformation can occur only as the Holy Spirit changes our thinking through consistent study and meditation on Scripture (Ps. 119:11; cf. Phil. 4:8; Col. 1:28; 3:10, 16). The renewed mind is one saturated with and controlled by the Word of God. good . . . acceptable . . . perfect. Holy living of which God approves. These words borrow from OT sacrificial language and describe a life that is morally and spiritually spotless, just as the sacrificial animals were to be (cf. Lev. 22:19–25).[169]

Below Jesus gives us the correct path, as well as exposing that we may believe that we are doing the will of the Father, when, in fact, we are not

[168] Or *well-pleasing*

[169] MacArthur, John (2005-05-09). The MacArthur Bible Commentary (Kindle Locations 52431-52439). Thomas Nelson. Kindle Edition.

doing the will of the Father. After reading Jesus' words, consider the questions that follow.

Matthew 7:13-25 Updated American Standard Version (UASV)

The Narrow and Wide Gates

13 "Enter through the narrow gate; for the gate is wide and the way is broad that leads to destruction, and there are many who enter through it. 14 For the gate is small and the way is narrow that leads to life, and there are few who find it.

Recognize Them by Their Fruits

15 "Beware of the false prophets, who come to you in sheep's clothing, but inwardly are ravenous wolves. 16 You will recognize them by their fruits. They do not gather grapes from thorn bushes, or figs from thistles, do they? 17 So every good tree bears good fruit, but the bad tree bears bad fruit. 18 A good tree cannot produce bad fruit, nor can a bad tree produce good fruit. 19 Every tree that does not bear good fruit is cut down and thrown into the fire. 20 So then, you will recognize them by their fruits.

21 "Not everyone who says to me, 'Lord, Lord,' will enter the kingdom of heaven, but the one who does the will of my Father who is in heaven. 22 On that day many will say to me, 'Lord, Lord, did we not prophesy in your name, and cast out demons in your name, and do many mighty works in your name?' 23 And then I will declare to them, 'I never knew you; depart from me, you who practice lawlessness.'

The Two Foundations

24 "Everyone then who hears these words of mine and does them will be like a wise man who built his house on the rock. 25 And the rain fell, and the floods[170] came, and the winds blew and beat on that house, but it did not fall because it had been founded on the rock. 26 And everyone who hears these words of mine and does not do them will be like a foolish man who built his house on the sand. 27 And the rain fell, and the floods[171] came, and the winds blew and beat against that house, and it fell, and great was its fall."

Leading Questions

These infer that there is but one correct answer and it guides the listener to that answer.

---

[170] Lit *rivers*

[171] Lit *rivers*

Q: After reading Matthew 7:13-14, does this not suggest there are two courses in life, one that leads to destruction, which many are on and one that leads to life, which few are finding?

A: Yes

Q: After reading Matthew 7:15, does this not suggest there will be some who appear as innocent as sheep, but really are false prophets to the point of being ravenous wolves?

A: Yes

Q: After reading Matthew 7:16-20, what is it that will help us identify these false prophets?

A: Their fruit

Q: After reading Matthew 7:21, who does Jesus say are the only ones who will enter into the kingdom.

A: Jesus said only those doing the will of the Father.

Q: After reading Matthew 7:22, will there be those who believe that they are doing the will of the Father?

A: Yes

Q: After reading Matthew 7:23, will Jesus accept their excuses for failing to do the will of the Father?

A: No

Clarifying Questions

These questions can be used in one of two ways. First, they can be used to clear up something that the listener said. Second, they can be used to clarify that the listener fully understands what something means.

NOTE/Q: The term prophet has two basic meanings. First, it means one who proclaims a message. Second, it means one who foretells the future. What does the term "prophet" mean here?

A: It means one who proclaims a message.

Q: What did Jesus mean by many being on the path of destruction? Was Jesus referring to his disciples (i.e., Christians) and those of religions other than Christianity?

A: The many Jesus referred to was his disciples, coming Christians.

Q: How do you know that the many who are on the path to destruction are the disciples of Jesus Christ?

A: Just after Jesus talks about the two paths, Jesus said 'be careful of false prophets.' Then, a few verses later he says "Not everyone who says to me, 'Lord, Lord,' will enter the kingdom of heaven ..."

Q: Are these false teachers found within Christianity and why are they so hard to recognize?

A: If it is the many Christian disciples, who are on the path to destruction; then, the teachers who taught them must have been Christian teachers. They are hard to recognize because Jesus compared them to sheep. In other words, they come across as innocent appearing.

Q: What did Jesus mean by the term "fruit"?

A: In other words, we would recognize them by their words and deeds.

Q: Based on who can enter into the kingdom, 'those doing the will of the Father,' what should we know?

A: What the will of the Father is?

Q: Did the many on the path to destruction believe they were doing the will of the Father?

A: Yes

Q: Jesus started out by talking about two paths and false teachers, correct?

A: Yes

Q: False teachers infer false teachings, correct?

A: Yes

Q: What did Jesus say he would say to those who thought they were doing the right thing or thought they were teaching the right thing but were not?

A: 'I never knew you; depart from me, you workers of lawlessness.'

Q: We have false teachers, who are difficult to recognize, as they appear as innocent as sheep. Recognizing them can only be accomplished by recognizing their fruit (words and deeds), as well as knowing the true will of the Father. Does it not then seem prudent on our behalf that we should apply 2 Thessalonians 2:10 and 2 Corinthians 13:5?

A: Yes, the ones, who are deceived by these false teachers, will perish because they refused to be receptive to the truth. Therefore, we need to be in a constant mode of examining ourselves, as well as our beliefs, to see whether we are really in the truth. We also need to test the beliefs of the church we attend, as well as the denomination.

2 Thessalonians 2:10 Updated American Standard Version (UASV)

[10] and with every unrighteous deception[172] for those who are perishing, because they did not receive the love of the truth so as to be saved.

2 Corinthians 13:5 Updated American Standard Version (UASV)

[5] Keep testing yourselves to see if you are in the faith. Keep examining yourselves! Or do you not realize this about yourselves, that Jesus Christ is in you, unless indeed you fail to meet the test?

Recognizing True Christianity by Their Fruits

In the above, we spoke of the importance of our using *discernment*. Does Scripture help us to be better at discerning, to obtain spiritual direction and understanding? The apostle Paul can help us in this matter. He gave the Thessalonians three command, which make obvious the necessities of a discerning mind. We considered these verses back in Chapter 5, which need revisited.

1 Thessalonians 5:21-22 American Standard Version (ASV)

[21] But examine everything carefully; hold fast to that which is good; [22] abstain from every form of evil.

(1) **examine** everything carefully

(2) **hold fast** to that which is good

(3) **abstain** from every form of evil

Bible scholar Knute Larson has it right when he says, "Paul advised the Thessalonians to **Test everything.** The word *everything* is universal; it leaves nothing free from examination by spiritual standards and understanding. Paul did not explain how to carry out this testing. But certainly the fire of the Spirit (his convicting, guidance, and illumination), the instructions from the apostles and missionaries, and the written revelation of God are the lenses through which we must scrutinize everything. The clear purpose of this testing was to **hold on to the good**, and to **avoid every kind of evil.**

[172] Lit *seduction*

The good has its origin in God; evil is a distortion of that good. Evil is twisting and destructive. We must not flirt with evil."[173]

While Larson is correct that the Greek word *panta* (everything) means that, we are to examine everything, leaving nothing free from examination. However, the 'everything examination' is within the context of the whole of Christianity: theological doctrine, ecclesiology, practices, and so on. Charles A. Wanamaker addresses more specifically. He writes, "In the context the [*panta*, ("everything")] almost certainly refers to manifestations of the Spirit in the words and deeds of the members of the church. People were capable of abusing the gifts of the Spirit in various ways, such as making unchristian pronouncements (cf. 1 Cor. 12:3; 1 Jn. 4:1–3) or even self-aggrandizing statements (cf. Did. 11:12) in the name of the Spirit. Thus Paul exhorts the community to evaluate what is said or done in the name of the Spirit or under the supposed influence of the Spirit (cf. 1 Cor. 14:29). He does not specify what criteria should be used in determining whether something is good or evil, but presumably, he expected his readers to weigh supposed Spirit-inspired words and deeds against the doctrinal and ethical norms they had received from him. While Paul does not say so here, it is the Spirit who enables a person to determine the genuineness of a word or deed done in the Spirit (cf. 1 Cor. 12:10)."[174]

Another identifying marker (fruit) of true Christianity is found at 1 John 5:3, which states: "For this is the love of God, that **we keep his commandments**; and his commandments are not burdensome." One of the commandments is, "You shall **love your neighbor** as yourself." (Matt. 22:39) In other words, regardless of racial, social, and national boundaries, we must love our neighbors. – Matthew 5:43-48; Romans 12:17-21.

Christian love is so exceptional that Jesus told us to "love your enemies and pray for those who persecute you." (Matt 5:44, ESV) It is a common expression to "love the sinner but hate the sin." Well, this is actually unbiblical. The fact is we are sinners. The apostle Paul stated: "for all have sinned and fall short of the glory of God." (Psa. 51:5; Eze. 18:4; Rom. 3:23; 5:12) Since "there is no man that does not sin" (2 Ch. 6:36), all of Adam's descendants can correctly be called "sinners" by nature. Nevertheless, in the

[173] Knute Larson, *I & II Thessalonians, I & II Timothy, Titus, Philemon*, vol. 9, Holman New Testament Commentary (Nashville, TN: Broadman & Holman Publishers, 2000), 75–76.

Did. Didache

[174] Charles A. Wanamaker, *The Epistles to the Thessalonians: a Commentary on the Greek Text*, New International Greek Testament Commentary (Grand Rapids, MI: W.B. Eerdmans, 1990), 203.

Scriptures "sinners" generally applies in a more precise way, designating those who practice or live in sin or who have a reputation of sinning.

When Jesus said that we were to love our enemy, he did not mean that we overlook the fact that he is an enemy of God. What he meant was that we see our enemy as a prospective brother or sister in the faith. In other words, we are loving them in the sense that if an evangelistic moment comes up, we would take it, hoping to convert them to Christianity, or even back to Christianity for those that have abandoned the faith. Trying to clarify even more, let us look at some common misconception. Scripturally, "sinners" are those living in sin. If they start attending our congregation regularly, they cannot become members until another member has studied with them.

If one is to be an effective, genuine, true Christian, he must have all three of the ingredients mentioned in this video:

(1) Knowledge

(2) Belief

(3) Obedience

To become a well-grounded Christian, you must,

(1) Obtain a good, deep knowledge of Bible truth (1 Timothy 2:3-4),

(2) Put faith in the things you have learned (Hebrews 11:6),

(3) Repent of sins (Acts 17:30-31), and

(4) Turn around in their course of life. (Acts 3:19);

(5) Then their love for God should move you to dedicate yourself to him.

Many liberal and moderate Christians, as well as Charismatic Christians, will try to argue that religious leaders condemned Jesus for associating with "tax collectors and sinners." (Matt 9:10-11) They use this rationale for not viewing others as "sinners." Yes, Jesus spent time with sinners, but this was not for recreational purposes. His objective was always about evangelistic purposes, i.e., looking for chances to convert them into his followers. Thus, we are looking to do the same.

Here is a typical comment about judging, "So the ones judging did not read that part of the Christian Bible that said 'do not judge." This judging comment is a tired argument, which is given so often, it needs to be dealt with here as well. We do not judge whether one is going to receive eternal life or not because there is but one judge, Jesus Christ. In other words, we do not condemn others.

However, the Bible is packed full of verses on how we are to decide if another Christian is a good associate or not. There are many Scriptures about false teachers, false prophets, false Christians and our obligation to identify such. Therefore, it is our responsibility to identify and recognize false teachers, false prophets, and false Christians. The characteristics of these false ones are identified in the Scripture as fingerprints identify who the criminal is. This book is just identifying these lines in the fingerprints of these false teachers. Judging in a condemnatory way is wrong, as this is Jesus job. Judging as an evaluator is what Jesus and New Testament writers commanded us to do.

If you do not know the Word of God accurately, it can be difficult to recognize the false ones. There are 41,000 different denominations, all claiming to be the truth and the way. Almost all are false based on Scripture. Jesus made it very clear to those who just go along thinking they are doing the right things. These ones say, 'but I do this and I do that and I ...' However, we have heard Jesus' words numerous times in this publication, "I never knew you; depart from me, you workers of lawlessness." (Matt. 7:23, ESV) Next, we will discuss the love we need to have for our brothers and sisters of the faith.

1 John 4:20-21 Updated American Standard Version (UASV)

[20] If anyone says, "I love God," and hates his brother, he is a liar; for he who does not love his brother whom he has seen cannot love God whom he has not seen. [21] And this commandment we have from him, that the one who should love his brother also.

John 13:35 Updated American Standard Version (UASV)

[35] By this all men will know that you are my disciples, if you have love for one another.

Particularly important is the love we have for our brothers and sisters in the faith. On the importance of such love David Walls and Max Anders, write, "God first loved us and made a relationship with him possible. The text drives home its refutation of the antichrists and false prophets. We cannot claim we love God and then show that we hate our brothers. This only proves one thing: we are liars. It's hard to prove whether or not we love God based on our actions toward him because we cannot see him. Love for God is reflected in love for his children, our brothers, and sisters, whom we can see. Therefore, God gave us this verifiable command: Whoever loves God must also love his brother. Jesus stated the principle in other words: whatever you did not do for one of the least of these you did not do for me (Matt. 25:40)."[175]

As one commentary puts it, this loving one another is a new commandment. "This is a new commandment and a new object. Not just "love God" or "love me," but **love one another.** In 1 John this theme of loving one another appears in 2:9–10; 3:11–18; 4:7–12, 19–21; and 5:1–3. It was not only a new commandment and a new object, but a new mode (**as I have loved you**) and, perhaps most difficult and shocking of all, a new judge. Verse 35 can be identified as the key verse of this chapter. God allows the world to judge whether people are truly Jesus' disciples by the way they behave toward one another. Sadly, the church has not done very well on this point. Perhaps this accounts for some of the struggles the gospel has had for almost two thousand years."[176]

Moreover, true Christians, who truly love one another, must be at unity with their brothers and sisters, for God's Word commands: "I appeal to you, brothers, by the name of our Lord Jesus Christ, that all of you agree, and that there be no divisions among you, but that you be united in the same mind and the same judgment." – 1 Corinthians 1:10.

This love and unity need to be maintained beyond an individual church. "The apostle began with a respectful but forceful appeal. In this verse and the next, he called his readers **brothers** to remind them of his intense familial affection for them. Paul also revealed the intensity of his concern by appealing to his readers **in the name of our Lord Jesus Christ**. By so doing, Paul reminded them that the authority of Christ himself stood behind his exhortations. The appeal divides into three parts. He asked the Corinthians to **agree with one another**, to eliminate **divisions**, and to **be perfectly united in mind and thought**. Each part says basically the same thing: the Corinthians needed to eliminate the divisions in their church. They needed to become like-minded with one another. Paul did not desire unity at the expense of truth (see 11:18–19). Paul himself stood against others in the church when the central truths of the gospel were at stake (Gal. 2:5, 11; 5:12). Here, he expressed plainly that Christian unity requires like-mindedness."[177]

---

[175] David Walls and Max Anders, *I & II Peter, I, II & III John, Jude*, vol. 11, Holman New Testament Commentary (Nashville, TN: Broadman & Holman Publishers, 1999), 211–212.

[176] Kenneth O. Gangel, *John*, vol. 4, Holman New Testament Commentary (Nashville, TN: Broadman & Holman Publishers, 2000), 255.

[177] Richard L. Pratt Jr, *I & II Corinthians*, vol. 7, Holman New Testament Commentary (Nashville, TN: Broadman & Holman Publishers, 2000), 8.

The Roots of the Lawless One

2 Corinthians 4:3-4 Updated American Standard Version (UASV)

[3] And even if our gospel **is veiled**, it is **veiled** to those who are **perishing.** [4] In their case the god of this world has **blinded the minds of the unbelievers**, to keep them from seeing the light of the gospel of the glory of Christ, who is the image of God.

2 Corinthians 3:12-18 Updated American Standard Version (UASV)

[12] Therefore having such a hope, we use great boldness in our speech, [13] and are not like Moses, who used to put a veil over his face so that the sons of Israel would not look intently at the end of what was fading away. [14] But **their minds were hardened**; for until this very day at the reading of the old covenant the same **veil remains unlifted**, because it is **taken away only by means of Christ.** [15] But to this day whenever Moses is read, a **veil lies over their hearts**; [16] but whenever one **turns to the Lord**, the **veil is taken away.** [17] ow the Lord is the Spirit, and where the Spirit of the Lord is, there is freedom. [18] But we all, with unveiled face, beholding as in a mirror the glory of the Lord, are being transformed into the same image from glory to glory, just as from the Lord, the Spirit.

Let us start by looking at an example of blind minds within Scripture. This was not a case of physical blindness, but mental blindness. There was a Syrian military force coming after Elisha, and God **blinded them mentally**. If it had been physical blindness, then each of them would have to have been led by hand. However, what does the account say?

2 Kings 6:18-20 Updated American Standard Version (UASV)

[18] And when the Syrians came down against him, Elisha prayed to Jehovah and said, "Please strike this nation[178] with blindness." So he struck them with blindness in accordance with the prayer of Elisha. [19] Then Elisha said to them, "This is not the way, nor is this the city; follow me and I will bring you to the man whom you seek." And he brought them to Samaria. [20] When they had come into Samaria, Elisha said, "O Jehovah, open the eyes of these men, that they may see." So Jehovah opened their eyes and they saw; and behold, they were in the midst of Samaria.

Are we to believe that one man led the entire Syrian military force to Samaria? If they were physically blind, they would have to have all held hands. Were the Syrian military forces not able physically to see the images that were before them? No, rather, it was more of an inability to understand them. This must have been some form of mental blindness,

---

[178] Or *people*

where we see everything that everyone else sees, but something just does not register. Another example can be found in the account about the men of Sodom. When they were blinded, they did not become distressed, running into each other.

Definitely, Paul is speaking of people, who are not receptive to truth, because their heart is hardened to it, callused, unfeeling. They are not responding because their figurative heart is opposed. It is as though, God handed them over to Satan, to be mentally blinded from the truth, not because he disliked them per se, but because they had closed their hearts and minds to the Gospel. Thus, no manner of argumentation is likely to bring them back to their senses.

However, at one time Saul (Paul) was one of these. Until he met the risen Jesus on the road to Damascus, he was mentally blind to the truth. He was well aware of what the coming Messiah was to do, but Jesus did none of these things because it was not time. Thus, Paul was blinded by his love for the Law, Jewish tradition, and history. So much so, he was unable to grasp the Gospel. Not to mention, he lived during the days of Jesus ministry, studied under Gamaliel, who was likely there in the area. He could have even been there when Jesus was amazing the Jewish religious leaders, at the age of twelve. Therefore, Saul (Paul) needed a real wake-up call, to get through the veil that blinded him.

Hence, a mentally blind person sees the same information as another, but the truth cannot or will not get down into their heart. I have had the privilege of talking to dozens of small groups of unbelievers, ranging from four people to ten people in my life. I saw this in action. As I spoke to these groups, inevitably, I would see the light going off in the eyes of some (they would be shaking their heads in agreement as I spoke), but others having a cynical look, a doubting look (they would be shaking their heads in disgust or disapproval), and they eventually walked away. This is not saying that the unbeliever cannot understand the Bible; it is simply that they see no significance in it, as it is foolishness to them.

1 Corinthians 2:14 Updated American Standard Version (UASV)

[14] But a physical man **does not accept** the things of the Spirit of God, for <u>they are foolishness</u> to him; and **he is not able to know [understand] them,**[179] <u>because they are examined spiritually</u>.

[179] "The Greek word *ginosko* ("to understand") does not mean comprehend intellectually; it means know by experience. The unsaved obviously do not experience God's Word because they do not welcome it. Only the regenerate have the capacity to welcome and experience the Scriptures, by means of the Holy Spirit."— (Zuck 1991, 23)

Hundreds of millions of Christians use this verse as support that without the "Holy Spirit," we can fully understand God's Word. They would argue that without the "Spirit" the Bible is nothing more than foolish nonsense to the reader. What we need to do before, arriving at the correct meaning of what Paul meant, is grasp what he meant by his use of the word "understand," as to what is 'foolish.' In short, "the things of the Spirit of God" are the "Spirit" inspired Word of God. The natural man sees the inspired Word of God as foolish, and "he is not able to understand them."[180]

Paul wrote, "But the natural man does not accept the things of the Spirit of God, for they are foolishness to him." What did Paul mean by this statement? Did he mean that if the Bible reader did not have the "Spirit" helping him, he would not be able to grasp the correct meaning of the text? Are we to understand Paul as saying that without the "Spirit," the Bible and its teachings are beyond our understanding?

We can gain a measure of understanding as to what Paul meant, by observing how he uses the term "foolishness" elsewhere in the very same letter. At 1 Corinthians 3:19, it is used in the following way, "For the wisdom of this world is foolishness with God." This verse helps us to arrive at the use in two stages: (1) the verse states that human wisdom is foolishness with God, (2) and we know that the use of foolishness here does not mean that God cannot understand (or grasp) human wisdom. The use is that He sees human wisdom as 'foolish' and rejects it as such.

Therefore, the term "foolishness" of 1 Corinthians 3:19 is not in reference to not "understanding," but as to one's view of the text, its significance, or better yet, lack of significance, or lack of value. We certainly know that God can understand the wisdom of the world, but condemns it as being 'foolish.' The same holds true of 1 Corinthians 1:20, where the verbal form of foolishness is used, "Has not God made foolish the wisdom of the world?" Thus, we have the term "foolishness" being used before and after 1 Corinthians 2:14, (1:20; 3:19). In all three cases, we are dealing with the significance, the value being attributed to something.

Thus, it seems obvious that we should attribute the same meaning to our text in question, 1 Corinthians 2:14. In other words, the Apostle Paul, by his use of the term "foolishness," is not saying that the unbeliever is unable to understand, to grasp the Word of God. If this were the case, why would we ever share the Word of God, the gospel message with an

---

[180] "I also believe that the role of the Holy Spirit, at least in His special work on believers related to Scripture, is in illuminating our understanding of the significance (not the meaning) of the text. The meaning is clear apart from any special work of the Holy Spirit."–Dr. Norman L. Geisler.

unbeliever? Unbelievers can understand the Word of God; however, unbelievers see it as foolish, having no value or significance. The resultant meaning of chapters 1-3 of 1 Corinthians is that unbelieving world of mankind can understand the Word of God, but views it foolish (lacking value or significance); while God, on the other hand, understands the wisdom of the world of mankind, but views it foolish (lacking value or significance). Therefore, in both cases, the information is understood or grasped; however, it is rejected because to the party considering it, believes it lacks value or significance.

We pray for the guidance of the Holy Spirit, and our spirit, or mental disposition, needs to be attuned to God and His Spirit through study and application. Now, if our mental disposition is not in tune with the Spirit, we will not come away with the right answer. As Ephesians shows, we can grieve the Spirit.

Ephesians 4:30 Updated American Standard Version (UASV)

[30] And do not **grieve the Holy Spirit** of God, by[181] whom you were sealed for the day of redemption.

How do we grieve the Holy Spirit? We do that by acting contrary to its leading through deception, human weaknesses, imperfections, setting our figurative heart on something other than the leading.

Ephesians 1:18 Updated American Standard Version (UASV)

[18] having the **eyes of your hearts** enlightened, that you may know what is the hope to which he has called you, what are the riches of the glory of his inheritance in the holy ones,

"Eyes of your heart" is a Hebrew Scripture expression, meaning spiritual insight, to grasp the truth of God's Word. So we could pray for the guidance of God's Spirit, and at the same time, we can explain why there are so many different understandings (many wrong answers), some of which contradict each other, as being human imperfection that is diluting some of those interpreters, causing them to lose the Spirit's guidance.

A person sits down to study and prays earnestly for the guidance of Holy Spirit, that his mental disposition be in harmony with God's Word [or simply that his heart be in harmony with . . .], and sets out to study a chapter, an article, something biblical. In the process of that study, he allows himself to be moved, not by a mental disposition in harmony with the Spirit, but by human imperfection, by way of his wrong worldview, his

---

[181] Lit *in*

biases, his preunderstanding.[182] A fundamental of grammatical-historical interpretation is that that we are to look for the simple meaning, the basic meaning, the obvious meaning. However, when this one comes to a text that does not say what he wants it to say, he rationalizes until he has the text in harmony with his preunderstanding. In other words, he reads his presuppositions into the text,[183] as opposed to discovering the meaning that was in the text. Even though his Christian conscience was tweaked at the true meaning, he ignored it, as well as his mental disposition that could have been in harmony with the Spirit, to get the outcome he wanted.

In another example, it may be that the text does mean what he wants, but this is only because the translation he is using is full of theological bias, which is **violating** grammar and syntax, or maybe textual criticism rules and principles that arrive at the correct reading. Therefore, when this student takes a deeper look, he discovers that it could very well read another way, and likely should because of the context. He buries that evidence beneath his conscience, and never mentions it when this text comes up in a Bible discussion. In other words, he is grieving the Holy Spirit and loses it on this particular occasion.

Human imperfection, human weakness, theological bias, preunderstanding, and many other things could dilute the Spirit, or even grieve the Spirit, so that while one may be praying for assistance, he is not getting it, or has lost it, because one, some, or all of these things he is doing has grieved the Spirit.

Again, it is not that an unbeliever cannot understand what the Bible means; otherwise, there would be no need to witness to him. Rather, he does not have the spiritual awareness to see the significance of studying Scripture. An unbeliever can look at "the setting in which the Bible books were written and the circumstances involved in the writing," as well as "studying the words and sentences of Scripture in their normal, plain sense," to arrive the meaning of a text. However, without having any spiritual awareness about themselves, they would not see the significance of applying it in their lives. 1 Corinthians 2:14 says, "The natural person does not **accept** [Gr., dechomai] the things of the Spirit of God." Dechomai means, "to welcome, accept or receive." Thus, the unbeliever may very well understand the meaning of a text, but just does not *accept*, *receive* or *welcome* it as truth.

---

[182] Preunderstanding is all of the knowledge and understanding that we possess before we begin the study of the text.

[183] Presupposition is to believe that a particular thing is so before there is any proof of it

Acts 17:10-11 Updated American Standard Version (UASV)

[10] The brothers immediately sent Paul and Silas away by night to Berea, and when they arrived, they went into the synagogue of the Jews. [11] Now these [the Beroeans] were more noble-minded than those in Thessalonica, for they received the word with great eagerness, examining the Scriptures daily to see whether these things were so.

Unlike the natural person, the Bereans accepted, received, or welcomed the Word of God eagerly. Paul said the Thessalonians "received [*dechomai*] the word in much affliction, with the joy of the Holy Spirit." (1 Thess. 1:6) At the beginning of a person's introduction to the good news, he will take in knowledge of the Scriptures (1 Tim. 2:3-4), which if his heart is receptive, he will begin to apply them in his life, taking off the old person and putting on the new person. (Eph. 4:22-24) Seeing how the Scriptures have begun to alter his life, he will start to have a genuine faith over the things he has learned (Heb. 11:6), repenting of his sins. (Acts 17:30-31) He will turn around his life, and his sins will be blotted out. (Acts 3:19) At some point, he will go to God in prayer, telling the Father that he is dedicating his life to him, to carry out his will and purposes. (Matt. 16:24; 22:37) This regeneration is the Holy Spirit working in his life, giving him a new nature, placing him on the path to salvation.—2 Corinthians 5:17.

A new believer will become "acquainted with the sacred writings, which are able to make [him] wise for salvation through faith in Christ Jesus." (2 Tim. 3:15) As the Bible informs us, the Scriptures are holy and are to be viewed as such. If we are to acquire an accurate or full knowledge, to have the correct mental grasp of the things that we carried out an exegetical analysis on, it must be done with a prayerful and humble heart. It is as Dr. Norman L. Geisler said, "the role of the Holy Spirit, at least in His special work on believers related to Scripture, is in illuminating our understanding of the significance (not the meaning) of the text. The meaning is clear apart from any special work of the Holy Spirit." What level of understanding that we are able to acquire is based on the degree to which we are **not** grieving the Holy Spirit with our worldview, our preunderstanding, our presuppositions, our theological biases. In addition, anyone living in sin will struggle to grasp God's Word as well.

No interpreter is infallible. The only infallibility or inerrancy belonged to the original manuscripts. Each Christian has the right to interpret God's Word, to discover what it means, but this does not guarantee that they will come away with the correct meaning. The Holy Spirit will guide us into and through the truth, by way of our working in behalf of our prayers to have the correct understanding. Our working in harmony with the Holy Spirit means that we buy out the time for a personal study program, not to mention the time to prepare properly and carefully for our Christian meetings. In these studies, do not expect that the Holy Spirit is going to miraculously give us some flash of understanding, but rather understanding will come to us as we set aside our personal biases, worldviews, human imperfections, presuppositions, preunderstanding, opening our mental disposition to the Spirit's leading as we study.

The Record of One Aspect of the Man of Lawlessness

The Christian religious leaders that make up the man of lawlessness have been very reprehensible in their shedding blood. They have used the name of God to commit some of the most atrocious crimes against humanity and against their brothers and sisters in the faith. We need look no further than the Crusades, other religious wars, inquisitions, and persecutions. The Crusades (a war or campaign that is religiously motivated) ran from the 11th to the 13th century. The result of the Crusades was horrific bloodshed and plundering in the name of God. Literally, hundreds of thousands were slaughtered. This also includes the Children's Crusade of the year 1212, where thousands of children were slaughtered as well.

The Roman Catholic Church formally authorized another God-dishonoring horror in the 13th century, the Inquisition. *The New Encyclopedia of Christian Martyrs* writes, "Of the multitudes who perished by the Inquisition throughout the world, no authentic record is now discoverable. But wherever popery had power, there was the tribunal. It had been planted even in the east, and the Portuguese Inquisition of Goa was, until within these few years, fed with many an agony. South America was partitioned into provinces of the Inquisition; and with a ghastly mimicker of the crimes of the mother state, the arrivals of viceroys, and the other popular celebrations were thought imperfect without an auto da fe. The Netherlands were one scene of slaughter from the time of the decree which planted the Inquisition among them. In Spain, the calculation is more attainable. Each of the seventeen tribunals during a long period burned annually, on an average, ten miserable beings! We are to recollect that this number was in a country where persecution had for ages abolished all religious differences, and where the difficulty was not to find the stake, but the offering. Yet, even in Spain, thus gleaned of all heresy, the Inquisition could still swell its lists of murders to thirty-two thousand! The numbers burned in effigy, or condemned to penance, punishments generally equivalent to exile, confiscation, and taint of blood, to all ruin but the mere loss of worthless life, amounted to three hundred and nine thousand. But the crowds who perished in dungeons of torture, of confinement, and of broken hearts, the millions of dependent lives made utterly helpless, or hurried to the grave by the death of the victims, are beyond all register; or recorded only before HIM, who has sworn that "He that leadeth into captivity, shall go into captivity: he that killeth with the sword must be killed with the sword."

The encyclopedia continues, "Such was the Inquisition, declared by the Spirit of God to be at once the offspring and the image of the popedom. To feel the force of the parentage, we must look to the time. In the thirteenth century, the popedom was at the summit of mortal dominion; it was independent of all kingdoms; it ruled with a rank of influence never before or since possessed by a human scepter; it was the acknowledged sovereign of body and soul; to all earthly intents its power was immeasurable for good or evil. It might have spread literature, peace, freedom, and Christianity to the ends of Europe, or the world. But its nature was hostile; its fuller triumph only disclosed its fuller evil; and, to the shame of human reason, and the terror and suffering of human virtue, Rome, in the hour of its consummate grandeur, teemed with the monstrous and horrid birth of the INQUISITION!"[184]

The Charismatic Movement

This author sees the Charismatic branch of Christianity as another facet of the man of lawlessness.[185] Sadly, this is the fastest growing segment of Christianity. Below is an introduction to the charismatic movement from *The Encyclopedia of Christianity.* Rather than indent, we will simply show the reader the Excursion and at the end, we will show the End of Excursion. Again, this author sees the charismatic branch of Christianity as a part of the body of the man of lawlessness.

> What would God say about those who blatantly misrepresent His Holy Spirit; who exchange true worship for chaotic fits of mindless ecstasy; who replace the biblical gospel with vain illusions of health and wealth; who claim to prophesy in His name yet speak errors; and who sell false hope to desperate people for millions of dollars? – John Macarthur

---

[184] Mark Water, *The New Encyclopedia of Christian Martyrs* (Alresford, Hampshire: John Hunt Publishers Ltd, 2001), 591–592.

[185] **Strange Fire: The Danger of Offending the Holy Spirit with Counterfeit Worship** Nov 19, 2013 by John F. MacArthur

EXCURSION: Definition and Terminology

The term "charismatic movement" refers to the currents of revival and renewal resulting from a transforming spiritual experience generally termed "baptism in the Spirit," which is associated with the reception and contemporary availability of the spiritual gifts of 1 Cor. 12:8–10 (esp. prophecy, healing, and glossolalia). While baptism in the Spirit and the spiritual gifts also characterize the Pentecostal movement, the charismatic movement with its many different strands is clearly distinct in theological framework, patterns of fellowship, and sociocultural ethos.

The term "charismatic movement" was coined by H. Bredesen and J. Stone in 1963 to designate what was at first called neo-Pentecostalism, that is, the occurrence of Pentecostal-type blessing within the historic Protestant denominations. This was the general connotation of "charismatic movement" in the mid-1960s. By the late 1960s, however, there were independent groups and ministries, often calling themselves nondenominational, that identified more with the charismatic movement than with Pentecostalism per se. These nondenominational currents, which spread in the 1970s and mushroomed in the 1980s, are now generally recognized as part of the overall charismatic movement, in which we may distinguish three major strands: (1) charismatic renewal in the historic Protestant churches (from the 1950s); (2) charismatic renewal in the Roman Catholic Church (from 1967); (3) charismatic renewal in the independent sector (from the late 1960s). In 1988 the numbers of those active in these three groups were estimated, respectively, at 10.9 million, 10.1 million, and 17.4 million.

2. Beginnings

The early stirrings of the charismatic movement lie in the 1950s in the United States, the Netherlands, and the United Kingdom, although only in the early 1960s did they enter public consciousness and acquire visibility as a movement. Important influences in its origins, all of which were operative in the 1950s, were groups praying for revival (e.g., Nights of Prayer for Worldwide Revival in the United Kingdom), circles ministering divine healing (e.g., the London Healing Mission, the key role of Agnes Sanford, often—despite its official disapproval—within the milieu of the Order of St. Luke in the United States), people studying the Book of Acts (e.g., the Methodist Tommy Tyson in North Carolina), and contact with Pentecostals (e.g., the healing campaigns of T. L. Osborn in the Netherlands and the major influence of the Full Gospel Business Men's Fellowship International; Pentecostal Churches). Some people and groups became charismatic without any evident outside influence.

The public emergence of a distinct movement occurred in the United States through national publicity in 1960 concerning the Episcopal priest Dennis Bennett (then of Van Nuys, Calif., and later of Seattle) and in Britain in 1963 through another Anglican priest, Michael Harper. Other major publicizing factors were David Wilkerson's biographical book *The Cross and the Switchblade* (1963) and John Sherrill's *They Speak with Other Tongues* (1964). Between 1962 and 1965 the charismatic movement spread to New Zealand, Germany, Kenya, South Africa, and Australia.

Like the meetings of Pentecostals, charismatic meetings were characterized by vocal praise, lengthy preaching or teaching, personal testimonies, and personal ministry. From the start, there was a strong lay character about the charismatic movement, with an emphasis on "every-member" ministry. This practice favored the discovery and use of gifts independent of ministerial ordination, though the mainline charismatics continued to recognize ordained ministry.

Charismatic renewal in Protestant traditions tended to produce either overtly charismatic congregations or congregations with a charismatic flavor, while charismatic Roman Catholic renewal typically gave rise to prayer groups, intentional (often covenant) communities, and centers for ministry and healing.

3. Developments Worldwide

3.1. *North America*

Between the mid-1960s and the late 1970s, the charismatic movement spread rapidly in the United States, helped by the homogeneity of language and culture, media publicity, mass conventions, and the influence of the Full Gospel Business Men's Fellowship. Since 1988, the impact of the movement has been uneven, except in the independent sector, which has continued to grow steadily.

Charismatic renewal in the mainline churches has generally struggled to have a significant influence on church life. Often just tolerated, sometimes given a limited welcome, charismatic renewal has lost many of its supporters to Pentecostal and independent charismatic churches, especially from Presbyterian, United Methodist, and Baptist ranks. In the 1990s an increasing liberalism in the liturgical churches has intensified the struggle of loyal charismatics. Some Episcopalians have

---

Calif. California

joined the Charismatic Episcopal Church, formed in 1992 by former independent charismatics and Pentecostals.

The spread of the charismatic movement to the Roman Catholic Church in 1967 produced a powerful new thrust toward church renewal, the beginning of Life in the Spirit seminars to prepare people for the baptism in the Spirit, and the establishment of local and national service committees for the renewal movement. This pattern soon spread to the Catholic renewal in other countries and influenced other major denominations in the United States such as the Episcopalians and Lutherans to establish their own renewal agencies.

Charismatic Roman Catholic renewal was marked in its early years by the forceful influence of the covenant communities, especially Word of God (Ann Arbor, Mich.) and People of Praise (South Bend, Ind.). Divisions between such communities and the challenge of those favoring parish renewal, represented particularly in the Association of Diocesan Liaisons, led to a more diverse but weakened charismatic Catholic renewal.

The tradition that has been most positively influenced by charismatic renewal seems to be the Mennonite/Anabaptist churches, whose denominational leaderships have taken the charismatic movement more seriously. Until recently, charismatic renewal among Episcopalians has maintained momentum, strengthening the evangelical strands in the Episcopal Church.

At its beginning, opposition to the charismatic movement was least in the Roman Catholic Church and greatest among the Presbyterians, in the Lutheran Church–Missouri Synod, and among the Orthodox. However, a leading Presbyterian scholar, John A. Mackay, with positive memories of Pentecostalism in Latin America, defended the Presbyterian charismatics and urged his church to study the question, leading to the important *Report on the Work of the Holy Spirit*, received by the United Presbyterian Church in 1978. The Lutheran Church–Missouri Synod has taken somewhat longer to come to terms with charismatic renewal, as have the Holiness churches such as the Church of the Nazarene, which opposed the Pentecostal movement at its beginning.

The independent, or nondenominational, groupings first came into prominence in the early 1970s with the impact of Christian Growth Ministries, based in Fort Lauderdale, Florida. Led by Derek Prince, Bob Mumford, Don Basham, Charles Simpson, and Ern Baxter, the group

---

Ann *Annales*
Mich. Michigan
Ind. Indiana

produced the magazine *New Wine* (1969–86) and until the mid-1970s were the main exponents of so-called discipleship teaching. Their teaching and practice became controversial, and the mid-1970s saw much effort in the United States to repair strained relationships and to moderate heavy forms of authority.

The independent charismatics have tended to form networks linked more by personal bonds between the leading pastors than by creed or style of church government. Their patterns of organization reflect secular patterns from the world of business enterprise, with the possibility of simultaneous association with more than one network. The major networks include International Convention of Faith Ministries (Tulsa, Okla.), Fellowship of Covenant Ministers and Churches (Mobile, Ala.), Liberty Fellowship (Birmingham, Ala.), People of Destiny International (Gaithersburg, Md.), and Vineyard churches (Anaheim, Calif.). In the United States, independent charismatics outnumbered all "denominational" charismatics by the early 1990s (14 million vs. 6 million).

The interdenominational character of the charismatic movement was fostered by major events such as the Kansas City conference of 1977. This ecumenical dimension weakened in the 1980s, though the formation of the North American Renewal Service Committee (1985) and their organizing of interchurch congresses (New Orleans, 1987; Indianapolis, 1990; Orlando, 1995) have given a new impetus. The monthly magazine *Charisma* serves all constituencies, coming out of a Pentecostalism reanimated through the charismatic movement plus a strong nondenominational impulse.

3.2. *Europe*

Charismatic renewal in European Protestant churches has been uneven. Variations reflect (1) church situations (minority churches may accept charismatic renewal as an agent of growth, as do, for example, the Baptists in France), (2) experience of revival movements (charismatic renewal is often stronger in regions with a history of revival, such as the Lutheran Church of Finland and the Evangelical Church in Wurttemberg), and (3) quality of leadership (Anglican charismatic renewal in England has benefited from responsible leadership, esp. of D. Watson [1933–84]). Charismatic renewal has had less impact on Methodism than on the Reformation churches. The

---

Okla. Oklahoma
Ala. Alabama
Ala. Alabama
Md. Maryland
Calif. California

renewal in the Evangelical Lutheran Church has been gaining ground, despite some defections to the independent sector.

The charismatic movement in France has been marked by the rise of strong communities (Emmanuel, Chemin Neuf, Lion de Juda [now Béatitudes], and Pain de Vie) that have spread to many other countries, especially in Africa. In Italy, the charismatic Roman Catholic renewal attracts huge numbers to its annual convention in Rimini. In Ireland it has faded; it is relatively small in Spain and Portugal. In Germany, theology has played a larger role, with a theological commission having been formed for charismatic Catholic renewal.

In Scandinavia, charismatic renewal has been strongest in Finland and Norway and weakest in Denmark. Lutheran renewal has struggled generally with the antienthusiastic strain in Luther's heritage.

The independent sector has grown the fastest. Britain has many networks, of which the largest are Pioneer (led by G. Coates), New Frontiers (led by T. Virgo), and Salt and Light (led by B. Coombs). The Ichthus churches of R. Forster have integrated charismatic and social concerns with a strong ministry to the inner city. The British independent sector has strong outreach to other lands and has pioneered the worldwide March for Jesus, held annually especially in the capital cities of the world.[186]

End of Excursion

Liberal Christianity or Theological Modernism

This author sees Liberal Christianity or Theological Modernism a movement within Protestant denominations as another facet of the man of lawlessness. Sadly, this is the fastest growing segment of Christianity, as it is intertwined with the charismatic aspect as well. Below is an introduction to the Liberal Christianity or Theological Modernism movement from Conservapedia.[187] Rather than indent the text, we will simply show the reader the Excursion and at the end, we will show the End of Excursion. Again, this author sees the Liberal Christianity or Theological Modernism within Protestant denominations as a part of the body of the man of lawlessness.

---

[186] Peter Hocken, "Charismatic Movement," *The Encyclopedia of Christianity* (Grand Rapids, MI; Leiden, Netherlands: Wm. B. Eerdmans; Brill, 1999–2003), 404–406.

[187] http://www.conservapedia.com/Liberal_Christianity

Excursion

Liberal Christianity or Theological Modernism is a broad term which basically refers to a movement within American Protestant denominations to stress the social role of Christianity, as in the Social Gospel of the early 20th century. This movement is characterized by a lack of emphasis on or denial of the plenary Divine inspiration and authority of the Bible, and commitment to doctrinal purity. Prevalent Biblical themes such as repentance from personal moral sin, hell and damnation for those who reject Christ, His blood atonement and His future literal reign are minimized, or militated against. In 1937, H. Richard Niebuhr summarized their basic gospel message as preaching that "A God without wrath brought men without sin into a kingdom without judgment through the ministrations of a Christ without a Cross."[188]

Theologically, Liberal Christianity stresses a basic continuity between man and God, emphasizing the immanence of God rather than His transcendence. It tends to see religious knowledge emerging from research and the use of reason, as superior to Biblical revelation. Thus the liberal idea of religion as a personal relationship with God is one which is not necessarily bound to a Biblical doctrinal basis. This stands in in contrast to salvation resulting from faith in the Biblically substantiated gospel of grace, and in conformity with orthodox theological beliefs.

Origins of liberal Christianity

The most influential liberal Christian theologians were 19th century Germans: Friedrich Schleiermacher and Albrecht Ritschl.

Schleiermacher emphasized that religion was a personal relationship with God, and downplayed historical Christian doctrines such as the doctrine of creation, doctrine of Incarnation, doctrine of eternal life, etc.

Schleiermacher sought to re-establish the importance of Christianity using Christian religious experience rather than scientific knowledge. Ritschl revised Schleirmacher's idea and tried to re-establish their authority using Kant's idea of moral experience and in the fulfillment of the Kingdom of God.[189]

Doctrines that did not relate well to religious experience or moral experience tended to disappear.

---

[188] he Kingdom of God in America (1937), New York: Harper and Row, 1959, p. 193

http://www.touchstonemag.com/archives/article.php?id=15-09-011-c

[189] Langdon Gilkey, *Naming the Whirlwind: The Renewal of God-Language*, (1969), 73, 74, and 75

Role of the Bible

Liberals view the Bible as the witness of God rather than the word of God. Strangely the view looks for support by a type of literal interpretation — though this should not be confused with the form of Biblical literalism found in fundamentalist and conservative churches — of the words of Paul in his second letter to Timothy:

2 Timothy 3:16 Updated American Standard Version (UASV)

16 All Scripture is inspired by God and profitable for teaching, for reproof, for correction, for training in righteousness;

Here some see Paul conveying that that scripture is a direct result of the authors contact with God ("witness"), whilst stopping short of claiming actual divine authorship ("word"). Conservative Christians would answer that Paul states here that the words which make up scripture are God-breathed, and that the Bible records God's promise to preserve His words, not merely His ideas.[190]

As a result Liberal Theologians view the Bible as a text to be interpreted in its historical context but through liberal critical analysis.[191] As a result, many hold that texts such as Genesis' early chapters or Old Testament miracles are poetry or fables — having a message, but not to be taken literally (in spite of the New Testament referring to such as literal events).[192] This approach began to dominate most Protestant denominations in the early 1900's, and was challenged by Neo Orthodoxy and Fundamentalism after 1940. Examples today include some churches within Anglican/Episcopalian, Lutheran, Methodist, Presbyterian, and United Church of Christ churches.[193] The word "liberal" in liberal Christianity does not refer to any political agenda or set of beliefs, although liberal theological beliefs will often form the basis of liberal political beliefs.

In addition, liberal Christians are seen taking an unwarranted pick-and-choose approach to the Bible, declaring that passages, which they favor, were intended by God to be followed today, while other parts are outdated or need to be reinterpreted, in order to conform with current

---

[190] http://www.chick.com/information/bibleversions/preserve.asp

http://www.biblebelievers.com/kam/kam_001.html

[191] http://home.earthlink.net/~gbl111/liberalism.htm

[192] http://www.gotquestions.org/liberal-Christian-theology.htm

[193] http://www.beliefnet.com/story/80/story_8028_1.html

trends. As needed, the spirit of the Bible is emphasized in such a way that its specific wording can be ignored or negated. As Machen comments,

> Admitting that scientific objections may arise against the particularities of the Christian religion—against the Christian doctrines of the person of Christ, and of redemption through His death and resurrection—the liberal theologian seeks to rescue certain of the general principles of religion, of which these particularities are thought to be mere temporary symbols, and these general principles he regards as constituting "the essence of Christianity.[194]

Rather than the Bible being wholly inspired by God, many liberal Christians believe that the Bible was the work of numerous editorial redactors[195] — homophobic ones in cases where pro-homosexual writers wish to see homoeroticism positively portrayed between Bible characters — or even that certain parts of the Bible that do not agree with liberal theology are later additions that do not belong in the Bible at all. In extreme cases, some liberal Christians even engage in politically correct censorship against those who quote Bible verses that tend to disprove a liberal Christian position. It may also esteem other books as works of God as well as the Bible. Some liberal Christians argue that correct Christian doctrine is whatever each individual believer deems it to be.

Most of those within mainline denominations evidence beliefs and its effects, which are at variance with Biblically, based historical Christian faith.[196] Two issues usually indicative of liberal denominations are support for abortion and homosexuality. For a more detailed treatment, see Homosexuality and Christianity.[197]

Some liberal Christians acknowledge that an omnipotent God could easily preserve His words and conclude that, for whatever reason, He has chosen not to do so, instead leaving us to our subjective impressions of God's will.[198]

---

[194] J. Gresham Machen, Christianity and Liberalism; Introduction
http://www.biblebelievers.com/machen/machen_introduction.html

[195] Documentary Hypothesis
http://ccat.sas.upenn.edu/rs/2/Judaism/jepd.html
http://www.ukapologetics.net/docu.htm

[196] http://peacebyjesus.witnesstoday.org/RevealingStatistics.html#Sec4

[197] http://www.conservapedia.com/Homosexuality_and_Christianity

[198] This note is by the author of this book. The original manuscripts are error free. However, over the centuries many copyist errors have slipped into the manuscripts. Nevertheless, over the past 500 years of textual studies, scholars have been able to restore the text to 99.99% of what would have been in the originals. A restored text is an exact

A few Christian denominations perform same-sex marriages. These include:

- The Episcopalian church
- The United Church of Christ
- The Presbyterian Church (USA)
- Evangelical Lutheran Church of America

End of Excursion

Exposing the Man of Lawlessness

We need to appreciate and apply the principle behind Paul's words to the Galatians. He wrote, "Do not be deceived: God is not mocked, for whatever one sows, that will he also reap." (6:7, ESV) Thus, God will hold the man of lawlessness accountable and any who have knowingly or unknowing support the lawless one's efforts. Again, Jesus will say to those who refuse the truth for the lie, "depart from me, you workers of lawlessness." (Matt. 7:23) He also said, "Every tree that does not bear good fruit is cut down and thrown into the fire [i.e., destroyed]."[199] Since the Second Coming of Christ is upon us,[200] all true Christians are obligated to expose the man of lawlessness and save those willing to accept the truth from the coming destruction. Jesus said, "If you abide in my word, you are truly my disciples, and you will know the truth, and the truth will set you free." (John 8:31-32, ESV) If we remain in or abide in the Word of God, we will recognize what facets of so-called "Christianity" is a part of the body of the man of lawlessness. That same Word of God can free others who have a receptive heart.

Conversation Evangelism

Evangelism[201] is the work of a Christian evangelist, of which all true Christians are obligated to partake to some extent, which seeks to persuade

---

representation of the original. A translation is the Word of God when the rendering in the receptor language is an equivalent of the original.

[199] WHAT IS HELL? Basic Bible Doctrines of the Christian Faith by Edward D. Andrews

http://www.christianpublishers.org/apps/webstore/products/show/5346167

[200] The SECOND COMING of CHRIST: Basic Bible Doctrines of the Christian Faith by Edward D. Andrews

http://www.christianpublishers.org/apps/webstore/products/show/5383701

[201] CONVERSATIONAL EVANGELISM, [Second Edition] by Edward D. Andrews

other people to become Christian, especially by sharing the basics of the Gospel, but also the deeper message of biblical truths. Today the Gospel is almost an unknown, so what does the Christian evangelist do? **Preevangelism** is laying a foundation for those who have no knowledge of the Gospel, giving them background information, so that they are able to grasp what they are hearing. The Christian evangelist is preparing their mind and heart so that they will be receptive to the biblical truths. In many ways, this is known as apologetics.

Christian apologetics [Greek: *apologia*, "verbal defense, speech in defense"] is a field of **Christian theology** that endeavors to offer a reasonable and sensible basis for the **Christian faith**, defending the faith against objections. It is reasoning from the Scriptures, explaining and proving, as one instructs in sound doctrine, many times having to overturn false reasoning before he can plant the seeds of truth. It can also be earnestly contending for the faith and saving one from losing their faith, as they have begun to doubt. Moreover, it can involve rebuking those who contradict the truth. It is being prepared to make a defense to anyone who asks the Christian evangelist for a reason for the hope that is in him or her. – Jude 1.3, 21-23; 1 Pet 3.15; Acts 17:2-3; Titus 1:9.

What do we mean by **obligated** and what we mean by **evangelism** are at the heart of the matter and are indeed related to each other.

EVANGELISM: An evangelist is a proclaimer of the gospel or good news, as well as all biblical truths. There are levels of evangelism, which is pictured in first-century Christianity. All Christians evangelized in the first century, but a select few fit the role of a full-time evangelist (Ephesians 4:8, 11-12), as Philip and Timothy.

Both Philip and Timothy are specifically mentioned as evangelizers. (Ac 21:8; 2 Tim. 4:5) Philip was a full-time evangelist after Pentecost, who was sent to the city of Samaria, having great success. An angel even directed

---

http://www.christianpublishers.org/apps/webstore/products/show/5749015

CHRISTIAN APOLOGETIC EVANGELISM: Reaching Hearts with the Art of Persuasion by Edward D. Andrews

http://www.christianpublishers.org/apps/webstore/products/show/7670559

THE CHRISTIAN APOLOGIST: Always Being Prepared to Make a Defense [Second Edition] By Edward D. Andrews

http://www.christianpublishers.org/apps/webstore/products/show/5273691

THE EVANGELISM HANDBOOK: How All Christians Can Effectively Share God's Word in Their Community, [SECOND EDITION], by Edward D. Andrews

http://www.christianpublishers.org/apps/webstore/products/show/4676258

Philip to an Ethiopian Eunuch, to share the good news about Christ with him. Because of the Eunuch's already having knowledge of God by way of the Old Testament, Philip was able to help him understand that the Hebrew Scriptures pointed to Christ as the long-awaited Messiah. In the end, Philip baptized the Eunuch. After that, the Spirit again sent Philip on a mission, this time to Azotus and all the cities on the way to Caesarea. (Ac 8:5, 12, 14, 26-40) Paul evangelized in many lands, setting up one congregation after another. (2 Cor. 10:13-16) Timothy was an evangelizer or missionary, and Paul placed special importance on evangelizing when he gave his parting encouragement to Timothy. – 2 Timothy 4:5; 1 Timothy 1:3.

The office of apostle and evangelist seem to overlap in some areas, but could be distinguished in that apostles traveled and set up congregations, which took evangelizing skills, but also developed the congregations after they were established. The evangelists were more of a missionary, being stationed in certain areas to grow and develop congregations. In addition, if we look at all of the apostles and the evangelists, plus Paul's more than one hundred traveling companions, it seems very unlikely that they could have had Christianity at over one million by the 125 C.E. This was accomplished because all Christians were obligated to carry out some level of evangelism.

OBLIGATED: In the broadest sense of the term for evangelizer, all Christians are obligated to play some role as an evangelist.

- *Basic Evangelism* is planting seeds of truth and watering any seeds that have been planted. [In the basic sense of this word (euaggelistes), this would involve all Christians.] In some cases, it may be that one Christian planted the seed, which was initially rejected, so he was left in a good way because the planter did not try to force the truth down his throat. However, later he faces something in life that moves him to reconsider those seeds and another Christian water what had already been planted by the first Christian. This evangelism can be carried out in all of the methods that are available: informal, house-to-house, street, phone, internet, and the like. What amount of time is invested in the evangelism work is up to each Christian to decide for themselves?

- *Making Disciples* is having any role in the process of getting an unbeliever from his unbelief state to the point of accepting Christ as his Savior and being baptized. Once the unbeliever has become a believer, he is still developed until he has become strong. Any Christian could potentially carry this one person through all of the developmental stages. On the other hand, it may be that several have some part. It is like a person that specializes in a certain aspect of a job, but all are aware of the other aspects, in case they are called on to carry out that phase. Again, each

Christian must decide for themselves what role they are to have, and how much of a role, but should be prepared to fill any role if needed.

• *Part-Time or Full-Time Evangelist* is one who sees this as their calling and chooses to be very involved as an evangelist in their local church and community. They may work part-time to supplement their work as an evangelist. They may be married with children, but they realize their gift is in the field of evangelism. If it were the wife, the husband would work toward supporting her work as an evangelist and vice-versa. If it were a single person, he or she would supplement their work by being employed part-time, but also the church would help as well. This person is well trained in every aspect of bringing one to Christ.

• *Congregation Evangelists* should be very involved in evangelizing their communities and helping the church members play their role at the basic levels of evangelism. There is nothing to say that one church could not have many within, who take on part-time or full-time evangelism within the congregation, which would and should be cultivated.

CHAPTER 14 The Mark of the Beast – 666

In our efforts to understand what is meant by the mark of the beast, the name, the number six hundred and sixty-six (666), we need to look for clues within the Scripture that will help us find the correct answer.

The Importance of Bible Names

If anyone has read much of Scripture, they will discover that Bible names play a significant importance, especially those handed out by God himself. On this Dr. Cornwall and Smith write, "Every Bible name has a meaning. So much so, that sometimes when God changed the nature of a person He also changed his or her name. For example, when Abram believed God's promise of a son, God changed his name to Abraham ["father of a multitude"] and changed his wife's name from Sarai to Sarah ["Princess"]. Years later, after the angel of the Lord had wrestled with him all night; Jacob's name was changed to Israel ["Contender with God"]. In the New Testament, Saul of Tarsus, whose name meant, "demanded," came to be known as Paul, which means "little." And this is what the greatest apostle became in his own eyes as he looked increasingly upon the greatness of Christ. It's amazing how often a Bible character lives up to the meaning of his or her name. Sometimes, as in the case of Paul, they deliberately took a name that meant what they wanted to be." (Cornwall and Smith 1998, Page viii)

We find this to be the case from Genesis to Revelation; therefore, the mark of the beast, the name, the number six hundred and sixty-six (666) given by God has to be in relation to the nature of the beast. If we are to understand the nature of the beast, we must identify the beat itself, so we can discover what we can about its undertakings.

The Beast Uncovered

We can actually discover much about the symbolic beast of Revelation by looking to the prophetic book of Daniel. In chapter 7 of Daniel, there are four beasts: a lion, a bear, a leopard, and "a fourth beast, terrifying and dreadful and exceedingly strong. It had great iron teeth; it devoured and broke in pieces and stamped what was left with its feet. It was different from all the beasts that were before it, and it had ten horns." (Daniel 7:2-7) If we look at verse 17 of chapter 7, Daniel tells us "These four great beasts are four kings who shall arise out of the earth." In verse 23 of the same chapter, Daniel says, "Thus he said: 'As for the fourth beast, there shall be a fourth kingdom on earth, which shall be different from all the kingdoms, and it shall devour the whole earth, and trample it down, and break it to pieces.'" In other words, these symbolic beasts represent kingdoms that were to rule over the earth.

Regarding the beast of Revelation 13:1-2, the *Holman New Testament Commentary: Revelation* states, "The monster appears even more royal than the dragon, wearing **ten crowns** (diadems) as compared to the dragon's seven (12:3). **The blasphemous name** on each head suggests a claim to divine status (vv. 5–6). The body parts of this brute are a composite of three of the four creature of Daniel 7:1–6, but in reverse order: body of **a leopard**, feet of **a bear**, and mouth of **a lion. In** Daniel's vision, these represented historical empires that opposed Judah, such as Babylon and Persia. Here they are all combined into one monster–raw political-military power. The Christians of John's day immediately grasped that the form of the monster current in their day was imperial Rome. Where did Rome's power come from? **The dragon gave the beast his power and his throne and great authority.** Although God has ordained that government be used for good (Rom. 13:1–7), clearly the devil has mastered the art of twisting what God means for good and turning it to evil."–(Easley 1998, p. 227)

Revelation 13:2 Updated American Standard Version (UASV)

[2] And the beast which I saw was like a leopard, and his feet were like those of a bear, and his mouth like the mouth of a lion. And the dragon gave him his power and his throne and great authority.

As we saw in the above, these symbolic beasts represent kingdoms that were to rule over the earth. However, what do these features denote? Regarding the characteristics of the beast of Revelation 13:1-2, the *Baker New Testament Commentary: Revelation* states, "The first portrayal is that of the leopard, noted for stalking its prey, its amazing speed in capturing prey, and its swiftness in dealing the deathblow. The second picture is that of a bear, which with its powerful paws is able to tear its victims apart. And third, the lion's mouth symbolizes cruelty as it kills and devours wild animals. The three pictures of these beasts are a depiction of force, speed, and savagery." (Kistemaker 2001, p. 379)

Revelation 13:1 Updated American Standard Version (UASV)

[1] And the dragon stood on the sand of the sea. Then I saw a beast coming up out of the sea, having ten horns and seven heads, and on his horns were ten diadems, and on his heads were blasphemous names.

What or who do these seven heads represent? The seven heads are seven world empires throughout Bible history that have had some kind of impact on God's people, five of which were before John's day: Egypt Assyria, Babylon, Medo-Persia, and Greece. The sixth of those world empires was in existence during John's day, Rome, with the seventh world empire, yet to come. Look at John's reference again in the same book.

Revelation 17:9-10 Updated American Standard Version (UASV)

[9] Here is the mind which has wisdom. The seven heads are seven mountains on which the woman sits, [10] and they are seven kings; five have fallen **[Egypt, Assyrian, Babylon, Medo-Persia, and Greece]**, one is **[Rome]**, the other has not yet come **[United States]**;and when he comes, he must remain a little while.

We can conclude that the first wild beast from the sea (vss. 1-10) and the second wild beast from the earth (vss. 11-18) of Revelation 13 represent two governmental powers. The first wild beast "the dragon **[Satan, Rev. 12:3, 9]** gave it his power and his throne and great authority." The second wild beast "exercises all the authority of the first beast on his behalf and compels the earth and those who live on it to worship the first beast." Therefore, these beasts or governmental powers are against Christ. Consequently, they are antichrists.

We must not overreact to this, believing that everyone within the government is somehow a tool, being possessed and used by Satan or his demons. We must realize that God uses the human governments for his own purposes as well. We have seen in the United States of late, what other countries have long known, without the law enforcement, a part of the government, there would be anarchy. Moreover, without the military might of the United States government, the world would be overrun by evil, such as Islam. If there were not legislatures, we would have no laws, which give structure to our human society. Some leaders and governments throughout human history have been used by Satan to try to stop pure worship, but others have protected the rights of its citizens, which include the freedom of worship. (Romans 13:3, 4; Ezra 7:11-27; Acts 13:7) Nevertheless, because of satanic influence and human imperfection, no human society has ever, nor will they ever bring true peace and security.[202]

The Number of a Man

Revelation 13:18 Updated American Standard Version (UASV)

[18] Here is wisdom. Let the one who has understanding calculate the number of the beast, for it is the number of a man, and his number is six hundred and sixty-six.[203]

---

[202] Because of Satan's influence over human governments, while Christians are to be in subjection to superior authorities (Rom 13:1), this is only as long as they do not ask anything that is in opposition to God's will and purpose. For example, if the government said, "no more evangelizing about the Bible," we would obey God rather than man. – Acts 5:29.

[203] One early MS reads 616

Our next clue is in the fact that the meaning of six hundred and sixty-six (666) lies in the fact that it "is the number of a man." "A man" is generic for humanity, i.e., a human number, and should not be taken as a reference to a specific man. (Luke 4:5-6; 1 John 5:19; Revelation 13:2, 18) What does the fact that it is a human number bring to the table? What do we know about humanity over the 6,000 plus years? Paul tells us, "all have sinned **[missing the mark of perfection]** and fall short of the glory of God." (Rom. 3:23) He also stated, "Sin came into the world through one man, and death through sin, and so death spread to all men because all sinned **[all are missing the mark of perfection, i.e., human imperfection]**." The world power governments mentioned above, the ones reflective in these symbolic beasts are made up of imperfect humans, name, sin, human imperfection. Jeremiah the prophet tells us why, "I know, O Jehovah, that the way of man is not in himself, that it is not in man who walks to direct his steps." – Jeremiah 10:23.

Biblical Numbers

Just as Bible names play a significant importance, this is also true of numbers. For example, the number seven is often associated with what is complete or perfect. On the number seven, the *Holman Illustrated Bible Dictionary* says, "God's work of creation was both complete and perfect, and it was completed in seven days. All of mankind's existence was related to God's creative activity. The seven-day week reflected God's first creative activity. The Sabbath was that day of rest following the workweek, reflective of God's rest (Gen. 1:1–2:4). Israelites were to remember the land also and give it a sabbath, permitting it to lie fallow in the seventh year (Lev. 25:2–7). Seven was also important in cultic matters beyond the Sabbath: major festivals such as Passover and Tabernacles lasted seven days as did wedding festivals (Judg. 14:12, 17). In Pharaoh's dream, the seven good years followed by seven years of famine (Gen. 41:1–36) represented a complete cycle of plenty and famine. Jacob worked a complete cycle of years for Rachel; then, when he was given Leah instead, he worked an additional cycle of seven (Gen. 29:15–30). A major Hebrew word for making an oath or swearing, *shaba*, was closely related to the word 'seven,' *sheba*. The original meaning of 'swear an oath' may have been 'to declare seven times' or 'to bind oneself by seven things.' A similar use of the number seven can be seen in the NT. The seven churches (Rev. 2–3) perhaps symbolized all the churches by their number. Jesus taught that forgiveness is not to be limited, even to a full number or complete number of instances. We are to forgive, not merely seven times (already a generous number of forgiveness) but 70 times seven (limitless forgiveness, beyond keeping count) (Matt. 18:21–22). As the last example shows, multiples of seven frequently had symbolic meaning. The year of Jubilee came after the completion of every 49 years. In the year of Jubilee, all Jewish bond slaves were released, and land which had been sold reverted to its former owner (Lev. 25:8–55). Another multiple of seven used in the Bible is 70. Seventy elders are mentioned (Exod. 24:1, 9). Jesus sent out the 70 (Luke 10:1–17). Seventy years is specified as the length of the exile (Jer. 25:12, 29:10; Dan. 9:2). The messianic kingdom was to be inaugurated after a period of 70 weeks of years had passed (Dan. 9:24)." (Brand, Draper and Archie 2003, p. 1201)

Simply put, six is one short of seven. If seven represents perfection and completion, it only seems reasonable that six falls short of that. On this, *The College Press NIV Commentary: Revelation* says, "*Six* is one less than seven; it does not 'measure up' to seven or attain to the fullness of seven. Six, then, symbolizes 'incompleteness,' "imperfection," and sometimes evil." (Davis 2000, p. 21) This really ties in well with the fact that, the number of the beast is a human number, being that we are under human imperfection. In short, what do we know? We know that "man" (Gk., *anthrōpos*), often signifies the whole of humankind, i.e., humanity. We also know that the number six in the Bible, one less than seven (perfect) can denote imperfection. We also know that when something is mentioned three times, it is a way of intensifying what is being said. Therefore, six hundred and sixty-six (666) could be signifying gross human imperfection.

AMERICA 15 Explaining Signs of the End of the Age

Matthew 24:4 Updated American Standard Version (UASV)

4 And Jesus answered them, "See that no one leads you astray.

Jesus' disciples, like any other Jew of the day, would have seen the destruction of Jerusalem in 70 C.E. as impossible. However, the first-century Jewish historian, Josephus, tells us 1,100,000 Jews were killed in the destruction of Jerusalem, with another 97,000 taken captive. (War VI. 9.3)[204] Therefore, here in advance (33 C.E.); Jesus wanted his disciples to be on the watch, to not be misled, as though the destruction of Jerusalem (66-70 C.E.) also meant "the end of the age," i.e., his second coming, the kingdom, and the millennial reign.

Matthew 24:5 Update American Standard Version (UASV)

5 For many will come in my name, saying, 'I am the Christ,' and they will lead many astray.

Yes, this would be one of the ways that many coming in Jesus' name would have led the disciples astray, claiming to be the Christ (Hebrew *Messiah*), namely the "anointed one." Therefore, it would not be Christians alone, who would be filling this role as false Christs/messiahs/anointed ones.

> "From Josephus it appears that in the first century before the destruction of the Temple [in 70 C.E.] a number of Messiahs arose promising relief from the Roman yoke, and finding ready followers ... Thus about 44, Josephus reports, a certain impostor, Theudas, who claimed to be a prophet, appeared and urged the people to follow him with their belongings to the Jordan, which he would divide for them. According to Acts v. 36 (which seems to refer to a different date), he secured about 400 followers. Cuspius Fadus sent a troop of horsemen after him and his band, slew many of them, and took captive others, together with their leader, beheading the latter ... Another, an Egyptian, is said to have gathered together 30,000 adherents, whom he summoned to the Mount of Olives, opposite Jerusalem, promising that at his command the walls of Jerusalem would fall down, and that he and his followers would enter and possess themselves of the city. But Felix, the procurator (*c.* 55-60), met the throng with his

[204] Flavius Josephus and William Whiston, *The Works of Josephus: Complete and Unabridged* (Peabody: Hendrickson, 1987).

soldiery. The prophet escaped, but those with him were killed or taken, and the multitude dispersed. Another, whom Josephus styles an impostor, promised the people "deliverance and freedom from their miseries" if they would follow him to the wilderness. Both leader and followers were killed by the troops of Festus, the procurator (60-62; "Ant." xx. 8, § 10). Even when Jerusalem was already in process of destruction by the Romans, a prophet, according to Josephus suborned by the defenders to keep the people from deserting announced that God commanded them to come to the Temple, there to receive miraculous signs of their deliverance. Those who came met death in the flames.

Unlike these Messiahs, who expected their people's deliverance to be achieved through divine intervention, Menahem, the son of Judas the Galilean and grandson of Hezekiah, the leader of the Zealots, who had troubled Herod, was a warrior. When the war broke out he attacked Masada with his band, armed his followers with the weapons stored there, and proceeded to Jerusalem, where he captured the fortress Antonia, overpowering the troops of Agrippa II. Emboldened by his success, he behaved as a king, and claimed the leadership of all the troops. Thereby he aroused the enmity of Eleazar, another Zealot leader, and met death as a result of a conspiracy against him (*ib.* ii. 17, § 9). He is probably identical with the Menahem b. Hezekiah mentioned in Sanh. 98b, and called, with reference to Lam. i. 17, "the comforter ["menaḥem"] that should relieve" (comp. Hamburger, "R. B. T." Supplement, iii. 80). With the destruction of the Temple the appearance of Messiahs ceased for a time. Sixty years later a politico-Messianic movement of large proportions took place with Bar Kokba at its head. This leader of the revolt against Rome was hailed as Messiah-king by Akiba, who referred to him. *The Jewish Encyclopedia* lists 28 false Messiahs between the years 132 C.E. and 1744 C.E.[205]

Matthew 24:6 Update American Standard Version (UASV)

[6] You will be hearing of wars and rumors of wars. See that you are not alarmed, for those things must take place, but the end is not yet.

There have been religious leaders that have been misled by the two Great Wars of the 20th century, World War I and II, associating each of them with the "end of the age." The First Jewish–Roman War (66–73

[205] Vol. X, pp. 252-255.

C.E.),[206] at times called The Great Revolt, could have misled the disciples into thinking that the end was imminent. Therefore, Jesus tells them that they should not be alarmed and that the end is not yet. This counsel of Jesus has had to be applied from First Jewish–Roman War to the two Great Wars of the 20th century, every time a war came along, which seems to be an end all for humanity. Nevertheless, this one sign alone is not enough to signal the end, because imperfect humans are prone to war.

Matthew 24:7 Update American Standard Version (UASV)

[7] For nation will rise against nation, and kingdom against kingdom, and there will be famines and earthquakes in various places.

Here Jesus expounds on his previous comments about war because the conflicts of humankind have been so pervasive that there was a need for a reference book, *Dictionary of Wars* by George C. Kohn. Therefore, while we should take note of current events, wars, rumors of wars and even kingdom against kingdom is not enough alone to suppose that the end is here. Therefore, Jesus adds yet another two signs, famines, and earthquakes. These two have also been a part of humankind's history. Of course, the impact is going to be far greater with seven billion living people on earth, as opposed to a hundred million in 100 C.E. Nevertheless, these are just the beginning.

Matthew 24:8 Update American Standard Version (UASV)

[8] But all these are but the beginning of the birth pains.

Wars, rumors of wars, kingdoms against kingdom, famines and earthquakes are just the beginning of the things to come. However, they are not the goal post that the end is imminent. Such tragedies being merely a "beginning of the birth pains," the end was "not yet." Men likely cannot appreciate this verse, because the woman only knows the pain of giving birth to a child. It is the most natural thing in her life and yet the most painful. Therefore, consider that what comes after this metaphorical concept is going to be far more painful for humankind. These pains will grow in severity until the birth of the end of the age, and the return of Jesus. Nevertheless, like any other birth that has finally reached the end, the joy of a newborn child makes one forget the past pains. This is true after the tribulation; the joys of the Kingdom will outweigh the previous pains.

---

[206] The Second Jewish–Roman War (132–135 C.E.) Simon Bar Kokba, who claimed to be the long awaited Messiah, led a revolt against Roman Emperor Hadrian (76-139), for setting up a shrine to Jupiter (supreme Roman god), on the temple site in Jerusalem, as well as outlawing circumcision and instruction of the Law in public.

Matthew 24:9 Update American Standard Version (UASV)

9 "Then they will deliver you up to tribulation, and will kill you, and you will be hated by all nations because of my name.

Verse 9 of the new section, 9-12, begins with "then" (Greek *tote*), which brings the reader into another section of signs, offering us more of the lines in the fingerprint, i.e., the full picture that we are in the time of to the end. "Then" can have the meaning coming *after, or at the same time*, or it could mean simply, *therefore*. It would seem that "then" is best understood as meaning 'at the same time,' because these signs, as well as those that we covered in 4-7, and those coming in verse 10 are of a composite sign. Meaning, we are looking for a time when they are all taking place and on a worldwide scale.

Who are "they" that deliver Christians up to tribulation? It would be those Christians of verse 5, who were led astray, abandoning the Christian faith. The last 50 years have truly brought about the abandonment of Christianity, as well as much tribulation for those that have remained faithful. This is primarily a reference to liberal Christianity (80 percent of Christianity), who has abandoned the biblical truth, for the lie so that they can maintain a good relationship with the world, and progressivism. Christianity has never been more hated than it is today. Sadly, conservative Christians have been deeply opposed and persecuted by liberal Christianity, atheists, not to mention Islam and other religions.

Verse 9 says "they will deliver you up" (ESV), or "they will hand you over" (HCSB), "to tribulation." If one is 'handed over,' he must first be seized and then delivered to those, who are seeking to do him harm, even death. Why are the Christians hated so? Former Christians (now agnostics and atheists), as well as liberal Christians, hate the stand that conservative Christians take as they truly live by God's Word, in the world that is anything but. Radical Islam[207] is simply trying to impose themselves on everyone who stands in their way of dominating the world. Thus, being handed over is a result of one's true faith in Jesus Christ.

Islamic Excursion

"There are about 1.6 billion Muslims, or 23% of the world's population, making Islam the second-largest religion. ... Muslims make up a majority of the population in 49 countries around the world." It has been

---

207 World's Muslim population more widespread than you might .., http://www.pewresearch.org/fact-tank/2013/06/07/worlds-muslim-population-more-wi (accessed December 23, 2015).

estimated that 5 to 15 percent of all Muslims are radical. However, let us be generous and say that it is only 01 percent. One percent of 1.6 billion is still 16,000,000 million radical Muslims. However, one must realize that in survey after survey, the majority of Muslims support radical views.[208]

Shariah Law is Islamic canonical law based on the teachings of the Quran and the traditions of the Prophet (Hadith and Sunna), prescribing both religious and secular duties and sometimes retributive penalties for lawbreaking. It has generally been supplemented by legislation adapted to the conditions of the day, though the manner in which it should be applied in modern states is a disputed between Islamic fundamentalists and modernists. Today Sweden is the rape capital of the world because of their Muslim population. Why? Under Shariah Law, it is not a sin or crime to force an infidel (i.e., non-Muslim) to have sex. This is what is missing from the debate. It is the culture, the worldview, the ideology, of the Muslim people that conflict with God's Word, the US Constitution, The UK, Canada, Germany, Sweden, namely, human moral values of a civilized society.

Under Shariah Law, women are viewed as property, not humans. A wife can be beaten for anything. She can be stoned to death for a number of things. A daughter could be killed for dating a non-Muslim, which is called an honor killing. A thief can have their hand or foot cut off. There are many horrific aspects of Shariah Law, but we will just look at honor killings as our example.

> An **honor killing** is the homicide of a member of a family by other members, due to the perpetrators' belief that the victim has brought shame or dishonor upon the family, or has violated the principles of a community or a religion, usually for reasons such as refusing to enter an arranged marriage, being in a relationship that is disapproved by their family, having sex outside marriage, becoming the victim of rape, dressing in ways

---

[208] UNDERSTANDING ISLAM AND TERRORISM: A Biblical Point of View by Kerby Anderson

http://www.christianpublishers.org/apps/webstore/products/show/7583136

IS THE QURAN THE WORD OF GOD? Is Islam the One True Faith? By Edward D. Andrews

http://www.christianpublishers.org/apps/webstore/products/show/7489030

A CHRISTIAN'S GUIDE TO ISLAM: What Every Christian Needs to Know About Islam and the Rise of Radical Islam by Daniel Janosik

http://www.christianpublishers.org/apps/webstore/products/show/5749263

which are deemed inappropriate, or engaging in non-heterosexual relations.

Refusing an arranged marriage is often a cause of an honor killing. The family which has prearranged the marriage risks disgrace if the marriage does not proceed. A woman attempting to obtain a divorce or separation without the consent of the husband/extended family can also be a trigger for honor killings. In cultures where marriages are arranged and goods are often exchanged between families, a woman's desire to seek a divorce is often viewed as an insult to the men who negotiated the deal. By making their marital problems known outside the family, the women are seen as exposing the family to public dishonor. In certain cultures, an *allegation* against a woman can be enough to tarnish her family's reputation, and to trigger an honor killing: the family's fear of being ostracized by the community is enormous. In many cultures, victims of rape face severe violence, including honor killings, from their families and relatives. In many parts of the world, women who have been raped are considered to have brought 'dishonour' or 'disgrace' to their families. This is especially the case if the victim becomes pregnant.

Central to the code of honor, in many societies, is a woman's virginity, which must be preserved until marriage. Suzanne Ruggi writes, "A woman's virginity is the property of the men around her, first her father, later a gift for her husband; a virtual dowry as she graduates to marriage."

Honor killings are often a result of strongly patriarchal views on women, and the position of women in society. In these traditional male-dominated societies women are dependent first on their father and then on their husband, whom they are expected to obey. Women are viewed as property and not as individuals with their own agency. As such, they must submit to male authority figures in the family – failure to do so can result in extreme violence as punishment. Violence is seen as a way of ensuring compliance and preventing rebellion. According to Shahid Khan, a professor at the Aga Khan University in Pakistan: "Women are considered the property of the males in their family irrespective of their class, ethnic, or religious group. The owner of the property has the right to decide its fate. The concept of ownership has turned women into a commodity which can be exchanged, bought and sold." In such cultures, women are not allowed to take control over their bodies and sexuality: these are the property of the males of the family, the father (and other male relatives) who must ensure virginity until marriage; and then the husband to whom his wife's sexuality is subordinated - a woman must not undermine the ownership rights of her guardian by engaging in premarital sex or adultery.[209]

We in the United States have known of Al Qaeda especially since September 11, 2001. Throughout 2014 to 2017, we have seen the rise of ISIS, whose slaughter of women, children, men, and older ones, anyone in their way has left us stunned. They have hung people on takes, put men in cages and set them on fire, put cages filled with people in a pool and filled it slowly with water, and have raped and killed a countless number of little girls. What do Al Queda, ISIS in Iraq and Syria, Boko Haram in northeastern Nigeria, Al-Shabaab, a Somalia-based cell of the Islamist militant group, and many others want?

They want an Islamic State, which is a type of government, in which the primary basis for government is Islamic religious law, i.e., Shariah Law. They want a caliphate, which is an Islamic state led by a supreme religious as well as a political leader known as a caliph and all the Prophets of Islam. The term caliphate is often applied to successions of Muslim empires that have existed in the Middle East and Southwest Asia.

Islam's eschatological (last days of humanity), belief is different from Christianity. Christians believe that an Armageddon (great was of God) is coming at the return of Christ but that Jesus determines when and how that return will take place. Islam, on the other hand, believes that one day Isa (Jesus) will return with their twelfth Imam.[210] They will rule the world from Jerusalem, where all are Muslims living under Shariah Law. Al Queda is trying to facilitate this through conversion, but also a slow process of turning countries into an Islamic majority state. They do so by growing the population until they reach the majority, who can then place Shariah Law on the same footing with whatever legal, governmental system that that country has. After that, the goal is to replace the governmental laws with Shariah Law. ISIS, on the other hand, believes they can simply conquer the lands through military might terrorism. They also believe that starting a World War III will facilitate the return of ISA and the twelfth Imam, i.e., their Armageddon.

The liberal-progressive world that we live in is a catalyst for Islamic growth. It is the political correctness run amuck that is aiding and abetting radical Islam and their silent supporters. Many of those liberals try to shift the blame over to the conservatives, by saying that the United States is

---

[209] Honor killing - Wikipedia, the free encyclopedia, https://en.wikipedia.org/wiki/Honor_killing (accessed December 23, 2015).

[210] An Imam is a leader of an Islamic community.

Islamophobic and that we are simply a recruitment tool for radical Islam by our identifying them by the phrase *radical Islamic terrorists.* What they fail to realize is that this eschatological belief of Islam is religious, ideological, and embedded in their very being, which has nothing to do with what anyone says. The liberal-progressive movement will be politically correct all the way up unto the end. Radical Islam and their silent supporters have a murderous hatred for the West, the United States and Israel especially, as well as Christians.

End of Excursion

Matthew 24:10 Update American Standard Version (UASV)

10 And then many will fall away,[211] will betray[212] one another, and will hate one another.

While early Christianity suffered horrible deaths through being martyred for simply being a Christian, the hatred today is just as vile by those that slaughter Christians around the world. Nevertheless, persecution through social media, news media, and by way of lawsuits, and protests in the streets, has become the new form of persecution in the Western world. Many have fallen away from Jesus, becoming apostates toward their former brothers and sisters, loathing their very existence.

Matthew 24:11 Update American Standard Version (UASV)

11 And many false prophets will arise and will lead many astray.

What is a prophet? The primary meaning is one who proclaims the Word of God, a spokesperson for God. Therefore, a false prophet would be a spokesperson giving the impression that he is a spokesman for God, but really he is far from it. These ones are very subtle and deceptive in their ability to present themselves as a person representing God. Some modern day examples would be, Jim Bakker, Kenneth Copeland, Benny Hinn, T.D. Jakes, Joyce Meyer, Juanita Bynum, Creflo Dollar, Eddie Long, Pat Robertson, and Joel Olsteen. Of course, these are just some of the televangelists, who are false prophets, with tens of millions of followers. Other false prophet religious leaders have tens of millions of followers as well. Then, there are charismatic Christian denominations that number over 500 million followers. These ones claim gifts of God (faith healing, speaking in tongues, etc.), which clearly are anything but. The true Christians are

[211] Lit *be caused to stumble*

[212] Or *hand over*

falling away in great numbers, being led astray by these false prophets, and those who have not fallen away, truly need to remain awake!

Matthew 24:12 Update American Standard Version (UASV)

[12] And because lawlessness will be increased, the love of many will grow cold.

The world we live in is overflowing with murders, rapes, armed robberies, and assaults, not to mention the wars between nations, as well as the war on terrorism. It has grown so pervasive that many have grown callused to seeing the newspapers, websites and television news filled with one heinous crime, one after another. In looking at just one city in the United States, in 2012, 532 people were murdered in Chicago, with a population of 2.7 million. However, in San Pedro Sula of the country Honduras, 1,143 people were murdered with only a population of 719,447. Statistics from the United Nations reported 250,000 cases of rape or attempted rape annually. However, it must be kept in mind that because of the savagery of the times, in "many parts of the world, rape is very rarely reported, due to the extreme social stigma cast on women, who have been raped, or the fear of being disowned by their families, or subjected to violence, including honor killings."[213]

Verse 12 says that the love of "the love of many will **grow cold**," and indeed, it has. There are atrocious crimes against individuals, groups, nations, which would cripple the mind of anyone living decades ago. However, because of seeing it every day, all day long, the world has grown hardened to the lawlessness that exists around them. Christians carry the hope of salvation in their heart, which Jesus addresses next.

Matthew 24:13 Update American Standard Version (UASV)

[13] But the one who endures to the end will be saved.

What are we to endure? We are to **endure while we** maintain our walk with God through false Christs who will lead many astray, the wars, and the natural disasters. We are to **endure while we** maintain our walk with God through the loss of many of our spiritual brothers and sisters who fall away, the betrayal of former Christians, and the hatred of humankind who is alienated from God. We are to **endure while we** maintain our walk with God through false prophets that have arisen and lead many astray, the increase of the lawlessness in this world, and the love of humanity growing colder. Yes, each of us, who survives to the end of the Christian era, to the return of Christ, will be saved from Jesus' destruction of the wicked. However, we are not to simply sit around; we have work to accomplish

---

[213] http://en.wikipedia.org/wiki/Rape_statistics

that is the last sign of the end of the age. We are to proclaim the good news, to teach biblical truths, as we make disciples.

Matthew 24:14 Update American Standard Version (UASV)

[14] And this gospel of the kingdom will be proclaimed in all the inhabited earth[214] as a testimony to all the nations, and then the end will come.

This is the last of the signs that Jesus gave that should concern us as it is directly related to the end of the age, and the return of Christ, namely '**the gospel of the kingdom being proclaimed throughout the whole world.**' Jesus makes it very clear what he meant by "the whole world," by then saying "all nations" (Gk., *ethnos*). What Jesus meant here was more directed toward all races, not so much the "nations" that we know the world to be divided into today. Therefore, Jesus speaking of the whole world was a reference to "**a body of persons united by kinship, culture, and common traditions, *nation, people.***"[215] Today, while, for the most part, nations are made up of different races, the world is also becoming a melting pot.

In the phrase "**testimony** to all nations," we find the Greek word *martyrion*, which was a legal term of "**that which serves as testimony or proof, *testimony, proof.***"[216] The testimony here that is to be shared by Christ's disciples has to with Jesus and the kingdom. Evidence, proof, testimony has the ability to overcome the false reasoning of those in the world, to win them over, as well as convict those who refuse to see the evidence for what it is. Elsewhere Jesus said very clearly,

Matthew 11:15 (UASV)	**Matthew 13:9** (UASV)	**Matthew 13:43** (UASV)
[15] He who has ears to hear, let him hear.	[9] He who has ears, let him hear."	[43] Then the righteous will shine like the sun in the kingdom of their Father. He who has ears, let him hear.

---

[214] Or *in the whole world*

[215] William Arndt, Frederick W. Danker, and Walter Bauer, *A Greek-English Lexicon of the New Testament and Other Early Christian Literature* (Chicago: University of Chicago Press, 2000), 276.

[216] IBID, 619.

John the Baptist Prepared the Way

As many are aware, John the Baptist was the fulfillment of a prophecy from Malachi 4:5–6, which reads, "'Behold, I will send you Elijah the prophet before the great and awesome day of the Lord comes. And he will turn the hearts of fathers to their children and the hearts of children to their fathers, lest I come and strike the land with a decree of utter destruction.'" Jesus well knew this, as is evidenced by his comments in verse 14 of chapter 11, "and if you are willing to accept it, he [John the Baptist] is Elijah who is to come." Nevertheless, many would refuse to accept that John was, in fact, the fulfillment prophecy about Elijah. Thus, Jesus says, "If you are **willing to accept it ... He who has ears to hear, let him hear.**"

Throughout Jesus' three and a half years ministry of teaching the people of Israel, bringing the truth to Israel, Jesus interpreted Scripture and told them many things that would be difficult for them to accept, because they conflicted with the religious leaders of Judaism. He did these things because he wanted to sift out those, who were not truly interested in the truth. Those who rejected Jesus and his teachings were unteachable because they lacked a receptive heart and mind. They had hardened hearts, to the point that they were beyond repentance, beyond being able to see the truth, regardless of whether it was the very Son of God explaining it.

Was John the Baptist some reborn Elijah? The Jews asked John who he was, "What then? Are you Elijah?" (John 1:21) John answered them quite plainly, "I am not." However, the angel, likely Gabriel, said to Zechariah [John the Baptist's father], before John was born, "Do not be afraid, Zechariah, for "he will be filled with the Holy Spirit, even from his mother's womb. And he [John] will turn many of the children of Israel to the Lord their God, and he will go before him **in the spirit and power of Elijah**, to turn the hearts of the fathers to the children, and the disobedient to the wisdom of the just, to make ready for the Lord a people prepared.'" (Lu 1:17; Mal. 4:5-6) In other words, John the Baptist was the new Elijah, or an Elijah-like one, who in a sense did a work very similar to what Elijah had done.

The baptism that John carried out in the Jordan was for the Jews to offer a public display of repentance over their individual sins against the Mosaic Law, a law that was designed to lead them to the first coming of the Christ. Luke writes, "As it is written in the book of the words of Isaiah the prophet, 'The voice of one crying in the wilderness [John the Baptist]: 'Prepare the way of the Lord.' (Lu 3:3-6; Gal. 3:24) Yes, John's work prepared the Israelites for the first coming of Christ.

In the Hebrew Scriptures (Old Testament), there is a very common phrase, "the day of Jehovah." (ESV, "the day of the LORD," LEB "the day of Yahweh", or ASV "the day of Jehovah") This day of Jehovah is detailed in the Scriptures as a time of battle, a day of distress and anguish, a day of darkness, a day of wrath and fierce anger, a day of wrath is that day, a day of distress and anguish, a day of ruin and devastation, and a day to destroy its sinners. – Amos 5:18-20; Isaiah 13:9; Zephaniah 1:15; Ezekiel 7:19; Zephaniah 1:18

The work that John the Baptist did was to prepare the Israelites to accept the Christ, as *a day of Jehovah* was very near. The apostle Peter quoted the prophet Joel right after Pentecost, explaining that the miraculous events they had just seen unfold, were a fulfillment of the words of Joel, i.e., a fulfillment of the words God's inspired Joel to pen. Peter showed that the words of Joel were to come to pass before "the great and glorious day of the Lord comes." (Acts 2:16-21; Joel 2:28-32) The prophecy of Joel was fulfilled in 70 C.E. when General Titus of the Roman army, destroyed Jerusalem, executing divine judgment on the nation of Israel for their centuries of rebellion, false worship, and finally, the rejection of the Son of God, in that they had him executed by way of the Roman government. – Daniel 9:24-27; John 19:15.

Peter's Sermon at Pentecost

Acts 2:16-21 Updated American Standard Version (UASV)

16 but this is what was spoken of through the prophet Joel

17 "'And it shall be in the last days, God says,
that I will pour out my Spirit on all flesh,
and your sons and your daughters shall prophesy,
and your young men shall see visions,
and your old men shall dream dreams;
18 and even on my male slaves and on my female slaves
I will pour out some of my Spirit in those days, and they will prophesy.
19 And I will show wonders in the heavens above
and signs on the earth below,
blood, and fire, and vapor of smoke;
20 the sun shall be turned to darkness
and the moon to blood,
before the great and glorious day of the Lord comes.
21 And it shall come to pass that everyone who calls upon the name of the Lord will be saved.'[217]

In all occurrences, prophecy proclaimed in Bible times had meaning to the people who heard it; it served for their guidance as well as each

[217] A quotation from Joel 2:28-32

generation up unto the time of its fulfillment. Usually, it had some fulfillment in that time, in numerous instances being fulfilled during the days of that same generation. In looking at Peters quote from Joel, it must be asked, 'did they see those cosmic events on Pentecost?' Yes, the cosmic terminology is expressing that God was acting on behalf of those first Christians. A new era was being entered, and God did pour out His Spirit, and sons and daughters did prophesy, both in proclaiming a message and in the foretelling of other events. However, let us delve even deeper into prophecy and how they are to be interpreted. Before moving on, let us briefly offer some insights:

- Judgment prophecies could be lifted, set aside if the parties affected repent and turnaround from their former course.
- On the other hand, if God has promised blessings, but then that person or group disobeys him and does evil, he will not do what he had said he would do.
- Then again, if one has repented, turned around, and a judgment prophecy has been lifted, it can be reinstated if that person or group return to their former evil ways.
- Prophets have a license to use prophetic language, cosmic terminology that evidences that God is working or acting within humanity.
- While we do not take cosmic terminology literally, we do discover its meaning, and this is what we are to take literally.

If we are to understand and interpret prophecy correctly, we must first have a grasp of the figurative language, types, and symbols. Walter C. Kaiser Jr. is distinguished professor emeritus of Old Testament and president emeritus of Gordon-Conwell Theological Seminary. He asks the following questions, which we will address at length,

> (1) the extent to which the NT authors also used ancient Jewish exegetical and interpretive methods in their use of the OT; (2) the NT authors' awareness or disregard of the larger OT context of the passages they quote; (3) the appropriate understanding of the function of typology; and (4) the question of whether contemporary interpreters may replicate the NT writers' techniques of appropriating and applying the OT Scriptures.[218]

---

[218] (2009-08-30). *Three Views on the New Testament Use of the Old Testament* (Counterpoints: Bible and Theology) (Kindle Locations 890-893). Zondervan. Kindle Edition.

See Interpreting New Testament Writers Use of the Old Testament

https://christianpublishinghouse.co/2016/12/07/interpreting-new-testament-writers-use-of-the-old-testament/

2 Peter 3:11-14 Updated American Standard Version (UASV)

[11] Since all these things are thus to be dissolved, what sort of people ought you to be in lives of holiness and godliness, [12] looking for and hastening the coming[219] of the day of God, because of which the heavens will be destroyed by burning, and the elements will melt with intense heat! [13] But according to his promise we are looking for new heavens and a new earth, in which righteousness dwells.

Do Not Be Led Astray

[14] Therefore, beloved, since you look for these things, be diligent to be found by him spotless and unblemished and in peace,

Is Peter's reference to a "new heavens and new earth" the same "new heavens and new earth" of which Isaiah spoke? It could be as we need to be cautious of being dogmatic. However, if Isaiah's was a prophecy that points to a remnant of restored Israelites, back from Babylonian captivity, who returned to pure worship, might this simply be Peter using Isaiah's prophecy to tack carry out an *Inspired Sensus Plenior Application*. It is hard to see Peter's use of Isaiah's words as a fulfillment of what Isaiah himself had meant because Isaiah was referring to the return of the Israelites to Jerusalem some 600 years before Peter's words about the new heavens and a new earth.

What we do know is that if Peter assigns a different meaning to Isaiah's words, it is his meaning, and it is subjective He has the authority to offer subjective meaning, as he was an inspired Bible writer, who had been moved along by Holy Spirit. Peter was not reiterating Isaiah's words with the same intended meaning that Isaiah had; he was giving us an *Inspired Sensus Plenior Application*, a new meaning of Isaiah's words. This author believes that Peter's "new heavens" is the Kingdom of God, of which Jesus is the King, and he has co-rulers. The "new earth" is a restored earth, which

---

[219] **Presence; Coming:** (Gr. *parousia*) The Greek word literally means," which is derived from *para*, meaning "with," and *ousia*, meaning "being." It denotes both an "arrival" and a consequent "presence with." Depending on the context, it can mean "presence," "arrival," "appearance," or "coming." In some contexts, this word is describing the presence of Jesus Christ in the last days, i.e., from his ascension in 33 C.E. up unto his second coming, with the emphasis being on his second coming, the end of the age of Satan's reign of terror over the earth. We do not know the day nor the hours of this second coming. (Matt 24:36) It covers a marked period of time with the focus on the end of that period. – Matt. 24:3, 27, 37, 39; 1 Cor. 15:23; 16:17; 2 Cor. 7:6-7; 10:10; Php 1:26; 2:12; 1 Thess. 2:19; 3:13; 4:15; 5:2.

Jesus will accomplish throughout his millennial reign. Peter did not mean that the earth was literally going to be destroyed, just the wicked. It is the same "new heavens" and "new earth," which the Apostle John actually beheld in a vision of a future time after the first century C.E. It is the same "new heaven and new earth" that Christians are awaiting today. In order to get us back on topic, we will repeat two paragraphs.

As we learned in the above, John the Baptist was the fulfillment of a prophecy from Malachi 4:5–6, which reads, "'Behold, I will send you Elijah the prophet **before the great and awesome <u>day of the LORD</u> comes**. And he will turn the hearts of fathers to their children and the hearts of children to their fathers, lest I come and strike the land with a decree of utter destruction.'" Joel tells us,

Joel 2:31 Updated American Standard Version (UASV))

[31] The sun will be turned into darkness and the moon into blood
Before the coming of the great and awe-inspiring **day of Jehovah.**

Peter quotes Joel, telling us,

Acts 2:17, 20 Updated American Standard Version (UASV)

[17] "'And it shall be in the last days, God says,
that I will pour out my Spirit on all flesh,
and your sons and your daughters shall prophesy,
and your young men shall see visions,
and your old men shall dream dreams;
[20] the sun shall be turned to darkness
and the moon to blood,
before the great and glorious **day of the Lord** comes.

Peter writes in his second letter,

2 Peter 3:10 Updated American Standard Version (UASV)

[10] But the day of the Lord will come like a thief, in which the heavens will pass away with a loud noise, the elements will burn and be dissolved, and the earth and its works will be exposed.[220]

In the Hebrew Scriptures (Old Testament), there is a very common phrase, "the day of Jehovah." (ESV, "the day of the LORD," LEB "the day of Yahweh", or ASV "the day of Jehovah") This day of Jehovah is detailed in the Scriptures as a time of battle, a day of distress and anguish, a day of darkness, a day of wrath and fierce anger, a day of wrath is that day, a day

---

[220] Gr *heurethesetai* ("will be discovered") is attested to by א B KP 424[c] 1175 1739[txt] 1852 syr[ph], [hmg arm] Origen. Gr *katakaesetai* ("will be burned up") is attested to by A 048 049 056 0142 33 614 Byz Lect syr[h] cop[bo] eth *al.*

of distress and anguish, a day of ruin and devastation, and a day to destroy its sinners. – Amos 5:18-20; Isaiah 13:9; Zephaniah 1:15; Ezekiel 7:19; Zephaniah 1:18

The work that John the Baptist did was to prepare the Israelites to accept the Christ, as *a day of Jehovah* was very near. The apostle Peter quoted the prophet Joel right after Pentecost, explaining that the miraculous events they had just seen unfold, were a fulfillment of the words of Joel, i.e., a fulfillment of the words God's inspired Joel to pen. Peter showed that the words of Joel were to come to pass before "the great and glorious day of the Lord comes." (Acts 2:16-21; Joel 2:28-32) The prophecy of Joel was fulfilled in 70 C.E. when General Titus of the Roman army, destroyed Jerusalem, executing divine judgment on the nation of Israel for their centuries of rebellion, false worship, and finally, the rejection of the Son of God, in that they had him executed by way of the Roman government.—Daniel 9:24-27; John 19:15.

Now, to tie all of this together, the day of the LORD (Jehovah) that took place in 70 C.E. when Jerusalem was destroyed was just one of many times of destructive judgment by God. For example, we had the first destruction of Jerusalem by the Babylonians. Malachi had prophesied that God would send the Jews Elijah-like prophet **before** the great and awesome **day of the LORD** comes. This came true with John the Baptist coming to prepare the way for Jesus, who prepared the way for the Christians, before the destruction of Jerusalem in 70 C.E., where one million Jews were killed and one hundred thousand taken captive. So, at that time a "day of the LORD" was near at hand. Joel tells us that there would be an outpouring of Holy Spirit before this same "day of the LORD," which Peter quotes. (Ac 2:17) Again, that "day of the LORD" came in 70 C.E. when God used the Roman army to execute divine judgment on the nation of Israel for their centuries of rebellion, false worship, and finally, the rejection of the Son of God.

However, there is another "day of the Lord" to come. The apostle Paul associated this "day of the LORD" with the second coming of Jesus Christ. Paul writes,

2 Thessalonians 2:1-2 Updated American Standard Version (UASV)

2 Now we request you, brothers, with regard to **the coming**[221] **of our Lord** Jesus Christ and our gathering together to him, [2] that you not be

[221] **Presence; Coming:** (Gr. *parousia*) The Greek word literally means," which is derived from *para*, meaning "with," and *ousia*, meaning "being." It denotes both an "arrival" and a consequent "presence with." Depending on the context, it can mean "presence," "arrival," "appearance," or "coming." In some contexts this word is describing the presence of Jesus Christ in the last days, i.e., from his ascension in 33 C.E. up unto his second coming, with the emphasis being on his second coming, the end of the age of Satan's reign of terror over the

quickly shaken from your composure or be disturbed either by a spirit or a word or a letter as if from us, to the effect that **the day of the Lord** has come.

The apostle Peter as we have mention associates this same "day of the LORD" with,

2 Peter 3:10-13 Updated American Standard Version (UASV)

[10] But **the day of the Lord** will come like a thief, in which the heavens will pass away with a loud noise, the elements will burn and be dissolved, and the earth and its works will be exposed.[222]

What Sort of People You Ought to Be

[11] Since all these things are thus to be dissolved, what sort of people ought you to be in lives of holiness and godliness, [12] looking for and hastening the coming of the day of God, because of which the heavens will be destroyed by burning, and the elements will melt with intense heat! [13] But according to his promise we are looking for **new heavens and a new earth**, in which righteousness dwells.

When we look at all of this, we can see a future "day of the LORD." We know that Elijah prepared the way for "the day of the LORD" in the first century, with his evangelism, as did Jesus. Moreover, Jesus said that Christians would do an even greater work that he (John 14:12). We do so because we are to prepare the way for the greatest "day of the LORD," namely, the return of Jesus Christ. Let us take a deeper look at the first century one, looking for correlations.

Excursion of "One Meaning"

The idea that the reader is the one who determines the meaning is known as the "reader response." For those who hold this position, all meaning is equal to another, and all are correct. We can have a set of verses, and 20 people may give us different interpretations, and many may seem the opposite of others. Those believing in the "reader "response" will say that all are correct. Under this position, the text allows each reader the right to derive his or her own meaning from the text. Again, this is where we hear "I think this means," "I believe this means," "this means to me," and

---

earth. We do not know the day nor the hours of this second coming. (Matt 24:36) It covers a marked period of time with the focus on the end of that period.–Matt. 24:3, 27, 37, 39; 1 Cor. 15:23; 16:17; 2 Cor. 7:6-7; 10:10; Php 1:26; 2:12; 1 Thess. 2:19; 3:13; 4:15; 5:2.

[222] Gr *heurethesetai* ("will be discovered") is attested to by א B KP 424c 1175 1739txt 1852 syrph, hmg arm Origen. Gr *katakaesetai* ("will be burned up") is attested to by A 048 049 056 0142 33 614 Byz Lect syrh copbo eth *al.*

"I feel this means to me." The problem with this is that the text loses its authority; God and his author lose their authority over the intended meaning of the text. When God inspired the writer, to express his will and purposes, there was the intention of **one meaning**, i.e., what the author under inspiration meant by the words he used. If anyone can come along and give it whatever meaning pleases them, then God's authority over the meaning is lost, and there is no real meaning at all.

The grammatical-historical method is a method, which attempts to ascertain what the author meant by the words that he used, which should have been understood by his first readers. It was the primary method of interpretation when higher criticism's Historical-Critical Method was in its infancy back in the 19th century (Milton Terry), and remains the only method of interpretation for true conservative scholarship in the later 20th century into the 21st century. The grammatical-historical method is objective, meaning that is free of any theological bias or prejudice caused by personal views.

Grammatical Aspect

When we speak of interpreting the Bible grammatically, we are referring to the process of seeking to determine its meaning by ascertaining four things: (a) the meaning of words (lexicology), (b) the form of words (morphology), (c) the function of words (parts of speech), and (d) the relationships of words (syntax). In the meaning of words (lexicology), we are concerned with,

(a) **Etymology,**[223] i.e., how words are derived and developed,

(b) **Usage**, namely, how words are used by the same author and other authors,

(c) **Synonyms and Antonyms**, that is how similar and opposite words are used, and

(d) **Context**, i.e., how words are used in various contexts, the words, phrases, sentences and paragraphs that surround them.

In discussing the form of words (morphology), we are looking at how words are structured and how that affects their meaning. For example, the word "eat" means something different from ate, though the same letters are used. The word "part" changes meaning when the letter "s" is added to it to make the word "parts." The function of words (parts of speech) considers what the various forms do. These include attention to subjects,

[223] This would be used on very rare occasions in the extreme, See etymological Fallacy in D. A. Carson's *Exegetical Fallacies.*

verbs, objects, nouns, and others, as will be discussed later. The relationships of words (syntax) are the way words are related or put together to form phrases, clauses, and sentences. (Zuck 1991, 100-101)

Historical Aspect

By "historical," we mean the setting in which the Bible books were written and the circumstances involved in the writing ... taking into consideration the circumstances of the writings and the cultural environment.

The context in which a given Scripture passage is written influences how that passage is to be understood. Context includes several things:

- the verse(s) immediately before and after a passage
- the paragraph and book in which the verses occur
- the dispensation in which it was written
- the message of the entire Bible
- the historical-cultural environment of that time when it was written. (Zuck 1991, 77)

Some of the truly conservative scholars who have remained faithful to the grammatical-historical method of interpretation are Bernard Ramm, Harold Lindsell, Gleason L. Archer, Robert L. Thomas, Norman L. Geisler, Thomas Howe, Roy, B. Zuck, David F. Farnell, among other select ones. Such ones are referred to as "fundamentalist Protestants," as though fundamentalism is now a dirty word. Some modern-day scholars believe that they can dip their feet in the pool of higher criticism, suggesting that they can use certain aspects of these forms of criticisms, without ending up doing any harm to the trustworthiness of the text, to inerrancy. This is very naïve, as some of them end up swimming in the deep end of higher criticism, while others walk along the edges of the deep end.

Here is just ten of the "tip-of-the-iceberg" of the things that these scholars would agree with:

- Matthew, not Jesus, Created the Sermon on the Mount.
- The commissioning of the Twelve in Matthew 10 is a group of instructions compiled and organized by Matthew, not spoken by Jesus on a single occasion.
- The parable accounts of Matthew 13 and Mark 4 are anthologies of parables that Jesus uttered on separate occasions.

- Jesus did not preach the Olivet Discourse in its entirety, as found in the of the gospel accounts.

- Jesus gave his teaching on divorce and remarriage without the exception clauses found in Matthew 5:32 and 19:9.

- In Matthew 19:16-17, Matthew changed the words of Jesus and the rich man to obtain a different emphasis or to avoid a theological problem involved in the wording of Mark's and Luke's accounts of the same event.

- The scribes and the Pharisees were, in reality, decent people whom Matthew painted in an entirely negative light because of his personal bias against them.

- The genealogies of Jesus in Matthew 1 and Luke 3 are figures of speech and not accurate records of Jesus' physical/and or legal lineage.

- The magi who, according to Matthew 2, visited the child Jesus after his birth are fictional, not real characters.

- Jesus uttered only three or four of the eight or nine beatitudes in Matthew 5:3-12[224]

The Original Meaning

The objective of the exegete in his use of the grammatical-historical method of interpretation is to discover what the author meant by the words that he used, as should have been understood by his originally intended audience. Each text has **one single meaning**. Milton S. Terry wrote, "A fundamental principle in grammatical-historical exposition is that the words and sentences can have but one significance in one and the same connection. The moment we neglect this principle we drift out upon a sea of uncertainty and conjecture." (Terry 1883, 205)

This author agrees with Robert L. Thomas and John H. Walton in the New Testament author's use of the Old Testament. I have no problem that the NT author either quote intending to convey the same meaning, i.e., there is but **one meaning** for the OT author, and the NT author is simply interpreting it as such. This author also uses Inspired Sensus Plenior Application (ISPA), in that, the NT author will use the OT author's verse, but not in a grammatical-historical sense (objective), but using his own meaning, which is subjective, and rightly so because he is inspired. Moreover, we do not copy the subjective interpretation process because

---

[224] (Thomas and Farnell 1998)

we are not inspired. All genuinely conservative should be completely of the one meaning camp.

This author ha revisited many author's chapters and papers that support one meaning and talk about NT author's use of OT authors. The main problem with Thomas' chapter, he does not give any real examples in the "one meaning" chapter, he just quotes all of those violating the rule and then says that they are wrong, and in some cases why they are wrong. When he does get to an example, it seems to close out our options of taking Jesus words of Matthew 24:3-28, as anything other than a first-century meaning, referent, and application.

For example, Thomas speaks of Zuck's saying that Psalms 8, 16, and 22 are David talking about himself, and then the NT author's use those verses, applying them to Christ, but differently from what David intended. Well, this is simply ISPA, in that they are giving what they mean by their use of David's words, which is fine, as they are inspired, and can be subjective. However, Thomas says Zuck's conclusions about these Psalm's are accurate to the meaning, but they cannot have more than one referent, as that would result in more than one meaning. In other words, David had applied them to himself, and he did not intend them to be prophetic, applying to Jesus. The NT author is using those words as he sees fit, and not acting as though that is what David meant, so the NT author's meaning of the words is his own, an entirely different referent, but belonging to the NT author. However, Thomas' words are true; words spoken or written by King David cannot have more than one referent unless David means to give them more than one referent.

Thomas gives another one, when he refers to Babylon in Revelation, and says some people interpret it as being Rome; others say it is literally Babylon while others claim it is Jerusalem, and even some saying all three and any other city that stands in the way of Christ and his disciples. Thomas goes on to say; it can only refer to one thing, either one of those cities, or a composite of any city in opposition. However, it cannot refer to each, i.e., Rome, Jerusalem and Babylon at the same time; otherwise, we would have more than one referent.

Now to our interpreting Jesus' prophecy of the desolation of Jerusalem in 66-70 C.E. and his second coming.

Did Jesus' prophecy (verses 3-28) about

- the signs of the end of the age,
- the abomination of desolation standing in the holy place,
- being cut short for the sake of the holy ones, false Christs, and false prophets,

- those on the housetops, in the field, in the winter, being pregnant, and the like,

Did these apply to what led up to 66 C.E. with General Gallus, his pulling away, and Titus coming back and destroying the temple Jerusalem in 70 C.E. by General Titus? Did these apply to the disciples he was speaking to and the events up unto the destruction of Jerusalem and the temple? If that is what Jesus was referring to; then, there cannot be a second referent, just before and up to the great tribulation, before the second coming of Christ, because we would then have two referents, i.e., two meanings. There are other options, without violating our single meaning, which will be discussed below.

The Coming of the Son of Man

Matthew 24:29-31 Update American Standard Version (UASV)

[29] "But immediately after the tribulation of those days the sun will be darkened, and the moon will not give its light, and the stars will fall from heaven, and the powers of the heavens will be shaken. [30] And then will appear in heaven the sign of the Son of Man, and then all the tribes of the earth will mourn, and they will see the Son of Man coming on the clouds of heaven with power and great glory. [31] And he will send forth his angels with a great trumpet call, and they will gather his chosen ones[225] from the four winds, from one end of heaven to the other.

The prophet is much like the poet, in that he is given a license to express himself in nonliteral language. Generally, he is working with images that are far more effective than words themselves.

The above cosmic terminology need not be taken literally. It is a part of their toolkit, which enables them to make it clear that God is acting in behalf of humans. (See Dan. 2:21; 4:17, 25, 34–35; 5:21) The sun is not going to be darkened, the moon will not stop giving its light, the stars are not going to fall from the heavens, nor will the heavens be shaken. What is being communicated here is that following the tribulation when God is going to judge humans, the righteous will receive life, and the unrighteous will cut off from life. (34-45) While we do not take cosmic terminology literally, we do discover its meaning, and this is what we are to take literally. Moreover, we do not want to be dogmatic in our interpretation either and will wait until the events have passed to see how much literalness

[225] Or *the elect*

there is from verses 29-31. Stuart K. Weber, in the *Holman New Testament Commentary*, offers some basic aspects that this author can get behind,[226]

> The Messiah's coming will be accompanied by supernatural manipulations of celestial bodies—or at least manipulations of their appearance, or their ability to give light. These signs in the sky will be such that all people of earth can see them and realize that the Messiah is coming, If only one of these, signs were given, it might be explained away as an eclipse or a meteor shower. But all of them together can be caused only by the hand of God. (Weber 2000, 404)

"Jesus now returns to the question of the sign of his coming. He will return "immediately after" the tribulation of the interadvent period." (Blomberg 1992, 362)

(Option A) the disciples asked three questions, "Tell us, **(1)** when will these things be, and **(2)** what will be the sign of your coming, and **(3)** of the end of the age?" (Matthew 24:3) Jesus words of verses 24:3-28 apply to what happened from his ascension up unto 70 C.E., and the destruction of the temple and Jerusalem; this answering question **(1).** He then began in verse 29 to talk about questions **(2)** and **(3)**, the second coming of Christ. This means that verses 3-28 would only have one referent, the first-century disciples.

(Option B) Jesus was applying verses 24:3-28 to what let up to 70 C.E., but he then made those words just as applicable to his second coming, starting verse 29. In other words, the disciples asked three questions, "Tell us, **(1)** when will these things be, and **(2)** what will be the sign of your coming, and **(3)** of the end of the age?" (Matthew 24:3) This author prefers option B.

The first question is legit about the destruction of the Temple complex, but the second and third is an assumption on their part of the disciples, because to them, if the temple and Jerusalem is being destroyed, the end has to be near and the second coming of Christ and his Kingdom must follow.

However, Jesus answered by giving them, in detail what would apply to them. When he uttered 3-28, he was talking about them, what was going to happen to them, which history bears out. Nevertheless, did he dragged those circumstances and events, which he had just spoken of (3-28), from

[226] He does make other comments, such as specifying that this cosmic show will last, i.e., "will extend over many hours."

the first century, to also applying just before his second coming. Is he the one that carried out an ISPA to his own words?

- Jesus words were for the end of the age of the Jewish age (Matt 24:3-28)
- Jesus gave the same words a Sensus Plenior Application, starting in verse 29 that were another end of the age, the end of wick humanity and the rule of age (era) of Satan.

If we remove the cosmic terminology, which is evidence of God acting on behalf of humankind, we have the following major points. 24:29-31 foretells us,

(1) the Son of Man comes immediately after the great tribulation,

(2) Jesus' second coming will be with great glory,

(3) as he will send forth his angels, and

(4) all the tribes of the earth will see him, in that they will perceive what is taking place, and

(5) Jesus will gather all of his chosen ones.

God will Gather the Remainder of His Chosen Ones Who Have a Heavenly Hope

Revelation 14:1-4 Updated American Standard Version (UASV)

14 Then I looked, and behold, the Lamb was standing on Mount Zion, and with him one hundred and forty-four thousand, having his name and the name of his Father written on their foreheads. [2] And I heard a voice from heaven, like the sound of many waters and like the sound of loud thunder, and the voice which I heard was like the sound of harpists playing on their harps. [3] And they sang a new song[227] before the throne and before the four living creatures and the elders; and no one could learn the song except the one hundred and forty-four thousand who had been purchased from the earth. [4] These are the ones who have not been defiled with women, for they are virgins. These are the ones who follow the Lamb wherever He goes. These have been purchased from among men as first fruits to God and to the Lamb. [5] And in their mouth no lie was found; they are blameless.

The whole of chapter 14 is proleptic. As a summary of the Millennium (20:4–6), the first five verses feature the Lamb in

---

[227] Two early MSS read *sing* something *like a new song*

place of the beast, the Lamb's followers with His and the Father's seal in place of the beast's followers with the mark of the beast, and the divinely controlled Mount Zion in place of the pagan-controlled earth (Alford, Moffatt, Kiddle).[228]

Revelation 7:4 Updated American Standard Version (UASV)

[4] And I heard the number of the ones who were sealed, one hundred forty-four thousand sealed from every tribe of the sons of Israel:

Various efforts have sought to determine the significance of the number 144,000. An understanding of the number as symbolical divides it into three of its multiplicands, 12 × 12 × 1000. From the symbolism of the three it is concluded that the number indicates fixedness and fullest completeness.[229] Twelve, a number of the tribes, is both squared and multiplied by a thousand. This is a twofold way of emphasizing completeness (Mounce). It thus affirms the full number of God's people to be brought through tribulation (Ladd). The symbolic approach points out the impossibility of taking the number literally. It is simply a vast number, less than a number indefinitely great (cf. 7:9), but greater than a large number designedly finite (e.g., 1,000, Rev. 20:2) (Lee). Other occurrences of the numerical components that are supposedly symbolic are also pointed out, 12 thousand in Rev. 21:16, 12 in Rev. 22:2, and 24, a multiple of 12, in Rev. 4:4. This is done to enhance the case for symbolism (Johnson). Though admittedly ingenious, the case for symbolism is exegetically weak. The principal reason for the view is a predisposition to make the 144,000 into a group representative of the church with which no possible numerical connection exists. No justification can be found for understanding the simple statement of fact in v. 4 as a figure of speech. It is a definite number in contrast with the indefinite number of 7:9. If it is taken symbolically, no number in the book can be taken literally. As God reserved 7,000 in the days of Ahab (1 Kings 19:18; Rom. 11:4), He will reserve 144,000 for Himself during the future Great

---

[228] Robert L. Thomas, Revelation 8-22: An Exegetical Commentary (Chicago: Moody Publishers, 1995), 189.

[229] Alford, Greek Testament, 4:624; Charles, Revelation, 1:206; Lenski, Revelation, p. 154.

Tribulation.[230] (Thomas, Revelation 1-7: An Exegetical Commentary 1992, 473-74)

These ones are made up of those under the new covenant, the Law of Christ, those called out of natural Israel, the new Israelites, also known as the Israel of God. They are a chosen number that are to reign with Jesus as kings, priests, and judges. Therefore, we ask, what is the other hope? What lies below was already mentioned in Chapter 3 but bears repeating again as a short repetition for emphasis as the thought are new to many minds.

The New Earth: The Earthly Hope

> In the O[ld] T[estament] the kingdom of God is usually described in terms of a redeemed earth; this is especially clear in the book of Isaiah, where the final state of the universe is already called new heavens and a new earth (65:17; 66:22) The nature of this renewal was perceived only very dimly by OT authors, but they did express the belief that a humans ultimate destiny is an earthly one.[231] This vision is clarified in the N[ew] T[estament]. Jesus speaks of the "renewal" of the world (Matt 19:28), Peter of the restoration of all things (Acts 3:21). Paul writes that the universe will be redeemed by God from its current state of bondage (Rom. 8:18-21). This is confirmed by Peter, who describes the new heavens and the new earth as the Christian's hope (2 Pet. 3:13). Finally, the book of Revelation includes a glorious vision of the end of the present universe and the creation of a new universe, full of righteousness and the presence of God. The vision is confirmed by God in the awesome declaration: "I am making everything new!" (Rev. 21:1-8).
>
> The new heavens and the new earth will be the renewed creation that will fulfill the purpose for which God created the universe. It will be characterized by the complete rule of God and

[230] Bullinger, Apocalypse, p. 282. Geyser is correct in observing that the predominant concern of the Apocalypse is "the restoration [on earth] of the twelve tribes of Israel, their restoration as a twelve-tribe kingdom, in a renewed and purified city of David, under the rule of the victorious 'Lion of the Tribe of Judah, the Root of David' (5:5; 22:16)" (Albert Geyser, "The Twelve Tribes in Revelation: Judean and Judeo Christian Apocalypticism," NTS 23, no. 3 [July 1982]: 389). He is wrong, however, in his theory that this belief characterized the Judean church only and was not shared by Gentile Christianity spearheaded by Paul (ibid., p. 390).

[231] It is unwise to speak of the written Word of God as if it were of human origin, saying 'OT authors express the belief,' when what was written is the meaning and message of what God wanted to convey by means of the human author.

> by the full realization of the final goal of redemption: "Now the dwelling of God is with men" (Rev. 21:3).
>
> The fact that the universe will be created anew[232] shows that God's goals for humans is not an ethereal and disembodied existence, but a bodily existence on a perfected earth. The scene of the beatific vision is the new earth. The spiritual does not exclude the created order and will be fully realized only within a perfected creation. (Elwell 2001, 828-29)

God created the earth to be inhabited, to be filled with perfect humans, who are over the animals, and under the sovereignty of God. (Gen 1:28; 2:8, 15; Ps 104:5; 115:16; Eccl 1:4) Sin did not dissuade God from his plans (Isa. 45:18); hence, he has saved redeemable humankind by Jesus ransom sacrifice. It seems that the Bible offers two hopes to redeemed humans, (1) a heavenly hope [i.e., the chosen ones], or (2) an earthly hope. It also seems that those with the heavenly hope are limited in number, and are going to heaven to rule with Christ as kings, priests, and judges either **on** the earth or **over** the earth from heaven. It seems that those with the earthly hope are going to receive everlasting life here on a paradise earth as originally intended.

---

[232] Create anew does not mean a complete destruction followed by a re-creation, but instead a renewal of the present universe.

Bibliography

Archer, Gleason L. *A Survey of Old Testament Introduction. Revised and expanded ed.* Chicago: Moody, 2007.

—. *The Expositor's Bible Commentary, Vol. 7: Daniel and the Minor Prophets.* Grand Rapids: Zondervan, 1985.

Arnold, Clinton E. *Zondervan Illustrated Bible Backgrounds Commentary: Matthew, Mark, Luke, vol. 1.* Grand Rapids, MI: Zondervan, 2002.

Arthur, Alexander. *A Critical Commentary on the Book of Daniel.* Edinburgh: Norman MacLeod, 1893.

Auberlen, Carl August. *The Prophecies of Daniel and the Revelations of St. John.* Edinburgh: T. & T. Clark, 1857.

Auchincloss, William Stuart. *The Book of Daniel Unlocked.* New York: Van Nostrand, 1905.

Barker, Kenneth L., and Waylon Bailey. *The New American Commentary: vol. 20, Micah, Nahum, Habakkuk, Zephaniah.* Nashville, TN: Broadman & Holman Publishers, 2001.

Barnes, Albert. *Daniel. Vol. 2. Notes on the Old Testament. Ed. Robert Few.* Grand Rapids: Baker, 1950.

Bauer, Walter. *A Greek-English Lexicon of the New Testament. William F. Arndt, Theodore Danker, and F. Wilbur Gingrich, trans. and rev., 3rd ed.* Chicago: University of Chicago Press, 2000.

Benware, Paul. *Understanding End Times Prophecy.* Chicago: Moody, 2006.

Black, Allen, and Mark C Black. *THE COLLEGE PRESS NIV COMMENTARY 1 & 2 PETER.* Joplin: College Press Publishing Company, 1998.

Blomberg, Craig. *The New American Commentary: Matthew.* Nashville, TN: Broadman & Holman Publishers, 1992.

Brand, Chad, Charles Draper, and England Archie. *Holman Illustrated Bible Dictionary: Revised, Updated and Expanded.* Nashville, TN: Holman, 2003.

Buter, Trent C. *Holman New Testament Commentary: Luke.* Nashville, TN: Broadman & Holman Publishers, 2000.

Campbell, Donald K., and Jeffrey L. gen. eds. Townsend. *A Case for Premillennialism.* Chicago: Moody, 1992.

Chouinard, Larry. *Matthew, The College Press NIV Commentary.* (Joplin, MO: College Press, 1997.

Easley, Kendell H. *Revelation, vol. 12, Holman New Testament Commentary.* Nashville, TN:: Broadman & Holman Publishers, 1998.

Elliott, Charles. *Delineation Of Roman Catholicism: Drawn From The Authentic And Acknowledged Standards Of the Church Of Rome, Volume II.* New York: George Lane, 1941.

Elwell, Walter A. *Baker Encyclopedia of the Bible.* Grand Rapids: Baker Book House, 1988.

Gangel, Kenneth, and Max Anders. *Daniel, vol. 18, Holman Old Testament Commentary.* Nashville, TN: Broadman & Holman Publishers, 2002.

Goldingay, John E. *Word Biblical Commentary Vol. 30, Daniel*. Nashville, TN: Thomas Nelson Inc, 1989.

Kistemaker, Simon J., and William Hendriksen. *Exposition of the Book of Revelation, vol. 20, New Testament Commentary.* Grand Rapids: Baker Book House, 1953–2001.

Larson, Knute. *Holman New Testament Commentary, vol. 9, I & II Thessalonians, I & II Timothy, Titus, Philemon.* Nashville, TN: Broadman & Holman Publishers, 2000.

Longman III, Tremper. *The NIV Application Commentary : Daniel.* Grand Rapids: Zondervan Publishing House, 1999.

MacArthur, John. *Because the Time Is Near.* Chicago: Moody, 2007.

—. *The MacArthur New Testament Commentary: Revelation 1–11.* Chicago: Moody, 1999.

—. *The MacArthur New Testament Commentary: Revelation 12-22.* Chicago: Moody, 2000.

Mangano, Mark. *Esther & Daniel, The College Press NIV Commentary (: , 2001).* Joplin, MO: College Press Pub., 2001.

Miller, Stephen R. *Daniel, vol. 18, The New American Commentary.* Nashville:: Broadman & Holman Publishers, 1994.

Montgomery, James A. *A Critical and Exegetical Commentary on the Book of Daniel (International Critical Commentary Series).* Edinburgh: Bloomsbury T & T Clark, 1926.

Morris, Leon. *The Gospel According to Matthew, The Pillar New Testament Commentary.* Grand Rapids, MI(; Leicester, England: W.B. Eerdmans; Inter-Varsity Press,, 1992.

Pentecost, J. Dwight, and ed. J. F. Walvoord and R. B. Zuck. *"Daniel," in The Bible Knowledge Commentary: An Exposition of the Scriptures, vol. 1.* Wheaton, IL: Victor Books, 1985.

Ryrie, Charles C. *Basic Theology.* Chicago: Moody, 1999.

—. *Revelation. rev ed.* Chicago: Moody, 1996.

Smith, J. B. *A Revelation of Jesus Christ.* Scottdale, PA: Herald, 1961.

Stein, Robert H. *A Basic Guide to Interpreting the Bible: Playing by the Rules.* Grand Rapids: Baker Books, 1994.

Terry, Milton S. *Biblical Hermeneutics: A Treatise on the Interpretation of the Old and New Testaments.* Grand Rapids: Zondervan, 1883.

Thomas, Robert L. *Revelation 8-22: An Exegetical Commentary.* Chicago: Moody Publishers, 1995.

Vine, W E. *Vine's Expository Dictionary of Old and New Testament Words.* Nashville: Thomas Nelson, 1996.

Walton, John H. *Zondervan Illustrated Bible Backgrounds Commentary (Old Testament): Isaiah, Jeremiah, Lamentations, Ezekiel, Daniel, vol. 4.* Grand Rapids, MI: Zondervan, 2009.

Walvoord, John. *Daniel (The John Walvoord Prophecy Commentaries)* . Chicago: Moody Publishers, 2012.

Weatherly, Jon A. *THE COLLEGE PRESS NIV COMMENTARY: 1 & 2 Thessalonians.* Joplin: College Press Publishing Company, 1996.

Weber, Stuart K. *Holman New Testament Commentary, vol. 1, Matthew.* Nashville, TN: Broadman & Holman Publishers, 2000.

Wilcock, Michael. *The Message of Revelation, The Bible Speaks Today, ed. John R. W. Stott.* Downer Groves, ILL.: InterVarsity, 1975.

Wood, Leon J., R. Laird Harris, Gleason L. Archer Jr., and Bruce K. Waltke. *Theological Wordbook of the Old Testament.* Chicago: Chicago: Moody Press, 199.

Zuck, Roy B. *Basic Bible Interpretation: A Prafctical Guide to Discovering Biblical Truth.* Colorado Springs: David C. Cook, 1991.